D0090211

SAVAGES AND SCOUNDRELS

Savages

AND

Scoundrels

The Untold Story of
America's Road to Empire
Through Indian Territory

Paul VanDevelder

YALE UNIVERSITY PRESS
NEW HAVEN & LONDON

Set in Linotype Century Expanded type by Duke & Company,
Devon, Pennsylvania. Printed in the United States of America by
Sheridan Books, Ann Arbor, Michigan.

Library of Congress Cataloging-in-Publication Data
VanDevelder, Paul
Savages and scoundrels : the untold story of America's
road to empire through Indian territory / Paul VanDevelder.
p.   cm.
Includes bibliographical references and index.
ISBN 978-0-300-12563-4 (alk. paper)
1. Indians of North America—Government relations.
2. Indians of North America—Land tenure.
3. United States—Territorial expansion—History. I. Title.

E93.V36 2009
323.1197—dc22   2008046683

A catalogue record for this book is available from the British Library.

This paper meets the requirements of ANSI/NISO Z39.48–1992
(Permanence of Paper). It contains 30 percent postconsumer waste
(PCW) and is certified by the Forest Stewardship Council (FSC).

10 9 8 7 6 5 4 3 2 1

for

FRANK &

MARY &

BRENDA &

ELLIE,

who held the lamp high
through the storms

Government is the potent, the omnipresent teacher.

For good or ill it teaches the whole people by its example.

Crime is contagious. If the government becomes a law breaker,

it breeds contempt for the law; it invites every man

to become a law unto himself.

Justice Louis Brandeis, U.S. Supreme Court

Justice. Justice shalt thou pursue.

Deuteronomy

 CONTENTS

INTRODUCTION
Kicking the Loose Stones Home

Like most American families whose widely flung ancestors arrived on these shores more than a generation or two ago, the thick trunk of my family tree is held upright by a tangled ball of far-ranging roots. Today, our family gene pool runs as deep and wide as the ocean our ancestors crossed to get here. In our case, most of our familial DNA is easily traced back to a point where the individual strands vanish in the mists of time in Holland, Belgium, England, Ireland, and Scotland. But thanks to reasons known only to my maternal grandmother Julia, who took those reasons with her to the grave, the origin of her own genetic makeup—one that produced high cheekbones, thick hair, great physical stamina, and us—was for many years an unattached limb on our family tree. Who are we, we wondered. Where did grandma really come from, and how did we get from there to here?

Throughout her life, Julia refused to claim a genetic (or cultural) heritage. Her silence was bolstered by an obdurate stubbornness, a brick wall if you will, one whose principal effect on her offspring was to excite and intensify their curiosity. Yet any suggestion that she might have Indian blood flowing through her veins was met with a flash of anger or mirthful disclaimers, depending on her mood. But Julia's lifelong denials were not enough to daunt her eldest daughter, my mother, who put much store in determining her own cultural identity. Having grown up in the South, my mother also knew enough about the lowly station of the Indians in the social pecking order of the early twentieth century (a full rung beneath that of blacks) to recognize a culturally reinforced stigma when she saw one. So, brushing aside her mother's once fierce protestations, on a fine June day in 1996, my mother, father, and I stepped into the small air-conditioned library beside the Eastern Band of the Cherokee Nation's tribal offices, in Cherokee, North Carolina, and proceeded to thread a thick coil of National Archives microfilm through the glass plates of the film reader. As the tribal archivist had explained minutes before, on this film were imprinted the names of every Cherokee tribal member born since the Indian removal era of the 1830s. If there were any clues to be found about our heritage in the Cherokee archives, this is where we would find them. But the task was formidable. The names numbered in the tens of thousands.

Having no particular strategy for finding our family's needle in the haystack, we probably did what most people do—we started walking backward from the present. Our eyes were soon bleary from staring at the screen. Each of us struggled to focus on the blizzard of names rolling past, and eventually the typewritten words became handwritten entries in photocopied ledger books. Discerning exotic-sounding names from the loops and scrawls of some long-dead government scribe quickly turned our search into a stupefying challenge. Then, with one slight twist of the knob, a page in the ledger book froze on the screen. My mother's finger reached out and pointed. Simultaneously, our three heads moved closer to the glass. Moments passed in silence as we searched each other's eyes with astonished smiles.

"That's your great-grandmother, when she was a little girl, and all her brothers and sisters," said my mother. "My mom's mom. Well how about that! We were Indians after all!"

Flush with elation at making such a momentous discovery, we rewound the spool of microfilm and walked back to the tribal headquarters through the late afternoon shadows. Strangely, the surrounding mountains suddenly seemed to have been transformed from a place vaguely alien into a world that was eerily familiar. These steeply walled valleys, these mountain streams and soaring ridgelines of the Great Smoky

Mountains, were home to my forbears. They had done well here. They had thrived. They had built a well-ordered agricultural civilization that prospered for countless centuries before the arrival of the first Europeans. As we drove off to find our motel, I looked out at those sunlit mountains in a state of mild bewilderment and unsettling wonder.

So there we were. Home. The last branch of our family tree was finally attached to its trunk. At the base of that tree sat an enormous and enigmatic ball of roots. In each of my mother's siblings, and in each of their children in turn, the people indigenous to this continent had been fused indistinguishably to the genealogy of countless immigrants. In its broader cultural context, this meant that my family was the genetic embodiment of our nation's story, and contained in that story were answers to the questions that had long eluded us: Where did we come from, and how did we get from there to here? That, it seemed to me, was a story worth telling, a crossing worth the inevitable storm.

If you happen to be an American with sensibilities shaped by the howl of a wolf, the pastoral tranquility of the Shenandoah Valley, or the spectral grandeur of Second Mesa, much of the narrative that follows is also your story. And it is the story of this nation, one that is animated by characters as colorful and wild as the country they founded, owned, or sought to tame. It has cowboys and Indians and aristocrats and common folk. It has legendary orators and egoistic geniuses, a "new world order" and lost causes galore. But the protagonist, as stated or unstated in all epic tales that are truly American, is the land itself, that unmapped landscape of paradoxes where boundless optimism and limitless possibility inevitably run up against a bulwark of human appetites, competing desires, and intractable conflicts. On the eve of his inauguration as our nation's first president, George Washington recognized in full measure the many fault lines that ran through our national character. As his biographer Joseph Ellis tells us, the Emperor of the Potomac foresaw with mounting dread that "what was politically essential for a viable

American nation was ideologically at odds with what it claimed to stand for." The nation's First Citizen correctly perceived that America was shaped at its moment of conception by antipodal ideals and paradoxes. The great and idealized aspirations of common men (and women) were underwritten by deep and worrisome contradictions in the citizenry's actions and behaviors. Somewhere along the way to full national maturity there would be a reckoning between what was "politically essential" for national survival, and what that nation "claimed to stand for."

If history could be used as a yardstick to measure the essential ingredients of human nature, for good and for ill, then for men such as Washington and Benjamin Franklin, a day was already marked in the future when the newly solemnized rights of "life, liberty, and the pursuit of happiness" would be vanquished by "venality, corruption, and prostitution of office for selfish ends." Though he would not live to see that day, Washington's predictions were soon borne out by a cataclysm of events in the nineteenth century. Flaws that the Founders had unintentionally embedded in the republican government's new concept of federalism would inevitably lead a strong central government to come to mortal blows with southern aristocrats who were deeply suspicious of the central government's authority. His Excellency's genius, concludes Ellis, was most clearly visible in his faultless judgments and predictions.

It was out of the fertile soil of idealism that collected in those fault lines and fissures that a lightning-struck sprig eventually grew into a nation. While young, that sprig was fertilized and shaped by great conflicts and ideological divisions that, in many respects, continue to shape our story to this day: promise and possibility, church and state, republicanism and egalitarianism, states' rights versus federal authority, betrayal and loss, and the ever hopeful quest for reconciliation. But to fully appreciate how all of this came to be in the first place—how we got from there to here—it is important to note that the great themes that would one day form the foundation for America's story were written three centuries before Columbus stepped ashore on the island of San

Salvador in 1492. It was in twelfth-century Europe that a succession of brilliant Catholic popes—men who wielded power like iron fists to rule and bring order to the geopolitical chaos known as medieval Christendom—also created the laws that enabled them to send crusading armies into the Holy Lands to confiscate territory from Muslim "heathens and infidels." Over the next five centuries those same laws would evolve through the discovery-era courts of Spain and Elizabethan England to eventually acquire the names by which we know them today: the doctrine of discovery and its more familiar offspring, eminent domain. More than half a millennium after the pope's Christian armies sacked Jerusalem, the medieval papacy's building blocks of empire would evolve into the legal fulcrums that the U.S. Congress used to open up western lands to migration and settlement—*our* story.

In our literature, which is a kind of safe-deposit box where we find the best and worst reflections of ourselves at a given point in time, the American epic took on unique shapes, sounds, and colors the moment James Fenimore Cooper turned Natty Bumppo loose in the primeval forest of his Leatherstocking tales. The path that Natty follows west across the wilderness of the continent marks a new frontier in European experience. This boundary separated the new "American story" from the stuffy parlor dramas of England and France. It was already clear to people like Cooper and Henry Thoreau (and soon to Mark Twain as well) that America's story lay beyond the western horizon. "Eastward I go only by force," wrote the bard of Walden Pond, "but westward I go free."

By the mid-nineteenth century, the story of going free had been spun through with enough romantic dust to lure a ceaseless procession of settlers toward the setting sun for the next half century. Wagon caravans cut ten-inch-deep ruts into limestone bedrock in eastern Oregon, grooves that are still visible today. And on they came, many tens of thousands of them, drawn toward Canaan by desires so fierce and a sky so vast that the unyielding silence drove many of our heartiest dreamers to whimpering madness. By 1845, trail bosses referred to the Oregon Trail as "the longest graveyard in the world." Yet onward they came, undeterred by the challenges and perils, boldly kicking loose stones toward a home they had never seen, toward a distant day when the dream would either materialize in glory or disintegrate into ashes scattered on the wind.

The title I have chosen for their adventure intentionally tethers this narrative to another era, to a time not so distant when words like *savages* and *nigger* were spoken by white men as common nouns, albeit nouns loaded with hatred, fear, and racial freight. Repeating "savages" in the text, over and over, reminds us how easily the cultural judgments of an entire civilization can be carried in a single two-syllable word that more often than not described its users. And while the title also insinuates events of enormous consequence in our nation's history, this narrative does not aspire to rewrite the literature of Euro-American settlement of North America. The story that follows attempts to recontextualize and realign some of the major themes in America's story that have been mythologized and embroidered in many of our familiar, widely read, and widely taught histories.

The conventional story of the Europeans' westward migration across the North American continent, for example, often begins in 1803 when President Thomas Jefferson arranged a treaty with Napoleon Bonaparte to annex the French territory of Louisiana. Generations of American schoolchildren have been taught that the United States government acquired nearly a million square miles of unsettled lands in the West through a deal known as the Louisiana Purchase. What the government actually bought from France amounted to a few dozen square miles of land beneath the port towns of New Orleans and St. Louis. The new republic also obtained the right to use the rivers that flowed through the territory for navigation and commerce—no trifling matter—and finally, it obtained the right to engage in negotiations for land cessions with the territory's owners, the American Indians. Although the nation's western boundary was moved on maps to the foothills of the Rocky Mountains, the government did not acquire the land itself. Despite the loftiest claims of generations of American historians, the U.S. Constitution, international law, and the U.S. Supreme Court all recognized the American Indians as the rightful owners of the million square miles of land that now fell within the nation's westernmost boundaries. Title to that land did not pass to the American people or the federal government. Title to that land remained with the Indians.

Consequently, the Euro-Americans' westward-looking ambitions in the nineteenth century first had to overcome the obstacle of Indian land ownership. This, too, was no trifling matter. The citizenry's elected representatives in Congress, and a succession of presidents, eventually did overcome that obstacle through masterful use of the government's favorite tools—treaty and breach, and executive orders. As seen through a lens brought to focus by the hundreds of treaties ratified during the "removal eras" of the nineteenth century—each one subsequently violated or abrogated in whole or in part by the federal government—the theocratically energized forces that converged in "the great migration" of Euro-Americans to the Pacific Ocean under the banner of Manifest Destiny begin to take on new aspects of meaning. The lawlessness of white men in Congress and on the frontier, and the officially sanctioned genocide of Indians that ensued, raise troubling questions about the widely accepted and sanitized theories of America's westward expansion.

Long-standing distortions of this magnitude have cascading effects. In the case of the Louisiana Purchase, the secular machinery of governance established by the Founders in the Commerce Clause of the Constitution, and in the Indian Trade and Intercourse Act that followed, proved too clunky and cumbersome in the first half of the nineteenth century to satisfy the new nation's rapacious appetite for land. By the mid-1840s, that secular machinery—and the nuts and bolts of the laws that held the machinery together—was all but officially replaced as an expansionist tool by a new set of loosely organized principles known as Manifest Destiny. As a political philosophy, Manifest Destiny arrived in the nick of time for President James K. Polk to justify the provocation of an illegal war with Mexico in order to fulfill the nation's expansionist dreams in Texas and California. As a social creed, Manifest Destiny asserted that Americans were distinguished as a morally superior race of people by the God who had chosen them to go forth and vanquish heathen races for the divinely ordained purpose of bringing civilization to the wilderness home occupied by "the wild and savage tribes." Through the legitimizing mechanism of Manifest Destiny, westward expansion was reconstituted on the same theocratic footing that had energized the Euro-Americans' crusading ancestors in their quest to conquer the Holy Lands five centuries earlier. But once Congress had overcome the obstacle of Indian land ownership, the vitalizing assets of Manifest Destiny made it too effective a tool of conquest to be set aside indefinitely. In a new guise, the doctrine's load-bearing principles reemerged a century later as the organizing credo of the neoconservative disciples of philosopher Leo Strauss.

As George Washington predicted in the closing days of his presidency, fatal flaws in federalism translated into incomprehensible misery for the American Indian. Nevertheless, as settlers gathered in increasing numbers on the western frontier and clamored for the right to subdue and populate the new Edens of California and the Oregon Territory— the treaty endured as the government's most reliable tool for securing a restless society's feverishly desired end. Throughout the half-century-long era of westward migration, many dozens of those treaties became the immigrants' stepping-stones to the Pacific at the same time they served as the government's stepping-stones to empire. This is the story of those stones, including one in particular, the Great Smoke at Horse Creek in 1851. This, *our* nation's story, seeks to explain the forces of governance that succeeded in laying those stones end to end, and the journey we made across them in order to fulfill our nation's perceived divinely ordained license to secure its "Manifest Destiny."

Even in the 1830s, James Fenimore Cooper could see how this story would play out. By the end of Natty Bumppo's life, in *The Prairie*, the famous frontiersman realizes that the freedoms he imagined, so beautifully symbolized by the vast and unfenced panorama of the American West, would inevitably be transformed into cruel illusions. When Natty lies dying on the prairie as an old man, what he hears as life runs out of him is the sound of wagon wheels approaching in the distance. No matter how far and how quickly Natty pushed west, Cooper knew that the wheels of civilization would soon follow. "The one true thing about every American frontier that seems concrete and immutable," writes the essayist Charles Pierce, "is that it does not last. Sooner or later, everything that makes it a frontier collapses into maps and charts and roads and cities, and it becomes a place where we all go and live."

It is in those places, those towns and cities where we finally ran out of wilderness, where we finally come face to face with one another, that we were compelled to reconcile the paradoxes that defined us and brought us together in the first place. Like the currents of the Mississippi, or the force of gravity, a young and restless American society could no more escape the violent pull of westward migration than it could avoid the consequences of betrayal and loss that forged that migration's end product. In the end, reconciliation, says the western writer William Kittredge, will be America's only way out of that legacy of dishonor, the only sensible path to a future worth living—our Last Chance Saloon.

The primary source material for this book would fill a small library. Those many and varied sources include the transcripts of hundreds of congressional hearings and reports from the first, second, and third removal eras, congressional debates, the papers of the Continental Congress, and the executive documents of presidents from George Washington to Benjamin Harrison. That library would also include the annual reports and letter books of dozens of Indian commissioners, field agents, and treaty commissioners, and the transcripts and rulings of hundreds of court cases heard in both federal courts and in the U.S. Supreme Court. Also, the contemporary segments of the narrative were drawn from many dozens of interviews, personal letters, journals, and memoranda written by the principals, and transcripts of dozens of court cases, congressional hearings and reports, all of which are listed and discussed more fully in the bibliography.

But for the weaver of tales that germinate in such storied soil, no source material, however hallowed and unimpeachable, can substitute for walking the frozen ground of the North Dakota prairie in a February wind, or for listening to the solitary voices of people whose bones were formed from the dust of prairie soil, or for the howl of a wolf, the trill of the loon, or the lilting melody of a meadowlark on a spring morning. In any search for the true and authentic America, one whose residue of betrayal and loss are redeemed by the endurance and perseverance of its resilient citizens, there are no proxies for the people whose lives and voices animate these pages.

ONE

Redeeming Eden

When morning broke bright and clear across the northern high plains, shot through with angular streamers of sunlight that ignited the greening crowns of cottonwoods along the big river and lit the wall beside her bed, nothing about the sound of the honkers feeding in the grain fields, or the yipping howls of the little wolves in the gooseberry creek bottom, keened for Louise Holding Eagle the last day of the world.

It was a frosty morning in late May 1951, just a few days after she and her husband, Matthew, and their two children, celebrated her twenty-first birthday with chocolate cake and homemade ice cream. She wore her birthday present, a new flannel robe, when she stepped into the chilly air to hunt for eggs in the chicken coop. Finding six, she gathered her skirt into a basket and collected the eggs carefully, one by one, then dashed back to the warmth of the kitchen to make coffee and breakfast. "I don't know what we would have eaten if it hadn't been for those eggs," she says half a century later, her eyes vivid with memory. "We always called the late spring the starving time. My birthday was a month away from diggin' prairie turnips, and a month from pickin' Juneberries. We were always hungry on my birthday."

Like many of their childhood friends who grew up in the semi-isolation of western ranch and farm country, Louise and her husband Matthew were born and raised just a few miles apart, but they didn't meet until high school. After a few awkward dates they started holding hands in public, eventually kissed at a school dance, and fell in love. Between football games and rodeos, school work, and the endless farm chores of branding calves and planting crops in the spring, harvesting in the fall, and hauling lignite by sled to keep the home fire burning through the frigid North Dakota winters, Matthew and Louise courted in stolen moments of semi-privacy in pickup trucks, at church, or down by the river when the weather turned nice. Then one evening, with high school diplomas in hand, they drove off into the prairie night beneath a cathedral of stars to find a justice of the peace, to get hitched. Their first child, a baby girl, came along a year later, and their second, another girl, a year after that.

By then, the foursome lived in a small white farmhouse on a quarter section (160 acres) of bottomland in the broad, meandering valley of the Upper Missouri River. Here, after being joined by the Yellowstone 150 miles upstream at the Montana border, the Missouri River valley broadened into a four-mile-wide belt of terraced woodlands, open pastures, and furrowed fields of dark fertile soil that produced bumper crops year after year. This was, by all accounts, the richest farmland in America, a lush anomaly of nature where mineralized alluvial silts were deposited by centuries of spring floods that carved a bountiful floodplain some eight hundred feet below the surrounding grasslands. For longer than anyone could remember, residents of the valley had called the treeless plains above them "on top," a deceptively simple shorthand for one of the harshest climates and the most marginal dry-land growing conditions in North America. Unless Louise and Matthew had to make a trip to the hospital in Bismarck, or visit the farm implement dealer in Minot, there was no reason to go "on top." Whatever was out there, beyond their hometown of Elbowoods, was an enormous blue void.

Surveyed by government engineers in the late nineteenth century, the incorporated town of Elbowoods was laid out on a grid of perpendicular lines in a swale of cottonwoods, oaks, chokecherry bushes, and willows, and set down on a piece of elevated ground at a ninety-degree bend in the Big Muddy, their nickname for the Missouri. A few miles downstream from Elbowoods was the river's confluence with the Knife, and a few miles upstream was the mouth of the Little Missouri. There was the town itself, with its eight hundred full-time residents and two churches, Catholic and Congregational, the school with the novelties of central heating and indoor plumbing, Simon's General Store, a country hospital with a doctor and a nurse, and the unassuming government buildings clustered beside the town square. Extending out from the town's tidy edges was a checkerboard of small family farms, a Norman Rockwell painting of the Jeffersonian dream at the heart of the continent. And like most of the folks who lived on that checkerboard, Louise and Matthew were self-sufficient from the first day of their marriage. Mostly, though, says Louise, they were too busy planting and harvesting and raising chickens and cows, goats, and pigs, to give it much thought. "If we didn't plant it, catch it, gather it, can it, or hunt it," says Louise, "we didn't eat. It was a hard life, and we didn't know how good we had it."

Even in a region accustomed to extremes, where the mercury could swing a hundred degrees in twenty-four hours, and forty below zero was an average day in February, the winter of '51 had been especially harsh. The Upper Missouri country of the Dakotas, Wyoming, and Montana had spent seven months in a deep freeze. Winter announced itself with a whiteout blizzard in late September and didn't release its grip until mid-April. A March storm dropped so much snow across the plains that the residents of Elbowoods were cut off from the world for almost three weeks.

Being snowbound in winter would not have posed a problem in most years, but this year was different. The Elbowoods Warriors, the boys' high school basketball team and the pride of the community, had a good shot at winning the state championship that year—but there was no way of getting out to play in the tournament. So, as the winds howled and the snow piled up faster than they could plow it, city fathers worked through the night of the storm and cleared four feet of the white stuff off Main Street. By morning they figured they had the storm licked.

The sun rose on the new Elbowoods airport—a landing strip that ran through the middle of town—just wide enough and long enough for a single-engine Piper Cub to land and take off again. On skis. The airplane, a "tin can" without a heater, flew two boys at a time out for their playoff game, and the half-frozen team was reassembled at the convention center in Minot minutes before tip-off. The Warriors thawed out enough in the first quarter to pull even with the boys from Parshall, and then went on to win the regional title. It was a game heard in every farmhouse from Sioux Falls to the Canadian border, wrote a reporter for the *Bismarck Tribune*.

By late May that year, the shelves in Louise's pantry were so bare that she and Matthew decided to dip into their emergency money and make a run to town to replenish their staples. After she made breakfast, mucked out the barn, and fed the pigs and chickens, Louise kissed Matthew and the kids goodbye and pointed the wheels of their Chevrolet pickup truck toward the grocery store in Beulah, thirty miles away.

The washboards of the farm road that skirted their property ran on for two jarring miles, but it was a beautiful spring day, the warmest of the season, with red-tailed hawks circling lazily overhead, and Louise was in such good spirits that she sang songs as she drove along. Finally she hooked up with the smoother surface of State Road Number 8. Turning west, the truck settled in to a pleasant hum and crossed the Four Bears Bridge over the roily Missouri, swollen now with melted snow from the distant Rockies, and swung left on the far side past a familiar granite obelisk. Erected on a freestanding abutment set into the hill beside the bridge, this was an eighteen-foot-tall monument honoring the Mandan, Hidatsa, and Arikara chiefs who, on horseback and foot, had made the eight-hundred-mile overland trek to the peace council at Fort Laramie in 1851, coincidentally, exactly a century earlier. It weighed more than five tons and was dedicated in 1934 by senators, governors, and men from Washington wearing suits and silk ties; some said that time and the river might one day sweep away the bridge, but the monument was a permanent fixture of the American landscape—as enduring as the treaty and the dust of the bones of the men who made it.

After filling up her truck with sugar, flour, beans, onions, penny candies for the girls, and four fifty-pound sacks of potatoes, Louise ran into some old high school friends at the gas station and agreed to join them for a dinner. After a delightful evening of catching up on gossip and chitchat about schoolmates, babies, and the price of spring wheat, she bade them farewell until next year and turned for home in the twilight. "Nobody had electricity back then, much less a phone, so I couldn't call my husband and let him know I'd be a little late," she remembers. "But Matthew was an easy-goin' kind of man, so I wasn't worried. I knew he wouldn't mind."

The road home was wide open for miles and miles. Out there in the Big Empty it was not unusual to drive for hours without seeing another car. Louise could find her way home with her eyes closed. She retraced her route in the fast-gathering twilight as scarlet fingers of light jumped from high spot to high spot, finally settling on the superstructure of the bridge as she recrossed the Missouri and dropped into the darkening bottoms. At the familiar intersection with the farm road she swung left and eased off the gas, not wanting to scatter her groceries across the countryside. When she reached the turn to her house a few minutes later, she realized she'd been daydreaming and made a mistake. Disoriented by the sudden darkness, she'd turned into the wrong driveway. She brought the truck to an abrupt stop at the edge of an empty field and just stared into the void beyond the beams of her headlights.

"I don't know how long I sat there before I realized I was home, all right. I was at the right place. This was our driveway. Everything was where it was supposed to be, the river, the fields. Except my house! Except the barn and chicken coop and my family. They were gone!"

While Louise was grocery shopping in Beulah, a crew of men hired by the Army Corps of Engineers had arrived at their farm equipped with crowbars, chains, hoists, hydraulic jacks, and flatbed trucks. Two hours later they drove off with her house, the two outbuildings, the farm animals, and her husband and two children. After calming her heart and collecting her wits, she jumped back into the truck and roared off down the farm road to State Road Number 8. She spent the next two frantic hours chasing her own headlights, and her house and her family, out of the bottomlands and across the prairie to the place "on top" where they were being relocated by the federal government.

"Most people didn't realize that when the big dams came to the Missouri River, what happened to me and my family happened to thousands, many thousands, of people," says Louise. "Until September 11th, people who didn't live through it really couldn't understand what happened to us. The trauma of losing everything. Everything! We know what that feels like."

In 1951, Louise's people were organized politically under the modern-day rubric of the Three Affiliated Tribes of the Mandan, Hidatsa, and Arikara nations. At the end of World War II, they were the only self-sustaining Indian tribes in the United States. The Mandan and Hidatsa peoples had made themselves famous in America's history books as the tribe that sheltered Lewis and Clark and the men of the Corps of Discovery through the bitterly cold winter of 1804–1805. Unlike tribes that had been pushed out of the woodlands by European interlopers, as the Sioux and Cheyenne were in the eighteenth and early nineteenth centuries, the Mandan people had migrated out of the crowded Mississippi River lowlands more than a thousand years before. Over the next several centuries they would meet and intermarry with members of the Hidatsa and Arikara nations, eventually blending their shared customs into a highly complex clan-based matrilineal society of farmers, warriors, and hunter-gatherers. Thanks to horticultural success resulting from favorable climate and the rich soil of the Upper Missouri River floodplains, these socially sophisticated peace-loving farmers and hunters would dominate native commerce on the northern plains for centuries to come.

So prominent was their reputation as masters of the deal that in 1682 the La Salle expedition, which had completed a survey of the Mississippi delta and thereby laid claim by right of discovery to the Louisiana territory for the French king, sent home word of a great trading bazaar at the villages of the "Mantannes Indians," far to the north near a big bend in the River of the West, the Missouri. Based on information contained in that report, the three tribes soon made their debut in western cartography. On maps drawn in 1718 by the leading French geographer of the day, Guillaume Insulanus Delisle, official cartographer to the court of Louis XV, the French crown laid claim to all the lands bordering those claimed for Spain a century earlier by Hernando de Soto, whose "discoveries" included the areas known today as Florida, Georgia, the Carolinas, Mississippi, and Louisiana. The French claims were based on the discoveries of the intrepid La Salle, whose men later reached the Gulf Coast of Texas. Emboldened by the remarkable accomplishments of his proxies, the king at Versailles claimed ownership of all the land south of Illinois between the English colonies on the east and the Spanish territory to the west.

The purpose of this claim was to open new commercial enterprises in hopes of one day reaching the rumored "Mer de l'Ouest," the Pacific Ocean. Almost by accident, the explorations that sought to establish trading routes to Spanish forts in Mexico resulted in the founding of the village of New Orleans, in 1718. This was the same year that Delisle placed the Mandan Villages inside the boundaries of French land claims on the Upper Missouri. With the eastern forests under the control of the British, and the Southwest in the hands of Spain, a ruthless and bloody battle to control the Indian fur trade in the Lake of the Woods region of Canada began. The natives had learned from the Dutch to take scalps for bounties, and as a result thousands of trappers and traders would lose their locks to woodland Indians. The severed heads of Englishmen who violated French territory were impaled on spikes—their blue eyes pecked out by ravens—as fair warning to their countrymen. For more than a century, no amount of murderous intrigue could fix trade boundaries in the north woods.

As battles raged in the forests of a distant continent, Delisle was only too happy to indulge his king's fantasies by fudging the geographic limits of the crown's claims. Such was the peerless mapmaker's standing in the international court of opinion that he got away with it. The boundaries inscribed on his 1718 map were still intact eighty-six years later when a new emperor named Napoleon decided to snub his British adversaries by selling France's New World possessions to the upstart Americans.

In pre-Columbian times, the Mandan people were able to exploit their horticultural success along the well-worn network of trade routes that linked them to the Pueblo and Hopi of the Southwest, and to the Cree and the Iroquois of the Northeast. By the time Columbus set sail from Gran Canaria, the Mandan had developed their own varieties of corn from seed they acquired from the Aztecs and the Maya. In the following centuries, crops grown in Mandan gardens—corn, squash, beans, and potatoes—became staple foods for people throughout the Americas. And the world: most seventeenth-century trade routes across the North American continent converged at the palisaded Mandan Villages. It was here, near the confluence of the Missouri and the Heart rivers in modern-day North Dakota, that the horse culture of the Comanche met the gun culture of the Cree in the mid-1700s. When the first European to visit the Mandan, the French fur trader and explorer Pierre Gaultier de Varennes, the Sieur de La Vérendrye, arrived in these villages on a mission of commerce and peace in November 1738, he was astonished to find the Mandan bartering trade goods manufactured in England, France, and Spain. "The Mantannes are much craftier in trade, as in everything else, than the Assiniboins, who are always being cheated by them," he wrote in his journal. "The Assiniboins, though numerous and strong and hardy men, are not brave; they greatly fear the Sioux, whom they consider brave. The Mantannes know their [the Sioux's] weakness and profit by it on occasion."

La Vérendrye was quick to recognize that the Mandan knew a good deal more about Europeans than Europeans knew about them. But what these Indians could not know, at the peak of their prosperity, was that they were hovering on the brink of catastrophe. In 1781, after traveling north from the central valley of Mexico into the American Southwest, the scourge of smallpox was carried to the Heart River villages by a Comanche trading party via a thousand-mile path no wider than a man's foot. In weeks, the vibrant villages of Mandan civilization were transformed into heaps of rotting bodies. Hundreds died every day. Mothers killed their own children to spare them from the wasting agony of the invisible curse. More than twelve thousand perished in "the time of one moon," twenty-eight days. Bewildered and terrified, the surviving leaders made a fateful decision to abandon the Heart River villages. But rather than disappearing into obscurity far out on the plains, the Mandan chose instead to join their good friends, the Hidatsa, at their villages upstream, at the confluence with the Knife.

When Lewis and Clark made their way up the Missouri River from St. Louis in 1804, Louise Holding Eagle's ancestors had already hosted twenty-six expeditions of French, Spanish, English, and Dutch traders. By then, Frenchmen were longtime residents of the villages and had spawned a subculture of mixed bloods known today as *métis*. Clever, wily, and shrewd by nature, the Mandan people were intimately familiar with the Europeans and had become very adept at pitting English, French, and Spanish interests against one another in order to increase their own profits. It was into this sophisticated commercial arena that President Thomas Jefferson sent his young emissaries to explore the "territories unknown" of the West. Unwittingly, says noted historian James Ronda, the Americans arriving at the villages on the Knife River on October 28, 1804, had sailed out of their depth. They brought with them a naive and simplistic diplomatic model that sought to reduce the tribes to a state of childlike servility to the Great White Fathers—a model that served neither the Indians nor the whites in any of their future dealings. "The captains were not the masters of Upper Missouri Indian affairs," writes Ronda. "They were simply players in a complex game made more intricate by their very presense."

A century and a half later, in 1951, agents of those same Great White Fathers were hoping to once again be met with childlike servility when they arrived at Louise Holding Eagle's home with crowbars and trucks. Before the sun went down, her land would be condemned and in the possession of the United States government. Without a word of warning, either spoken or written, her house, her family, and all their worldly possessions, were unceremoniously hauled away and deposited on a barren piece of wind-scoured ground—"on top." In the months that followed, Louise and Matthew and thousands like them slowly discovered that there was nothing they could do. The taking, it seemed, was beyond appeal, legal or otherwise.

"We certainly didn't need anybody to tell us that was our land," says Louise, gazing abstractly out a window at the rolling plains. "That land was ours forever. Then one day, just like that, they came and took it and it was gone."

For most of the nineteenth century, European civilization bypassed the plains. Until the killing of Sitting Bull and the massacre of Big Foot's band of Sioux by the Seventh Cavalry at Wounded Knee Creek in 1890, the two million square miles of short-grass country, the northern plains, belonged to the Indians. It was a formidable place, one that compelled its endemic creatures to either conform to its rigorous conditions or perish. It put horns on frogs, forced deadly snakes to slither sideways to keep from being swallowed up by sand, created grasshoppers that would fly five miles to eat a blade of grass, and gave one of the fastest animals on earth, the pronghorn antelope, the ability to live for months without a drink of water. From the hundredth meridian west to the high Sierra of California and the Cascades of the Pacific Northwest, average annual rainfall for the entire region seldom topped twelve inches.

For dry-land farmers, fifteen inches of "god-water," rain, marked the boundary between school shoes for the kids and a one-way trip to the nearest asylum.

When the first wave of homesteaders stepped out of the northern forests onto the open prairie in the late 1800s, one look at that sky, one moment surrendered to that awesome silence, dispelled any illusion that turning the Great Plains into a Garden of Eden would be a simple task. Its stark contrast to the East began in topography, continued in climate and vegetation, and closed the circle in its unique cultural history. At no point on that circle was there a match, a familiar connection, with the world these immigrants had left behind. This place was so different from the tidy pettiness of the eastern seaboard, or from the familiar farms of Norway or Sweden, that no sane man setting foot onto the prairie could pretend to have dominion over the earth. Old Testament conceits were mocked by its pitiless sky, its unreachable edges. "Above its vague and receding horizons forever broods a pathetic solemnity," wrote one homesteader, John J. Ingalls. "It is a place born of distance, silence, and an unnerving solitude."

That fabled solitude began yielding to the white man's will in the late 1870s, when lawmakers in Washington, D.C., realized they had a problem out there in the Big Empty. Despite their fiercely held differences of opinion about basic human nature, the nation's founders had been unified in their belief that ownership of property was the proven antidote to the dreaded ills of European society—an elite class of layabouts addicted to luxuries made possible by masses of peasants forever indentured to their whims and needs. Since power always followed property, the success of the American experiment would flow from the distribution of land to as many citizens as possible. In the wilderness lay deliverance from the chains of servitude.

By the 1870s, American society was growing by leaps and bounds along both coasts, but the middle was an enormous void. Hoping to forestall just that emerging problem, Congress had passed the Homestead

Act of 1862 with an eye to opening public domain on the prairies to new settlements. The government's difficulty from the beginning was that eastern lawmakers who had never traveled more than fifty miles west of Boston, Baltimore, or Charleston could not comprehend that the success of their land programs east of the Mississippi had more to do with growing conditions and the availability of water than with the mettle and spirit of the settlers. Out there in the "territories unknown," farmers would have to contend with a new set of challenges, such as short growing seasons and chronic aridity, fierce heat and withering winds, killer frosts, hailstones bigger than turnips, tornadoes, swarms of locusts, dust storms, and wild beasts.

Nevertheless, eastern bureaucrats and politicians seemed to think that once they had filled the surveyors' "little squares with people," success would take care of itself. The long-term benefits to the nation, said Congress, would be manifold. Chief among them was the notion that the homestead acts would relieve population pressures in eastern cities and bring the industry, enterprise, and commerce of a new agrarian economy into the continent's Big Empty. The census of 1870 revealed that fewer than twenty-five hundred adventurous pioneers were settled and farming the fertile prairie of eastern North Dakota. The homestead acts of 1870 and 1887 and a succession of executive orders (many of them later ruled illegal by courts, and subject to compensation) would increase that number a hundredfold in less than thirty years. By the 1890s, landless masses were arriving by the tens of thousands at the stepping-off points of Fargo, Minneapolis, and Sioux Falls. They came by train and on foot, astride horses and driving wagons. The swelling flood of humanity was further bolstered by the railroads that now saw a golden opportunity to redeem their construction investments by selling lands awarded to them by Congress when they laid the transcontinental tracks in the 1870s.

The Northern Pacific's hard sell in Europe of an Eden-like paradise lured thousands of stouthearted blond and blue-eyed migrants across the North Atlantic from Norway, Sweden, Switzerland, and Germany. Many were the second sons and daughters of yeoman farmers, born with no hope of inheriting the family farm or staking a claim to a piece of land they could call their own. With their life savings in one hand and a cardboard suitcase in the other, wave after wave of immigrants set sail from the Old Country determined to redeem a future from the virginal paradise in "the land of milk and honey." The voyages were arduous, and the journey across half a continent often took months. What awaited them when they climbed down from the train was a silent, semi-arid landscape of grass, endless grass, bluestem grass, needle grass, wheat grass, and buffalo grass. Beneath an inscrutable sky and a blistering sun, they encountered an environment that would humble the strong, punish the weak, and take pity on no one.

Vaguely aware that it was asking for superhuman efforts from mere mortals, Congress commissioned the famous one-armed geologist and river runner John Wesley Powell to travel through the West and report back on what he found about the prospects for agriculture on the high plains. In Powell's groundbreaking *Report on the Lands of the Arid Region of the United States*, in 1879, lawmakers got more than they bargained for. He told them that the first requirement for turning the West into a Garden of Eden would be to reframe their thinking about the homestead laws. The Jeffersonian equation of a gentleman farmer and his family on a 160-acre rectangle of land might have worked very well in the East, but it had no place in the West. Also, said Powell, sustained agriculture on the northern plains would demand a massive investment of federal dollars in public waterworks. He urged Congress to scrap the eastern homestead model entirely and replace it with pasturage districts on non-irrigable lands. Land units in irrigation districts should not exceed 80 acres, whereas units in pasturage districts should be a minimum of 2,560 acres.

Powell's report came with a bold-faced warning. If Congress failed to move quickly to take ownership of the water that flowed freely over streambeds and into rivers, the West would soon be monopolized by big business. This would create an intolerable set of conditions for the homesteader, conditions that would almost certainly reward his best efforts with failure. Water must be regarded as a commons, like public land. Otherwise, said Powell, the demise of individual homesteaders might quickly grow into a national disaster that would follow a predictable pattern: speculation, water monopoly, land monopoly, erosion, corruption, and widespread bankruptcy.

Having made his appeal on behalf of future homesteaders, Powell remained a hard-eyed pragmatist. He had little faith that Congress would take the steps necessary to preempt the inevitable water wars. His arid lands report was so brilliantly conceived, and such a radical departure from the familiar geometry of eastern land programs, that it was destined to become a leitmotif for congressional behavior throughout the water wars of the twentieth century in the West: identify a problem, commission a report, ignore its recommendations, and by doing so condemn the innocent, naive, and unwitting to demoralization, failure, and bankruptcy.

Without knowing it, Congress had already set Powell's disaster scenario in motion when it passed the Desert Lands Act on March 3, 1877. Among other things, this act established the arid-region doctrine and relied on the law of prior appropriation—an edict with roots in Roman times—to establish and enforce ownership of water in the arid parts of the West, a law that remains in place to this day in many western states. In practical terms, this doctrine held that a farmer who owns the headwaters of a stream could legally divert its cargo into a holding pond and leave his downstream neighbors, with bank foreclosures in hand, gazing at a bed of rocks. Moreover, individually or collectively, downstream farmers would be powerless to stop it. The Desert Lands Act was narrowing the homesteader's odds of success before his two-bottom plow ever cut its first furrow into prairie sod.

Wedged without appeal between a rock and a dry place, first-generation homesteaders abandoned three hundred thousand family farms on the high plains. Climatic realities beyond the hundredth meridian combined with the Desert Lands Act to morph Jefferson's vision of a nation of gentleman farmers from a bucolic mythology into a vast and silent graveyard. Only one out of five homesteaders survived the first three years. At forty below zero, dreams dissolved into fragments of madness as arctic winds howled through the deafening silence of ten thousand kitchens. A writer for the *Atlantic Monthly*, E. V. Smalley, reported that insanity on the Great Plains was more common than the common cold. Scandinavians, by far, were furnishing "the largest contingent to the asylums." Today, bullet-riddled windmills pump sand beside broken-down pickups rusting to air where they ran out of gas seventy years ago. It would take the dust bowl disaster of the 1930s to chasten an intractable Congress, but by then it was too late. Half-hearted measures by long-winded politicians "out East" were not going to restore people in those asylums to sanity or bring back their dreams.

There was nothing harder to kill in Washington than a well-funded bad idea, but the widespread failure of private agricultural enterprises in the West would finally drag a reluctant government into the business of making water. Since turn-of-the-century lawmakers were hesitant to take the blame for the failed policies of an earlier generation, a Congress favorably impressed by the Mormons' successful irrigation projects in the Utah desert finally acted on Powell's long-dormant suggestion, in 1902, by creating the Bureau of Reclamation. The new agency's mission was to bring relief—cheap irrigation—to long-suffering farmers in the Big Empty. In the ensuing decades the Bureau of Reclamation fulfilled its mission with breathtaking efficiency and zeal. Engineers rerouted rivers, such as the Colorado and the Columbia, once thought too wild to tame. They built the largest dams in the world, constructed tens of thousands of reservoirs, and turned millions of sun-baked acres of desert wasteland into landscapes green with vegetables and fruit. Despite these grand successes, the one region that went begging for relief (though not for lack of trying by farmers and politicians) was the million square miles of the northern plains that straddled the Upper Missouri River.

Throughout the 1920s, congressmen from states bordering the Upper Missouri—Colorado, Wyoming, Montana, and the Dakotas—did everything in their power to strong-arm the Bureau of Reclamation into building a region-wide irrigation system. But civilian engineers were every bit as reluctant to tangle with "that mad elephant of a river," as they called it, as their counterparts in the military, the U.S. Army Corps of Engineers, who had not forgotten their own fifty-year battle to keep the river open to steamboat traffic in the 1800s. For half a century, the river scorned the engineers' efforts to protect navigation and commerce with aloof contempt. Its ferocious currents and invisible underwater hazards claimed hundreds of steamboats and thousands of human lives. When railroads ended the age of the paddle-wheeler in the 1880s, the corps reported to Congress that the Missouri River, left to its own demonic devices and lethal hydraulics, could be expected to return to its "former state of uselessness" in short order. For its part, the Army Corps of Engineers intended to let it do just that, cheerfully waving a white flag and moving on to tame rivers it deemed more worthwhile and less formidable.

What the army's engineers said of the river was true enough. None of the West's great rivers were more contemptuous of man's vanity, pride, and industry than the Missouri. This was a river like no other. At times it seemed to be a living thing, with a will and a temper uniquely its own. From Fort Benton, Montana, to St. Charles, Missouri, it defied all efforts to shackle its energy, or predict its moods, with haughty disregard for human life. "Of all the variable things in creation," wrote an editor for the *Sioux City Register*, "the most uncertain are the actions of a jury, the state of a woman's mind, and the condition of the Missouri."

Braided together from the icy yarn of Rocky Mountain runoff near Three Forks, Montana, the Missouri gradually weaves itself together and flows another five hundred miles before joining its partner, the Yellowstone. There its volume suddenly doubles, and the river shakes free of the bluffs and sandstone pillars of the Badlands and bends southward for its long meandering run across the high plains. At 2,540 miles from head to tail, it is the second longest river on the continent, and along the way to its eventual meeting with the Mississippi, a few miles upstream from St. Louis, the Missouri picks up the freight of hundreds of streams and tributaries. Flash floods on any of those tributaries can cause the river's main stem to leap out of its bed at a moment's notice, hundreds of miles away. In fact, the river's upstream antics often had lethal consequences in downstream farm states. A million acre-feet pouring out of the Little Missouri in North Dakota could easily drown schoolchildren in Omaha, or carry away entire towns in Iowa, with little or no warning. It was the hydrologic tantrums of the river's unruly relatives that gave the Big Muddy its reputation for frightening ferocity.

The Army Corps of Engineers agreed to maintain dikes and levees on the lower portion of the river, but when it came to the Upper Missouri, above Sioux City, Iowa, the engineers resisted pleas from politicians and got busy elsewhere. Then came the devastating 1927 floods in Iowa and Missouri, which once again swept away tens of thousands of farm animals, destroyed hundreds of homes, and annihilated crops. Shocked, frustrated, and desperate for answers to these chronic insults, Congress asked the corps to prepare a formal study of the river and to report the findings as soon as possible. Lawmakers were finally running out of patience with this river. They wanted real-world solutions to head off future tragedies.

The Army Corps' chief engineer, General Lytle Brown, viewed this request from Congress as an opportunity to end, once and for all, the senseless hydrologic adventures promoted by Missouri River politicians and farmers. On February 5, 1934, General Brown presented lawmakers with the most comprehensive report ever compiled on an American river. This 1,245-page study, five years in the making, drew a number of unexpected—and dramatic—conclusions. In short, he told Congress that spending taxpayers' money to control floods on the Missouri would be an egregious abuse of public trust. Although hydroelectric facilities might one day be feasible on the lower river, the site often proposed for such a dam, near the Mandan Bluffs, at Garrison, North Dakota, would be unwise from every vantage point. The river's underlying geology, mostly sandstone, would not support a dam large enough to generate hydropower, and furthermore, heavy upstream siltation would be forever compromising the dam's effectiveness. General Brown concluded by saying that the Army Corps of Engineers could not recommend building water projects above the Iowa border. It would be like asking taxpayers to stand in a cold shower and tear up thousand-dollar bills for the next hundred years.

Congress accepted the general's recommendations and tabled the Missouri—until the next catastrophe. The lawmakers didn't have long to wait. In May 1935, a storm struck the Republican River with such ferocity that 105 Nebraskans were swept to their deaths in a matter of minutes. Most of the victims probably never knew what happened. As the bodies were floating toward the Gulf of Mexico, survivors described to the press "a river falling from the sky." Congress responded to the tragedy by passing the Flood Control Act of 1936. This feeble remedy ended up accomplishing little, but it was followed three years later by a more muscular bill, the Reclamation Project Act of 1939, which gave farmers of the high plains the renewed hope that help, in the form of irrigation, was finally on the way.

With the corps' seminal report of 1934 now gathering dust on congressional bookshelves and its well-founded recommendations officially forgotten, the 1939 law, more comprehensive than its predecessors, instructed the Bureau of Reclamation to prepare a new plan that would include flood-control measures on the Upper Missouri. Coincident with this request, the flood-control problem was already being studied by a young engineer in the Bureau of Reclamation's office in Billings, Montana. His name was Glenn Sloan, and as a longtime admirer of John Wesley Powell and an avid student of his work, he was convinced that he had found a way to bring the "mad elephant" to heel.

Once the Reclamation Project Act of 1939 was approved and signed into law by President Franklin D. Roosevelt, Glenn Sloan presented a sketch of his ideas to his superiors at the Bureau of Reclamation office in Billings. They were intrigued. His plan, if it worked, would eventually irrigate two million acres of short-grass prairie. Additionally, it would control flooding on the lower river without incurring the exorbitant expense of building large dams. At the core of Sloan's plan was an organic logic that was brilliant, deceptively simple, and seemed to grow out of the ground itself—not out of a policymakers' briefing book in Washington, D.C. He was a bit of a loner, this Sloan fellow, a freelancing oddball with a talent for provoking the wrath of higher-ups by thumbing his nose at convention, but his idea had great merit. So, without consulting midlevel bureaucrats in Washington where the idea was certain to spend two years in limbo, his superiors gave Sloan the go-ahead to develop his plan.

Sloan brought enthusiasm, diligence, and know-how to the project. He had driven the length of the river in his car and had studied the army engineers' 1934 report backward and forward. Between its stiff dusty covers was a treasure of information: flow rates, porosity and evaporation tables, data and stream profiles on hundreds of tributaries, all valuable information he would need to complete his own plan. Soon, word filtered up through channels to Harold L. Ickes himself, President Roosevelt's good friend and secretary of the interior, that an engineer in Billings was drafting a promising solution to their Missouri River woes. But when the Japanese attacked Pearl Harbor on December 7, 1941, all of the pent-up urgency in Congress about the Missouri vanished overnight. Undaunted, Sloan pressed ahead and was nearly finished with the master plan when Mother Nature again proclaimed her dominion over the frail endeavors of humanity. In the spring of 1943, a unique convergence of climatic events unleashed a trio of back-to-back hundred-year floods on the lower Missouri River.

At first, nothing about the March deluge over the Midwest seemed that unusual. A low-pressure system drifted north from the Gulf of Mexico just as warm Chinook winds brought a sudden thaw to the northern plains states, a thousand miles upstream from Omaha. Rapidly melting snow in the Rocky Mountains had already pushed the Upper Missouri over its banks, but downstream this wasn't a problem. The swollen river was easily contained by hundreds of miles of levees that had been built up over the previous thirty years by the Army Corps of Engineers.

Then came the downpour. The first flood breached levees in Iowa and inundated river towns as well as thousands of acres of low-lying farmland. The next flood, in late May, swept entire towns down the river and dumped them into the Gulf of Mexico. Farm animals from Nebraska came to rest on courthouse lawns and in treetops in Baton Rouge and New Orleans. When the river crested a third time, in early June, millions of acres of farmland and hundreds of towns, including Omaha, Nebraska, and Sioux City, Iowa, disappeared underwater.

An incensed Congress vowed that this was the last time it would be humbled by the Big Muddy. President Roosevelt put out an urgent call to the federal government's two water agencies, the Bureau of Reclamation (responsible for irrigation and hydroelectric generation) and the Army Corps of Engineers (charged with flood control and navigation) to come up with a plan that would end this river's tyranny once and for all. The nation was fighting Hitler in Europe and Tojo in the Pacific. What its leaders wouldn't tolerate was another enemy in its midst.

Glenn Sloan's unfinished master plan was presented to President Roosevelt by Harold Ickes himself. After studying the nascent scheme, Ickes had concluded that it exuded brilliance because at its heart lay the genius of John Wesley Powell. By constructing eighty-nine small- to medium-sized reservoirs across the entire breadth of the river basin, just as Powell had recommended, the impoundments could collect fifteen million acre-feet of water, the average annual flow of the Colorado— more than twice the amount of storage needed to prevent floods on the lower Missouri—and put the Missouri's tributaries out of the business of killing people. As an added benefit, the redistributed groundwater would stabilize fifty-three thousand existing farms on the northern plains and increase crop values by an estimated $130 million a year. Profits, in turn, would increase the region's farm population by 250,000. Capturing water in Sloan's constellation of collection basins before it reached the river's main stem would help to "desilt" the Missouri and arrest the ever escalating costs of dredging for downstream navigation.

President Roosevelt was an instant convert and enthusiastic supporter of the Sloan Plan. It had many things in common with his pet project, the Tennessee Valley Authority, a creative hydrologic brainstorm that had brought flood control and cheap hydroelectric power to the entire southeastern United States. But unknown to either man, Sloan's scheme was secretly being preempted in Congress by a hot-tempered autocrat in the Army Corps of Engineers by the name of Colonel Lewis Pick. Pick, who had been severely reprimanded just two years earlier for botching the construction of an airfield, had since been reassigned to the corps' Omaha office to do professional penance and ponder his transgressions. As the floodwaters rose in the streets outside his office at the height of the March flood, the diminutive colonel leaped onto a desk and bellowed to his subordinates, "I want control of the Missouri!" He then commanded every engineer in the office to drop all other projects at once, and to work double shifts until they came up with a comprehensive plan to tame the Big Muddy.

In contrast to the Sloan Plan, Pick's proposal, a scant ten pages long when it was secretly distributed to Congress by the corps' director, General Raymond A. Wheeler, called for the construction of twenty-five hundred miles of new levees, fourteen catchments, and five major dams. To accomplish the engineering feats envisioned by Pick and Wheeler,

Congress would have to condemn many hundreds of thousands of acres of prime agricultural bottom land along the river and many of its tributaries. The fact that most of the proposed "takings land" was owned by Indians and held in permanent trust for the tribes by the federal government was a legal conundrum that Pick and Wheeler temporarily finessed, emphasizing instead the plan's high-value selling points. The dams, rising across the continent's high plains like stair steps, would transform the river's main stem into a series of enormous reservoirs. The crown jewel of Pick's plan, surrounded by a cluster of smaller baubles, would be set at the Mandan Bluffs, near Garrison, North Dakota. Four miles wide at the crown and 220 feet high, the completed multipurpose dam would be the largest rolled earth structure in the world, equivalent to twenty Giza pyramids. The five dams proposed by Pick would at long last put the forces of the imperious Missouri under human control.

As soon as he got wind of Wheeler's legerdemain, Secretary Ickes launched an all-out attack on the corps' preemptive plan. He started by accusing its mastermind of having a legendary reputation for arrogance, and of making dismissive remarks about the Sloan Plan that revealed "an obduracy that is beyond belief." At best, charged Ickes, Colonel Pick's proposal was half-baked and professionally negligent. Roosevelt agreed, though in less strident terms, and told Congress that the plan was too sketchy and vague in its current form and seemed to have purposefully left important questions unanswered. Flowage estimates, for example, were entirely missing from its calculations, as were tables calculating the rates of power generation. Personally, he told them, he would like to see another Tennessee Valley Authority on the Missouri. In addition to bringing effective flood control to the southeastern states, TVA dams had efficiently transformed the taxpayers' money into an abundant source of cheap electricity that was owned and distributed from a public trust, the Tennessee Valley Authority. It was a proven winner.

States' rights groups immediately mounted campaigns against what they called "the specter of an MVA," a Missouri Valley Authority. Despite the TVA's widely heralded success, political conservatives lambasted the scheme as a socialist boondoggle and were determined not to concede any more authority over the nation's rivers to the federal government (even though the government—that is, the people—owned the water). The TVA had proven to be a formidable bulwark against the privatization of public resources. Attempts to break the government's monopoly on southeastern rivers and to privatize electric utilities had failed. While this political storm was raging in the back rooms of state capitols, the president learned that Colonel Pick had upstaged him by meeting privately with influential members of the Missouri River States Commission. Roosevelt was furious. Without consulting Ickes, he called an impromptu meeting with the press and accused the corps of attempting to make national policy independent of Congress and the White House. Here was an indication of just how rancorous the war at home was about to become.

As lawmakers acquainted themselves with the particulars of each plan in the months that followed, a public relations battle between the two agencies reached feverish intensity. By the late summer of 1944, both plans had won staunch advocates. Upstream politicians favored the Sloan Plan, while downstream states formed a solid bloc behind Colonel Pick. The National Farmers' Union, always suspicious of the army engineers' inclination to put navigation ahead of irrigation, backed the Sloan Plan as the economically sensible approach. Two senators from Wyoming and Colorado, Joseph O'Mahoney and Eugene Milliken, threatened to block the entire Flood Control Act of 1944 in committee unless the lower states agreed to make irrigation a priority over navigation. The lower states, backed by powerful lobbyists in the transportation industry, fought back, but O'Mahoney and Milliken had enough seniority to make the threat stick. It was finally agreed, over Pick's objections, that in low-flow years the irrigation needs of upstream farmers would trump the desires of barge owners downstream. Despite this compromise, months wore on as enthusiasm in Congress faded first to ambivalence, then to stalemate. Somehow, lawmakers had worked themselves into the very position they sought to avoid—hostages to competing water bills and two fiercely competitive agencies. It was a contest tailor-made for the feisty Ickes, who sharpened his attacks as the struggle wore on by accusing the corps of being "a willful, self-serving clique in contempt of the public welfare." To a degree that was unconscionable, said Ickes, the corps had grown accustomed to spending money faster, and with greater waste, than any agency in the history of the country. "No more lawless or irresponsible group than the Army Corps of Engineers has ever attempted to operate in the United States either outside of, or within, the law. It is truly beyond imagination."

But Colonel Pick, a fearless operator in the corridors of power, believed he had a trump card that would tip the public relations war in his favor. As lawmakers dug out from under a blizzard of acrimonious letters from ill-informed midlevel bureaucrats and politicians in Missouri River states, Pick went on the offensive by portraying the Missouri as a great unused highway that could easily bring long-desired economic vitality to the nation's ailing midsection. He had proof to show that approving the Sloan Plan would be an inexcusable waste of taxpayers' money. If members of Congress would look closer at the corps' proposal, they would quickly realize that the bulk of the "land takings" on the Upper Missouri would be borne by Indians. The Sloan Plan, by contrast, would take most of its land from white farmers and ranchers. In other words, the cost for the five big dams would be carried by twenty-three Indian nations, not the legislators' constituents.

Almost all of the tribes that stood to lose land to the corps' plan, from the Northern Cheyenne and the Crow at Lame Deer and Lodgegrass to the Assiniboin, Blackfeet, Arikara, Hidatsa, Mandan, and Sioux, from Wolf Point to Standing Rock, were signatories to the Treaty of Fort Laramie, the result of a peace council in 1851 that formally recognized the Indians' ownership of more than a million square miles of the Great Plains. If the land owned by individual tribes could be assembled into a monolithic block, it would comprise most of the Louisiana Purchase, plus another two hundred thousand square miles of land once owned by the Spanish and the English. Of the eight hundred square miles of bottomlands slated to disappear beneath the new reservoirs, whites owned less than 8 percent. All of the white communities on the river had been carefully spared inundation. The cost for taking the Indian lands, as opposed to the white lands that would be taken by the Sloan Plan, should tip the debate in the corps' favor.

As an engineer, Colonel Pick failed to appreciate the legal paradox he had just illuminated. In fact, many of the legislators had been wrestling with the question of Indian lands since the passage of the Reclamation Project Act of 1939. The federal government had a solemn trust relationship with all of the tribes on the Missouri, but it was not at all clear who exactly held title to the treaty-protected Indian lands. Much of that territory had been cut up into little squares, or "checkerboarded," by homesteading acts and executive orders in the late 1800s. If Congress, the Indians' trustee, attempted to take that land away under eminent domain, would it be in violation of its constitutional obligations? How could the government legally square the taking of six hundred square miles of Indian lands with its solemn fiduciary responsibilities to the tribes' well-being? And assuming that knot could be cut, who, then, would decide what that land was worth?

These questions animated committee rooms and private conversations throughout the months of 1944, but since Congress was high-centered between the two proposals, lawmakers were content to finesse the task of divining definitive answers for another day. In the meantime, another long-avoided moment finally arrived. The congressional deadlock forced Roosevelt to play King Solomon, but even the president faltered. Rather than cut the infant in half, he called Secretary Ickes and General Wheeler into his office and told them to come up with a compromise that could act as a centerpiece for the Flood Control Act of 1944. And remember, he cautioned, the expense of building Hoover Dam had nearly bankrupted the treasury. The corps' plan alone would be the equivalent of *five* Hoover dams. Adopting either plan was going to put a generation of American citizens in debt before they were even born. Therefore, above all else, the compromise needed to be a sober-minded, fiscally responsible blending of the two proposals.

Ickes nominated Glenn Sloan to negotiate the compromise for the Bureau of Reclamation. No one was more familiar with every line item and nuance of the 211-page proposal than its principal architect. Sloan made the five-hundred-mile flight from Billings to Omaha on October 15, 1944. Pick was in absentia, having been sent to Burma to finish the Ledo Road, but his surrogates had promised to fight for every item in the corps' proposal. The meeting began on schedule at 9 a.m., and before the attendees had halted for their first break at midmorning, each side recognized its own obstinacy in the other's position. With nothing to lose and everything to gain by digging in their heels, as they worked their way through the projects it became clear that neither side was going to concede a single drop of water. By midafternoon, they agreed to "reconcile" the two plans and send "it" back to Congress.

No attempt was made in Omaha to consolidate line items, or justify costs. Of the 113 proposed water projects, 110 survived the "compromise." The two schemes were simply added together into one. Colonel Pick had somehow persuaded Congress to ignore the scientific findings of his own agency, convincing the legislators instead to make Garrison Dam the key to flood control for the entire Missouri River. The resulting "Pick-Sloan Compromise" was signed into law by President Roosevelt on December 22, hailed as the largest public works project in the nation's history. It would take twenty years to build, and its projected price tag, $2.5 billion, would double three times. Two hundred feet below the surface of Pick-Sloan's showcase reservoir, Lake Sakakawea, sat Louise Holding Eagle's farm and the entire town of Elbowoods.

The day after the bill was signed into law, the president of the National Farmers' Union, James Patton, certain that the corps would begin construction of a big dam and ignore the pressing needs of farmers, told the press that the government had just performed a "shameless, loveless shotgun wedding" on the Upper Missouri. And like all such marriages, promised Patton, this one was destined to end in disaster.

TWO

Savages and Scoundrels

As waterlogged citizens of Iowa and Nebraska were mopping up and counting livestock in the days that followed the March flood of 1943, an Army Air Corps enlistee named Martin Cross was headed home to Elbowoods on a Greyhound bus from his training camp in the state of Washington. It was a two-day trip from downtown Seattle to the one-room café and bus depot in the railspur community of Garrison, North Dakota. Martin Cross stepped down off the bus into a beautiful spring day. He threw his duffel over his shoulder and walked the five blocks to the U.S. Post Office, then waited for a ride on the afternoon mail truck to take him the last forty miles home.

In the patriotic aftermath of Pearl Harbor, Martin Old Dog had been one of 280 men from the Three Affiliated Tribes to enlist in the armed forces. Fearful that his name would be an embarrassment or make him the butt of jokes in the rank and file, a few days before he left he stopped by the tribal court and changed it from the Hidatsa surname of his father, a revered chief and judge, to the Anglo-Saxon sounding Cross. "A lot of guys in Dad's generation thought that was the best way to close the gap between the Indian and the white man," says Martin's son Alfred, a college history professor in San Jose, California. "It's a real insight into their thinking, because that would never happen today."

In order to enlist from Elbowoods, young men like Martin Cross had to walk, ride a horse, or hitch a lift to Garrison on the mail truck, then hop on a bus the following day for the 250-mile drive to the nearest enlistment center, in Fargo. For many, leaving home to fight in World

War II was their first adventure "on top," in the white man's world. They left behind nine communities where everyone spoke a native language and subsisted on barter, and entered a foreign English-speaking world where the coin of the realm jangled in their pockets. In a number of respects, the exigencies of war lifted many reservation tribes, including the Crow, Sioux, Arapaho, Navajo, and Cheyenne, out of the cultural isolation that had carried over from the nineteenth century. The census of 1940 found that the Three Affiliated Tribes had grown from a low of 960 members, in 1900, to 1,854, a number not seen since the smallpox epidemic of 1837 killed many tens of thousands of native people on the high plains. With most of their families still dependent on a subsistence economy for sustenance and well-being, the sudden departure of so many men placed a heavy burden on the women and children they left behind.

"That was the toughest year of our childhoods," remembers Martin's eldest son, Crusoe. "Going to bed hungry when it's thirty below zero outside, after you've hauled coal on a sled all afternoon, isn't something you ever forget."

The house they lived in was built by their grandfather, Old Dog, and sat on a block-and-sill foundation at the end of a country lane about a mile from town. With neither indoor plumbing nor electricity, it was a twelve-hundred-square-foot clapboard dwelling with a hip roof, single-pane windows, and a copper wire that ran from an RCA radio in the living room to a windmill beside the stock tank. Most nights that wire would pull in Louis Armstrong from New York City, or their mom's favorite, the Carter Family Singers broadcast from a 100,000-watt border station at Del Rio, Texas. But this was a rare "luxury." Martin's sudden departure for the war left his wife, Dorothy—a dark-haired, high-spirited only child of Norwegian immigrants—alone to raise their five school-age children, with a toddler balanced on each hip and an eighth child bulging under her apron. After getting the kids dressed and fed and out the door to school every morning, Dorothy had the hay fields and two acres of garden to plant, the animals to feed, doctor, and butcher, crops to harvest and can, and meals to cook after she split wood for her kitchen stove. Despite the wartime hardships, the enlistment widows harvested record crops while their men were away, and the default rate on federal loans to farming wives of the Three Affiliated Tribes was the lowest in the nation. But as the birth of their eighth child approached, Dorothy wrote to Martin that she thought his warrior days were over. He needed to come home and help her raise their family and operate the ranch.

Martin received her letter just days before he was scheduled to ship out for his first overseas post. When his commanding officer discovered that the tall, soft-spoken, broad-shouldered airman from North Dakota had a wife and seven children back home, Martin Cross was immediately issued a hardship discharge, slapped on the back, and driven to the nearest bus station.

As things turned out, when he hopped off the mail truck in Elbowoods and started down the road on the last mile home, Martin's warrior days had not ended. They had just begun. He was no sooner home than elders started dropping by the house, urging him to run for tribal chairman in the upcoming elections. Something was afoot out in the world beyond the valley bottoms, they told him. The *Sanish Sentinel* newspaper had recently published a story, longer on rumors than facts, that told of government engineers poking around the Mandan Bluffs by the river near Garrison. A few weeks later, the *Sentinel* raised more questions than it could answer, with a headline reading "A Dam Question," and then ruefully confessed that "there was big news in the air . . . but we cannot get at it." The elders, however, sensed that something of consequence was brewing behind these headlines, and if history was a guide, whatever that might be was likely going to affect the tribes.

Martin shrugged off their prodding invitations with good-natured laughter. Week by week, the pressure to step into the shoes vacated by his father's death fifteen years before eroded his resistance. When the war finally ended and the boys came home, "they came walking in over the hills, or down State Road Number 8," remembers Crusoe, "with a duffel on their shoulder and pockets full of cash." For the first time in the history of the three tribes, the men all spoke English when they gathered on the town square. They read newspapers, had hard currency in their billfolds, and were well acquainted with the world "on top." At thirty-eight, Martin Cross was seen by young and old members alike as a man with one foot in the traditional world and one in the future.

Just as they had in 1781, tribal elders recognized that the world had changed. Like it or not, the future was upon them. The ethnocentric isolation of Chief Old Dog's era had protected them from the cultural ravages that devastated many other tribes early in the twentieth century. Those tragedies had been well documented in the now famous Meriam Report of 1928, the first official investigation ever conducted into living conditions in Indian country. Investigators for the Institute for Government Research concluded that the Dawes Act of 1887, and subsequent homesteading acts made both by Congress and by executive order, had been disastrous for the tribes. Indians had been neither set free from reservation-induced cycles of poverty, as lawmakers had predicted, nor assimilated into white society. The fact was, all things Indian had not gone according to plan. Lawmakers voting for homestead acts in the 1870s and '80s could not have imagined, much less seen the need for, a Meriam Report half a century later. At that time, the government's commissioner of Indian affairs, Amasa Walker, spoke for most Americans and their elected officials when he declared in his 1872 annual report to Congress: "What shall be done about the Indian as an obstacle to the progress of settlement and industry? He is a recognized evil, and never was an evil so gigantically environed, invaded, devoured by forces so tremendous, so appalling in the celerity and the certainty of their advance. They must now either yield or perish . . . because they occupy a position altogether barbarous and incompatible with civilization and social progress."

Like Walker, lawmakers of the day imagined the Indian race to be in its final days of fast-fading glory. The only disquieting question in the minds of congressmen was how many white people would perish as the Indian's swan song was playing out. There existed little doubt in Washington that century's end would find the Indians either vanquished or, for those few that survived, assimilated. Gone would be the formidable nuisance of Chief Justice John Marshall's federal trust doctrine, the legal fiction devised in the first decades of the century to formalize the government's binding partnership with sovereign "domestic dependent nations" living in its midst. Gone would be the tedious and cumbersome obligations Congress had solemnly assumed through ratified treaties with 371 tribes. Hoping to hasten that day, Congress approved the Dawes Act in 1887 and, concluded the Meriam Report, sanctioned the theft of hundreds of millions of acres of treaty-protected land. Along with that act, and in violation of the establishment clause in the Constitution separating church and state, lawmakers also approved the Indian Religious Crimes Code, a law inspired by Methodist missionaries forbidding Indians from performing their traditional religious ceremonies. The U.S. government also gave missionaries license to abduct Indian children from their parents' homes and ship them away to boarding schools. This was all done, said the Meriam investigators, in hopes of "killing the Indian to save the man."

The findings detailed in the Meriam Report resulted in a public fury concerning the plight of the Indians, and the Roosevelt administration seized the opportunity. Formulated by the new commissioner of Indian affairs, John Collier, the Indian Reorganization Act of 1934 sailed through Congress uncontested. Early in 1936, the Three Affiliated Tribes were among the first in the nation to disavow the chronic failures of federal paternalism, and to turn about and face the modern era. Overwhelmingly, natives embraced Collier's invitation to embark on a return to self-governance by adopting a tribal constitution, with the guidance of Collier's brilliant Indian law attorney, Felix Cohen.

By the time the end of World War II drew near, the Mandan, Hidatsa, and Arikara tribal government was intact and growing stronger, and the elders believed the tribes were ready for the next step forward. Martin Cross, the generous and outgoing successful cattle rancher and son of Old Dog, was the man to help take them there. Long lines of leaders distinguished both sides of Martin's family. The names in his family's lore reached back into the mists of time. His great-grandfather Cherry Necklace, the legendary chief who had captured a young Shoshone girl named Bird Woman, or Sakakawea, and brought her back to the Knife River, later decided to send the war chief Four Bears with Father Pierre De Smet to treat with representatives of the Great White Fathers at the Fort Laramie Peace Council of 1851. The resulting Treaty of Fort Laramie, also known as the Horse Creek treaty, formally recognized the three tribes' aboriginal title to twelve million acres of land from the Yellowstone to the Missouri. Now, these many years later, after their lands had been reduced by successive acts of Congress to less than a million acres, Cherry Necklace's great-grandson Martin Cross was stepping into his forefather's shoes. Crusoe remembers those years as a lonely and difficult time for his father. After dinner he would sing the little children to sleep with Hidatsa lullabies. Then, Crusoe would see the ember of his father's cigarette where he sat in the moonlight on the back porch, playing Hoagy Carmichael's "Stardust" on his tenor sax.

"He was in that first group of our leaders to realize that the American Indian was at a crossroads," says Crusoe. "Dad knew it, but knowing didn't make it any less lonely. It wasn't an easy thing being Martin Cross."

As committees in Congress were polishing the final version of the Flood Control Act of 1944 for President Roosevelt's signature, Martin Cross was sworn in as the new chairman of the Three Affiliated Tribes at the tribal offices in Elbowoods. In the weeks since the October elections, details of the federal government's plans had started leaking out to communities on the Upper Missouri. By the time the geese headed south and the first snows streaked across the plains, it was all the talk in cafés and bars, from Minot to Bismarck, that nine Indian communities —Elbowoods, Nishu, Charging Eagle, Lucky Mound, Shell Creek, Red Butte, Independence, Beaver Creek, and Square Butte—would be inundated under a lake created by a new dam to be built at Garrison. Along with those communities would vanish 156,000 acres of the most productive farm and ranch land on the Great Plains.

Although it was true that the natives were not entirely ignorant of what was happening in Washington, it was also true that no one from the Army Corps of Engineers, the Department of the Interior, or the Bureau of Reclamation ever contacted the tribes or bothered to inform their leadership about what was coming. If there was any truth to the rumors circulating in white communities "on top," Martin Cross knew there was no time to waste in mounting a defense. A few weeks after Cross was sworn in, he called the new governor of North Dakota, Fred Aandahl, and requested a meeting. The encounter in Bismarck was brief, sobering, and one-sided. The two men were no sooner seated than Governor Aandahl made a peremptory declaration. He knew why Martin had come to see him, but it would do no good. His appeals would be wasted words. The governor was foursquare behind the corps' plan to build a dam at Garrison, and he recommended that the new tribal chairman accept the outcome as inevitable and start making plans to move the tribes to new homes "on top."

Martin Cross drove home a chastened but wiser man. Arriving back in Elbowoods, he sent a telegram to William Brophy, President Roosevelt's new commissioner of Indian affairs, telling him: "We Indians on the Fort Berthold Reservation oppose the construction of the Garrison Dam one-hundred percent. Can you come and conference with us?"

Commissioner Brophy declined the invitation, citing scheduling conflicts, but he realized that due to all the bureaucratic shuffling and legislative turmoil caused by the Pick-Sloan Plan, something had gone awry.

After consulting his own letter book, and then those of his agents in the field, Brophy's suspicions were confirmed. He quickly dictated a letter to Senator O'Mahoney, the chairman of the Senate Select Committee on Indian Affairs, to alert him to the bureaucratic bungling that had prompted the urgent telegram from Cross. Apparently, no one in the government had ever bothered to inform the Three Affiliated Tribes about Pick-Sloan. These people, thousands of them, were about to lose their world and everything in it. Something, in the name of human decency, had to be done.

Commissioner Brophy made two copies of the letter to O'Mahoney; one he kept for his files, and the other he sent to Chairman Cross. With it he enclosed a personal note advising Cross to work with sympathetic senators on O'Mahoney's Indian committee. Since President Roosevelt's recent death, Brophy confessed to being distracted by an unexpected battle of a different nature. The president had no sooner died than western Republicans launched a full-scale offensive against the Bureau of Indian Affairs. Hearings were set to begin on the removal of federal protection from tribal trust lands on reservations across the West. In Brophy's opinion, this was the same sort of sinister business that seemed to be promulgated by private business and state governments at least once a generation. Here it was again, a thinly veiled attack on the legal bulwarks that held Indian-owned resources in trust, such as timber, gold, uranium, copper, silver, and coal. Brophy suspected correctly that the ultimate aim of these congressmen was to dismantle the bureau altogether. With apologies, there was nothing more he could do, and he wished Cross the best of luck.

If the meeting with Governor Aandahl was sobering, the letter from Commissioner Brophy sent shock waves through the tribal council. Their ace in the hole, their point man in Washington, the commissioner of Indian affairs, had surrendered before the battle was even begun. After absorbing this news and pondering the tribes' options, Cross called a meeting of the council and proposed a bold new strategy. It was something unthinkable for an Indian, a tactic unheard of in recent memory, but since they had lost their principal ally in Washington, they should attack Colonel Pick on his own ground. They should go to Washington and make the case themselves. The council's approval was unanimous.

"Not one of those guys had a stitch of clothes he could wear to a hearing in Congress," remembers Crusoe. "Dad and I drove all over the country in our old green truck, going from church to church, digging through mission barrels for suits, hats, shoes, shirts, and socks, anything we could find to make those guys look halfway presentable in Washington."

The Empire Builder passenger train left daily from the Northern Pacific station in Minot, connecting dozens of small farming communities across the upper Midwest to Fargo, Minneapolis, Chicago, and finally, three days later, to Washington, D.C. Eager to make their guests feel at home in the big city, Secretary Ickes and his assistant solicitor general, Felix Cohen, met the four-member contingent from Elbowoods at Union Station, then escorted them to the New Ebbits Hotel, at Tenth and H streets, within walking distance of Capitol Hill. Cohen, a thirty-seven-year-old Jewish lawyer from New York and a rising star in the secretary's inner circle, held a doctorate in philosophy from Harvard and a law degree from Columbia, and had recently published the *Handbook of Federal Indian Law*, a legal opus written at the request of his boss. At 10:25 a.m. on October 9, 1945, the bespectacled Cohen held open the door to hearing room 424 of the Senate Office Building, then followed Martin Cross and the three tribal councilmen in to face O'Mahoney's Senate Select Committee on Indian Affairs.

The committee chairman rapped the gavel as the minute hand struck twelve, and opened the hearing. O'Mahoney, the senior senator from Colorado, was a powerful, trench-hardened veteran of many Depression-era legislative battles on Capitol Hill. As his adversaries had discovered during the wrangling over irrigation and navigation in the Pick-Sloan

Plan, he was not a man to be trifled with. Officially, this hearing was scheduled at the request of the Three Affiliated Tribes, who had sent their leaders to Washington with a message: "Garrison Dam, the construction of which is embodied in the engineering plan for the development of the Missouri River . . . will, if constructed, take or inundate 221,000 acres of Indian lands in violation of the treaty between the United States and these Indians." Off the record, Congress viewed the hearing as a polite formality conducted to humor the complainants. Cross raised his right hand and promised to tell the truth and then took his seat and listened while the chairman made a brief statement outlining the purpose of the hearing. The senator welcomed the tribal councilors who had traveled all this way from Elbowoods to have their day in court, so to speak, and then noted for the record the presence of Felix Cohen, solicitor for the Department of the Interior, also acting as counsel to the Indians. Then, as the committee stenographer's finger came expectantly to rest on the keys of her recorder, O'Mahoney turned to the prepossessing Indian seated before him and invited him to speak.

"Mr. Chairman, Senators," began Martin Cross, "the Corps of Engineers seems to think that the Indian land in the flooded area can be acquired by eminent domain, if necessary. We question the legality of this process on the grounds that the treaty law between the United States government and the Indians is binding, and not subject to eminent domain. Since I have no legal talent I must rely on others to interpret these legal points. I want to come out openly against the construction of the Garrison Dam, not only from the legal standpoint but from destructiveness and the setback of our Indian people. I believe that this group of men, composing this honorable body, are adamant foes of abuse and, being such, that they will not permit the Army engineers to carry out their program, their plan."

Senator O'Mahoney gently interrupted, asking Cross to clarify a point. Was Cross saying that the dam, if constructed, would flood a large amount of their land? That was correct, said Chairman Cross. And what is the character of that land, asked O'Mahoney, leading Cross to his next appeal. Cross explained that this was the best farming land on the Great Plains, and that the tribe would lose 95 percent of its homes.

O'Mahoney scribbled a note to himself, then shot a glance at Felix Cohen before returning to Chairman Cross.

"Do these Indians raise agricultural crops?"

"We raise spring wheat, oats, corn, potatoes, squash, beans, and a little alfalfa. We have a thriving cattle cooperative."

"And how much of your land do you use for grazing?"

"Well, I would say out of the six hundred thousand acres, about half of it is used for grazing."

"I see. What is the value of this land, per acre? Have you any idea?"

"I'm not permitted to say that," said Cross. "In my personal opinion, I would say around $150 per acre. But we're not here on the question of selling our land. We want to keep it."

"You say you were not permitted. By whom?"

"We're not here on the question of selling our land. We want to keep it."

A murmur rippled through the audience. The committee chairman adjusted his glasses on the bridge of his nose as he pondered the impasse.

"You mean . . . the Indians did not want to disclose the value of their land?"

"That's right!"

Senator William Langer of North Dakota, growing more frustrated by the minute, now blurted a question: "It's not for sale at all?"

"That's right," said Cross with a steady voice. "Senator, with all due respect, I am not here to sell land. Again, I am here to keep it."

"How long have your ancestors been living there?" asked Langer.

"From time immemorial we have been living there," answered Cross.

At this point Senator O'Mahoney turned his attention from the tribal chairman and asked the committee's counsel, Mr. Cohen, for an explanation of the corps' rationale for building the dam and a brief review of its costs. After the committee heard a sketchy reappraisal of the corps' approach to flood control on the Missouri River, the committee's chairman pinched the bridge of his nose, took a moment to absorb what he had just heard, then trained his eyes on Felix Cohen.

"Nothing can be done to dispossess these Indians without a formal taking of this land," stated the senator.

"It raises pretty much a legal question," interjected Senator E. H. Moore of Oklahoma.

"Well, considering the general disregard of Indian rights, which has characterized our dealings with Indians, I think it's a very important question," said O'Mahoney in a tone that had turned from lightly inquisitive to grave. He knew his committee was about to broach that thorny unresolved question about all those little squares, those checkerboard lands on the Great Plains that Congress had been so careful to finesse during the hearings on Pick-Sloan. "At this point, I think I'd like to hear from Mr. Cohen on the question of treaties, and the federal trust responsibilities, et cetera. Mr. Cohen? You're the expert in these matters. Please . . ."

Felix Cohen rose, pledged to tell the truth, and then took a seat beside Martin Cross. He looked at each of the committee members, individually, before beginning.

"Mister Chairman, members of the committee, these Indians were at their present location one hundred forty years ago, when Lewis and Clark went through that country," he began. "Their ownership of this land has been formally recognized and ratified by this body, the United States Congress, in the treaty made at the peace council near Fort Laramie, at Horse Creek, in 1851. On the specific question of eminent domain, the fact is, regardless of whatever moral obligations we may have with respect to the homes of the Indians, Congress has the authority to condemn allotted [privately owned] lands."

However, he added, this was not an end point in this discussion, but rather a beginning. "That's why the business of treaties gets so sticky," said Cohen. He then explained that Congress had made a very bad decision when it turned its back on John Marshall's trust doctrine, in the 1880s, and opened Indian lands to private ownership by both Indians and whites. The Dawes Act, passed by Congress in 1887, effectively divided the ownership and legal status of aboriginal territory into three categories: private land owned by Indians, private land owned by whites, and lands held in trust for the tribes by the federal government. As a result, the three kinds of titles were now hopelessly intermingled in what was formerly looked upon as the exclusive domain of the Indian.

"You see," said Cohen, "Congress can condemn privately owned land. It doesn't need anyone's permission to do that. It doesn't need to go to the courts, or obtain permission from the owners. It can just take it. But that's not the case we're discussing. What is at stake here are trust lands, and Congress cannot take trust lands." As trustee for those lands, Cohen explained, Congress had a fiduciary duty to the owners that superseded its plenary power to abrogate treaties under extraordinary circumstances. Trust lands were protected by virtue of the government's solemn agreements with the tribes, agreements protected by the U.S. Constitution as "the supreme law of the land."

"Which is the whole problem here," said Senator Moore, with mounting exasperation. "We can't very well inundate allotted lands without inundating trust lands, can we?"

"No sir. As far as I've been able to determine," said Cohen, "Congress has never authorized condemnation of tribal trust lands. It's just not legally possible."

Each member of the Senate Select Committee on Indian Affairs was a lawyer. To varying degrees, each was well versed in the arcane world of federal Indian law, though none could claim the expertise of the man sitting before them. O'Mahoney's committee knew that the U.S. Supreme Court had always held Congress and the president to the highest fiduciary standards in their dealings with Indian tribes. Therefore, the taking was not possible because Congress would run into a dead end when it followed the logic of its legal justifications back to King George III, whose preemptive rights over Indian lands had passed to the new American government at the end of the Revolutionary War. Given that legal encumbrance, the federal government could make this "taking" only by sawing through one of the load-bearing beams supporting the house of democracy—its fiduciary responsibilities to the descendants of the treaty makers.

Members of O'Mahoney's committee were keenly aware of a series of high-court decisions from the late nineteenth and early twentieth centuries that had set clear benchmarks and bright lines for Congress to follow when navigating the metaphorical wilderness of federal Indian law. Since treaties were written in the language of the white man, they should always be interpreted as the Indians themselves would have understood them. The high court also ruled that ambiguous expressions of language should always be resolved in favor of the tribe's descendants. Whenever duty to the public threw Congress into conflict with its fiduciary responsibility to the tribes, the interests of the former should be set aside in order to fulfill the superior trust obligation to the Indians.

Before his death in 1953, at the age of forty-six, Cohen would write an epigram that has since become a monument of words to these same principles: "Like the miner's canary," he reminded Congress, "the Indian marks the shifts from fresh air to poison gas in our political atmosphere; and our treatment of Indians, even more than our treatment of other minorities, reflects the rise and fall in our democratic faith."

Now, the stenographer's fingers tapped out Felix Cohen's final words, "not legally possible," then paused on the keys. She took a deep breath, reassembled her ankles beneath the chair, then scanned the room in the awkward silence, glancing from face to face. Felix Cohen had dared to lay bare the unmentionable enigma that had confounded lawmakers since 1776. How could the federal government take trust lands it was sworn, as a trustee, to protect, and then, as if by magic, turn that land into public domain? Beyond the obvious legal imperatives, in 1851, Congress assumed a moral obligation to these tribes that was annealed in time and anchored by words laden with sacred meaning on which the republic had been founded. The metronomic insinuations of a clock, a muffled sneeze, the tapping of counsel's pencil, punctuated a silence that held fast to the question that could not be spoken. But this was the knot that must be cut, the very question that bedeviled the republic's Founders. If, by building these dams on the Missouri we willfully violate our most sacred trust as a republic in order to secure a material objective of our exclusive desires and self-interests, who are we after that choosing? What is this stuff that we are made of, as a nation, as a people?

"Thank you, Chairman Cross, Mr. Cohen. At this time," said Senator O'Mahoney, giving the gavel a sharp rap, "this committee will stand adjourned."

In her 1994 memoir, *True North*, historian Jill Ker Conway recalled with bemused astonishment that the debates among eighteenth-century political theorists about human nature were entirely absent from her undergraduate studies back home in Australia. Her stodgy Anglophile professors, she decided, must have been reluctant to guide young minds through the treacherous shoal waters of human nature, so they steered around it altogether. It was only by crossing the Pacific Ocean to attend graduate school at Harvard that the future president of Smith College learned "that [Enlightenment-era] political institutions were derived from a definition of the human predicament, a predicament from which the state or the ruler might [or might not] offer release."

Pluck and curiosity led Conway to encounter the Big Question that had energized political debates in the public houses of Boston, Williamsburg, and Philadelphia throughout the enervating months leading up to the Constitutional Convention in the summer of 1787: *Once freed from the manacles of despots and monarchs, who are we? What is our nature?*

Divining an answer to such a question from the checkered history of their European ancestors was roughly equivalent to predicting a baby elephant's behavior in the wild by watching its mother performing tricks under a circus big-top. A century before, John Locke had attempted a similar trick when he published his revolutionary ideas on the intersection of human nature and civil government in two landmark works: *An Essay Concerning Human Understanding* and the *Second Treatise of Government*. What, he asked, was man capable of becoming outside the bonds of oppression? Now, colonial leaders found themselves marooned on that very question. Could Locke's idealized man be entrusted with self-rule? If yes, what should self-rule look like? If the power of government was to be derived from the consent of the governed, how could that power best be exercised to advance the ambitions of the majority without abridging the liberties of minorities?

The Founders' initial attempt at self-governance sought to sidestep the prickliest aspects of these questions. The result was a soon-to-be-forsaken compact known as the Articles of Confederation, a feeble arrangement that deservedly fell in tatters into history's dustbin after attempting to divide power equally among thirteen masters. Formidable states' rights advocates despaired of its demise, while budding Federalists like John Adams and James Madison (the father of the Constitution—an apt tribute) saw in the rubble an opportunity to press for a government with a unified center, a gravitational core around which the states would orbit. If nothing else, the failed Articles had proved that building a new government from a blueprint of universal truths about human nature was a long way from the lively arguments about Locke's ideas at Chownings Ale House on Market Square in Williamsburg.

Europeans, after all, had been doffing their hats to kings and queens since the beginning of memory. The master-to-servant relationship of European society had been reinforced by centuries of conditioning as commoner to king, serf to prince. Since the end of the Middle Ages, commoners had paid in countless gallons of blood to learn that clergymen were as jealous of liberty as kings and princes. To Madison, an Anglican pragmatist and the author of the "disestablishment" legislation that severed official ties between the Church of England and the state of Virginia, whether clergymen took the form of popes or parish priests was immaterial. The end of oppression would not come until, in a paraphrase of Denis Diderot, the last king had been strangled with the entrails of the last clergyman. Both were antipodal to liberty, and neither could be trusted by free men. Yet as dangerous as clergymen were to civil liberty, banishing religion from society was neither practical nor prudent. The vacuum that resulted from its absence would invite rule by despots. Therefore, reasoned the young Virginian, the only sensible political solution was to let all religions through the gate and hope that time would achieve the same end when each neutralized the other's influence.

We know from the Founders' private letters and diaries that the frontier of ideas from which they milled the laws to build the new republic was far more inscrutable than the frontier of trees to the west, that region on maps labeled "territories unknown." That was Indian Territory, and by 1787, with the exception of the Five Civilized Tribes that lived south of the Mason-Dixon Line, the eastern forests had been more or less ethnically cleansed of sylvan gypsies and savages. Solutions to the inevitable "Indian problem" farther west would have to be postponed until a future day. For the time being, it was out of that trackless realm of ideas that the young James Madison began to envision a representative republic, a secular government of semi-autonomous institutions, the executive, the legislative, and the judicial, which would exercise power through civil laws and the administrative machinery of checks and balances. Madison's co-conspirator at the Constitutional Convention in Philadelphia, Benjamin Franklin, would forcefully defend the three-sided scheme by reminding the assembly that, although it was new to Europeans, the three-cornered government structure was, in fact, home grown. A local idea, if they would. In fact, this very model of government had proved itself resilient in keeping peace among the six great nations of the Iroquois Confederacy since the days of Hiawatha.

Madison, Franklin, and the Emperor of the Potomac, the peerless Mr. Washington, understood that success in the business of nation building would turn on a shrewd reading of human nature. But in postcolonial America, this was a rose with many thorns. During his seven long years as the commander of the Continental Army, George Washington had looked on with helpless and ever-mounting frustration as his army foundered for want of simple necessities, clothing and food, while the "single head" of the government fractured into thirteen impotent ones. By war's end, the general was a confirmed federalist. Dealing with the confederacy of sovereign states had convinced him that the only way to consolidate the political gains of the revolution was through an enlargement of federal power. But this, he suspected, would require a crisis, and things were bound to get worse before they got better. "I believe all things will come out right at last," he reflected, "but like a young heir, come a little prematurely to a large inheritance, we shall . . . run riot until we have brought our reputations to the brink of ruin."

Of the three, Franklin's views on his fellow man were the most foreboding, and he assumed that one day "the people shall have become so corrupted [by liberty] as to need despotic government, being incapable of any other." The general, whose assessment of his fellow citizens had grown more caustic with the passage of time, saw in the aristocracy a "venality, corruption, and prostitution of office for selfish ends, abuse of trust, perversions of funds from a national to a private use," all of which diminished whatever attributes might have redeemed them. The preeminent legal historian Robert A. Williams has noted that "few legislative bodies in American history have so mired themselves in corrupted self-interest parading as principle as did the Revolutionary-era American Continental Congress." Across the ocean, even King George III, who was given to spells of dark brooding about the war's outcome, was eventually restored to sanity by a more cheerful outlook:

"Knavery seems to be so much the striking feature of its [America's] inhabitants that it may not in the end be an evil that they have become aliens to this kingdom."

Before the Founders assembled their new government, Madison wanted to know if the darker angels of human nature would take flight in the absence of tyranny, or whether they simply came from within, and remained in spite of externalities. Which characteristics would strengthen individual liberty: Property ownership? The right to vote? And which innate weaknesses, if left unchecked, would corrode liberty over time: Venality and avarice? The promotion of material self-interest at the expense of community welfare and happiness, and liberty for one's fellows? As beings who derive their identity from membership in society, who should prevail in a contest of wills—the group or the individual?

When Madison left his father's home in Virginia to join Washington and Franklin in Philadelphia in May 1787, the grave uncertainties that lay ahead cast the thirty-six-year-old political wunderkind into a gloomy state of mind. This short, aristocratic hypochondriac—who would never tip the scales past a hundred pounds—emerged finally from his monkish seclusion and confided to members of his family on the eve of his departure that he was likely embarking on a fool's errand. He had spent the previous six months exiled to a room in his father's grand manse at Montpellier, carefully assembling and testing his model government against imagined storms. Beginning with Thucydides and Xenophon, Plutarch and Tacitus, he read everything (in the original Greek and Latin) that had been written on the Greco-Roman experiments in republican government and democracy. In two thousand years, he decided, little had changed. The central problem of governance in a republican society was still a profoundly human one: how to divide power without creating fatal jealousies among "equal" states, equal persons? If there was to be life for the republic after the Articles of Confederation, this was the insurmountable difficulty that must be solved.

As the day of reckoning approached, it was not the delegates from the

North that worried the future president. Madison fretted most about his neighbors, men like Patrick Henry, who had achieved celebrity status by railing against the evils of monarchy. For Henry and his friend Thomas Jefferson, the distance between the tyranny of King George and a strong central government in Philadelphia was but a short step. Henry and Jefferson built up their political fortunes by depicting the monarch as the root of all evil, and by advancing their favorite nostrums to any who would listen: that educated free men were entirely capable of self-restraint and self-governance. Since these truths were self-evident, said they, the highest calling of government would be to protect individual liberty—an argument that played well among southern aristocrats—so long as it didn't apply to Negroes, women, or savages.

In the early decades of the republic, Jefferson's states' rights faction came to be known as Republicans. Those in favor of a strong central government, the Federalists, were led by Madison, John Adams, and Jefferson's nemesis, Alexander Hamilton. "I must own to you that the daring traits of ambition and intrigue, and those unbridled rivalries which have already appeared, are the most melancholy and alarming systems that I have ever seen in this country," wrote Adams of the gulf between Republicans and Federalists. A portly man with a robust constitution and an insatiable appetite for knowledge, the Massachusetts farmer's lifelong study of history and literature had convinced Adams that humans' essential flaws were biblical in nature. Men were a baneful stew of impulses that ran to greed, gluttony, and a quenchless thirst for power. The best government, said Adams, would protect liberty at the same time it applied the regulatory correctives necessary to keep a rascal citizenry's self-aggrandizing behaviors in check. Under the Republicans, he warned, dissolution of the union was only a matter of time. The liberties of all would soon be trampled by the excesses of the few (read: aristocrats).

As the wheels of Madison's carriage rolled toward destiny at a canter, the young Virginian wondered if his imagined experiment in self-governance could possibly work. Would Americans speak out of altruism but act out of self-interest, as Machiavelli had predicted three centuries before? Or could Locke's idealized man, on the first day of the new world, be brought into a state of enlightenment sufficient to accept certain limits on personal liberty and financial aggrandizement in deference to the greater good of the republic?

In 1787, time and experience would be needed to answer such a slippery question. As one L. W. Hastings wryly observed about Americans in their first century, "All appeared to be determined to govern, but not to be governed." What was clear to the delegates arriving in Philadelphia was that a sea of perils ran between the speculations of genius and the bloody anvil of governance, literally and figuratively. Jefferson and Adams were away in Paris arranging a treaty, so both men placed fate in the hands of their proxies and sat back patiently to await news from home.

When Madison arrived in the City of Brotherly Love, he quickly forged an alliance with the city's first citizen, the wise old fox Ben Franklin. Franklin brought along his friend and protégé, a shrewd back-room operator named James Wilson. One of the hallmarks of genius is the ability to see it in others, and after several clandestine meetings with Madison, Franklin confided to Wilson that he was certain that a model of the republic he envisioned already resided behind the dome of Madison's forehead. In order to give the model form in the real world, the trio settled on a deceptively clever ploy to slip the ideological noose that was being prepared for them by Patrick Henry and his confederacy of southern delegates. When the doors closed behind them in Convention Hall, their principal strategy was to avoid getting baited into trivial contretemps with the fulsome orator from Williamsburg, and patiently wait for an opening of substance.

The opportunity to preempt the southerners came earlier than they expected. On a sweltering afternoon in early June, Franklin rose to make an appeal to the entire assembly. Because the stifling humidity had become so unbearable inside the cloistered room, and because the issue at hand was such a minor item of housekeeping on the division of power between the states and the proposed central government, the elder statesman urged the delegates to assign to the federal government the exclusive right to make treaties with foreign governments. After all, such a proviso could not be construed as abridging the sovereignty of the states. There was no harm, since no foreign country could be expected to make thirteen separate treaties.

Concealed behind the veil of Franklin's charm, Madison's initiative was now poised to breach the walls of the southern aristocracy's resistance to a strong national government. The motion was approved with nary a vote against. Disguised as a minor legal device borrowed from Hugo Grotius and Emmerich de Vattel's recently codified law of nations, this minor cession of power to the central government would be regarded by all thirteen states as the supreme law of the land. On this basis alone, the central government could claim a power of governance superior to that of its many fathers.

By the convention's end in mid-September, many of the weaknesses that doomed the Articles of Confederation had been skillfully corrected in the new compact. Rather than risk losing three months of hard work in which they had won the majority of the battles, Madison and Franklin chose to leave other issues—including the most contentious, such as slavery, and the finer points of dividing power between the states and the central government—to the wise leaders of a future day. The delegates called for their carriages and set off down autumn roads in thirteen directions, well satisfied that they had made for themselves, and their fellow citizens, a bold new nation.

The Founders' best ideas succeeded in lifting up to the world a new model of self-governance that would be a shining city on a hill. The drafters of the Constitution believed they had conceived a government as sure-footed and balanced as any imagined by Locke. The document that was put to the thirteen legislatures for ratification was an achievement of revolutionary consequence for the people of the world to follow. If they dared. Not least among these consequences was the irony that the price for this great adventure would be underwritten, in large part, by the American Indians. For more than a century, the continent's native people proceeded to give up life, land, liberty, and happiness to sate the material cravings of their European neighbors, until there was nothing left for them to concede. The document produced in Philadelphia made scarce mention of the continent's original inhabitants, an oversight that commanded the attention of the U.S. Supreme Court in more than fourteen hundred cases over the next two hundred years. In the meantime, the legal instruments used to solemnize the Europeans' steady march to the Pacific Ocean were safely built into the new Constitution with a pair of tools: the Indian Commerce Clause, which gave the federal government the exclusive right to regulate trade with the Indian nations, and Madison and Franklin's clever ploy to subvert the rule of the states, in the supremacy clause of Article VI, known to us as the power to make treaties.

Between 1778 and 1871, the federal government ratified 369 treaties with Indian tribes. By means of this sometimes cruel, sometimes amicable legal instrument, the United States acquired 1.85 billion acres of Indian-owned land. Nineteenth-century land cessions by the Indians made the United States government "the largest real estate broker in the world." This was the natural outcome of Revolutionary-era debates over the status and rights of natives in their lands, debates in which the rights of whites, and expedience, always won out. Neither "the rule of law or even the opinions of learned jurists would ultimately determine whether the Indians enjoyed the same rights as white men in America." Increasingly, those rights were defined by, and subordinated to, the appetites of the natives' European neighbors.

The first treaty, with the Delaware nation, was similar to the last, with the Nez Perce: both compacts called for earlier hostilities to be "mutually forgiven, and buried in the depth of oblivion, never more to be had in remembrance," thereby sealing a solemn pact of friendship and cooperation between the tribes and "the Great White Fathers." From first to last, the treaties formally recognized the inherent governmental sovereignty that adhered to each party, or each signatory nation, as many treaties included several nations. But as to the inherent sovereignty of the Indian nations, there could be no question that it was grounded in the law or the Constitution. As early as 1705, the Mohegan Indians turned to an English court to seek relief from whites invading their lands in violation of their treaty with the crown. A royal commission rendered its final verdict in 1743, ruling: "The Indians, though living among the king's subjects in these countries, are a separate and distinct people from them, they have treaties with us as such," and "they make peace and war with any nation of Indians when they think fit, without control from the English." Further, the royal commission ruled that the crown recognized the Indians as having the property and the soil of the countries, and that their lands were not "by his majesty's grant of particular limits of them for a colony, thereby impropriated in his subject till they have made fair and honest purchases of the natives." A century later, in response to southerners who were seeking to place limits on tribal authority, the United States attorney general, William Wirt, echoed the English court. "If it be meant to say that, although capable of treating, their treaties are not to be construed like the treaties of nations absolutely independent," wrote Wirt, infuriating the states' rights bloc, "no reason is discerned for this distinction in the circumstances that their independence is of a limited character. If they are independent to the purpose of treating, they have all the independence that is necessary to the argument."

As Madison rode away from Philadelphia in the fall of 1787, he was well aware that the final status of Indians in the scheme of federalism was an open question. Like slavery and states' rights, "the Indian problem" was put aside. For the moment, the facts before the nation's first and most reluctant president, George Washington, were plain and pressing enough. As was the case with his own private enterprises in Virginia and Ohio, in 1790, the new government teetered from one day to the next on the precipice of financial ruin. Before the republic's first government had even been convened, the treasury was bankrupt. The only means Congress had of retiring the debts to foreign governments it had incurred during the War for Independence was through the sale of land. And since the government had no army capable of taking that land by force, the only option left to it was the treaty.

Reports from Indian country on these prospects were not auspicious. The war with England was no sooner over than Americans started pouring over the nation's western boundaries into the Ohio and Kentucky valleys, incensing the tribes. In 1789, an exasperated George Washington requested an audience with the Senate in order to bear upon those fine gentlemen a matter that troubled him greatly. The Treaty of Hopewell with the Cherokee nation was in danger of being shredded into legal nonsense. Lawless Americans were sacking Indian towns in Georgia and North Carolina. "The [republic's] treaty with the Cherokees has been entirely violated by the disorderly white people on the frontiers," declared the president. Marauding frontiersmen had killed hundreds of Indians in unprovoked attacks. Something had to be done to prevent all-out war. Just a year earlier, Congress had authorized the secretary of war, Henry Knox, to run white intruders off by whatever force was necessary, but now North Carolina was showing reluctance to ratify the Constitution. Rather than inflame prejudices, troops were never actually sent. After North Carolina relented, Washington's diatribe prompted the First Congress to authorize a renegotiation of the Treaty of Hopewell, replacing it with the Treaty of Holston in 1791.

It could not be said of the early pioneers that their spirits were burdened by altruism and virtue or that their outposts were centers of civilization and good deeds. Major Caleb Swan reported to Congress in 1790 that, taken as a whole, white settlers in Indian country "are the most abandoned wretches that can be found, perhaps, on this side of

Botany Bay; there is scarcely a crime but some of them has not been guilty of." Washington, who had fought with and against the tribes of the Old Northwest in the French and Indian War, had good reason to fear their martial might. The reports from the wilderness left the president deeply concerned. If the new republic's outcasts and rabble provoked war with the powerful savages of the Ohio Valley, the new nation could easily be driven into the sea.

To prevent that from happening, the First Continental Congress had created two Indian departments, for north and south, and sent eleven commissioners into the field "to treat with the Indians . . . in order to preserve peace and friendship and to prevent their taking any part in the present commotions," meaning the war with England. The first treaty ratified by the new government was a compact of friendship and mutual protection with the Delaware nation. Twelve more soon followed, but the Continental Congress had left itself open to trouble with the states. In the government's founding charter, Congress encumbered its own authority by including a proviso that gave states the right to manage relations with tribes inside their own borders. Southern states like Georgia and South Carolina, which were home to the Cherokee, Chickasaw, and Choctaw, "civilized tribes" with large land holdings, interpreted this as a reservation of authority over Indian lands within their own boundaries. Congress, invoking long-established guidelines in the law of nations, rejected this interpretation out of hand and in 1783 declared that any gift or cession of land secured in violation of the exclusive relationship Congress had with the natives would be considered null and void. In 1790, the new republic's First Congress passed the Indian Non-Intercourse Act and claimed an exclusive right to sanction all transfers of Indian lands regardless of where they lay.

Southern landowners, speculators, and lawmakers were outraged by the government's meddling. For forty years this issue smoldered in the delicate fabric of federalism. Chief Justice Marshall, that "principal inventor of the nation," commenced the task of mending this flaw in

1831, in *Cherokee Nation v. Georgia,* by observing that the nation's first treaty with the Delaware was "in its language, and in its provisions . . . as near as may be, the model of treaties between the crowned heads of Europe." By invoking the memory of kings and queens, he was sending an important message to state legislatures about the preeminence of the federal government in the regulation of Indian affairs. Since the founding of Jamestown on the James River, a transfer of Indian land from one party to another required the approval of the "sovereign" in whose name the lands had been "discovered." This long-settled preemptive right of kings was recognized by all European sovereigns under the law of nations. When George III's subjects won their independence, the king's preemptive power over native lands was transferred to the new government. In the case of the Delaware treaty, said Marshall, that sovereign was the Continental Congress. It was in this regard, and because of that sovereign-to-sovereign relationship, the chief justice wrote, that "the condition of the Indians in relation to the United States is perhaps unlike that of any other two people in existence."

John Marshall, as it turned out, was the wise middle-aged country gentleman to whom Madison and Franklin were entrusting the decisions of the future. In the waning days of the checkered presidency of John Adams, the beleaguered bookworm from Quincy, Massachusetts, nominated Marshall to lead the Supreme Court through the inevitable and imminent storms already building. Adams, who was still carrying wounds from his ruthless battle with the Republicans during the election of 1800, held the tall, forty-five-year-old Federalist from Fauquier County, Virginia, in the highest esteem. The two men, while polar opposites in appearance and points of origin, saw the world as if through the same pair of eyes. Marshall, born in a log cabin near Germantown, Virginia, inherited his lanky frame and vigorous athletic constitution from his father's English genetics. To his mother, who gave birth to fifteen children, all of whom survived to adulthood, Marshall owed his droll wit and good nature. He spent his youth being tutored by his father,

Thomas, and roaming widely in the foothills of the Appalachians with his brothers and sisters. At twelve, he transcribed the whole of Alexander Pope's *Essay on Man* and was reciting from memory the poets of the Old English school, particularly John Milton. As with Adams, who was said to have walked from his crib to his grave, Marshall's habit of walking, especially before breakfast when he did his thinking on questions before the court, was one he followed until the end of his days.

The maligned second president saw this appointment as just deserts for Jefferson, his successor (and Marshall's distant cousin, a blood tie that brought no comfort to either man). Among all his remarkable achievements, for John Adams the eleventh-hour appointment of Marshall to the high court left the most lasting imprint on the country he helped found. Daniel Webster once described the chief justice as having a legal intelligence that was as faultless as his moral compass. "I have never seen a man of whose intellect I had a higher opinion," wrote Webster. When the words "it is admitted" were uttered by the chief justice at the conclusion of a hearing, Webster once remarked to Justice Story, "I am preparing for a bomb to burst over my head and demolish all my points."

Over the course of thirty-four years, Marshall wrote dozens of landmark opinions that continue to guide the ship of state and protect the civil rights and liberties of individual citizens. Of these, none have had a greater impact on the American Indians than his opinions in *Cherokee Nation v. Georgia*, *Johnson v. McIntosh* (1823), and *Worcester v. Georgia* (1832). These cases are known as the Marshall trilogy, and they not only laid the foundation for federal Indian law but, through their application to the unfinished project of federalism, initiated a vital realignment of the government itself. A generation earlier, James Madison had constructed a new republic from a frontier of ideas. To turn that revolutionary idealism into the practical machinery of government, Marshall had to find a way to make that republic work on the frontier.

Hoping to prevent the first spark from igniting a powder keg in the western wilderness of the Ohio River valley, Washington told his secretary of war, Henry Knox, that making peace with the tribes would be his administration's top priority. Knox, who helped draft the Indian Non-Intercourse Act passed by Congress in 1790, recommended that the government build a string of posts in order to coerce the ungovernable frontier whites into compliance with the law. "The angry passions of the frontier Indians and whites, are too easily inflamed," wrote Knox, "and are too violent to be controlled by the feeble authority of the civil power." For Washington, Adams, and Knox, the sovereign status of Indian nations was long-settled business. In 1785, Washington had urged the Continental Congress to reassure the Indians that their title to lands, and sovereignty, were inviolate in the eyes of the new government. Congress approved the Northwest Ordinance, also written by Knox, which stipulated the manner in which settlers on the frontier could turn the wilderness into states, and, in turn, sought to reassure the tribes of the Ohio Valley "that the utmost good faith shall always be observed towards the Indians; their land and property shall never be taken from them without their consent; and in their property, rights and liberty, they shall never be invaded, or disturbed, unless in just and lawful wars authorized by Congress."

Despite the saber rattling implied in the act's final clause, this was much too generous to the natives to sit well with Thomas Jefferson and the Republicans. Intensely jealous of the new federal government's power, these fierce defenders of states' rights were not about to concede so much as the dust of sovereignty to "the wild savages of the forest." But Jefferson's summary rejection of Indian sovereignty was legally groundless. His own state of Virginia had come into existence through treaties with Indians, treaties that acknowledged their inherent sovereignty by way of the law of nations. European governments had recognized the Indians' natural law claim to aboriginal title for two centuries. This was the thorn in the Constitution that the states' rights advocates could not remove. As Marshall later explained in *Cherokee Nation v. Georgia,* treaties formally recognized each participant as "a distinct political society, separated from others, capable of managing its own affairs and governing itself." No political philosophy or legislative agenda could overcome the supreme law of the land's protection conferred on treaties, or change the fact that these nations of savages were formally recognized as sovereign and fully "capable of maintaining the relations of peace and war."

The nation had no sooner given birth to itself than the consent of the governed began to waver. Southern legislatures cavalierly ignored the prerogatives of Congress stipulated in the Indian Commerce Clause. State governors and lawmakers routinely violated treaties by encouraging white citizens to commit violent provocations in Indian towns. As rumors of widespread fraud, bloodletting, and foul trickery reached New York from the South, Vice President Adams despaired. Here was the fatal schism he had dreaded, the one that would not be vanquished by tightly constructed words on a piece of paper. In a letter to his friend William Tudor, Adams noted that the first line of the Constitution, "We the people, in order to form a more perfect union," should have settled the states' rights question once and for all. It was clear, however, that Jefferson and his cohorts were going to press their case until a day of reckoning engulfed the nation in turmoil. Adams, for one, was ready to settle that question now, before it had a chance to destroy the union. "The fate of this government," he wrote, "depends absolutely upon raising it above the state governments."

But fate intervened, if only temporarily, on behalf of Jefferson and the Republicans. When Jefferson took up residence in the White House in 1801, southern Republicans were free to press their case on the frontier without having to worry about consequences. The new president, who had a flair for all things literary, was a master at applying a "philosophical gloss on the violently partisan." On April 24, 1802, he committed the federal government to a deal with the Georgia legislature, known as the Georgia Compact, in which the state ceded a parcel of land, soon to become Alabama and Mississippi, to the United States. Later it was discovered that speculators had colluded with Georgia state legislators to illegally arrange for the purchase of Indian lands, for pennies an acre. To complete the extortion, state legislators acted as brokers between speculators and the federal government, and pocketed the ill-gotten profits.

In exchange for this cession of land, and without consulting the tribes, Jefferson promised to extinguish Indian title to Cherokee and Choctaw lands within the Georgia state boundaries. The timetable and procedures for "removal" were left open-ended, and Jefferson quickly assured the tribes that their relocation from their treaty-protected lands would only occur at their pleasure and on their terms. But Georgia had the agreement it wanted and a timetable of its own—one it could push through a loophole that gave the state the right to defend itself against Indian depredations. Since the Georgia Indians were peaceful, accelerating that timetable was a simple matter of provoking war.

When the Indians raised protests against white depredations, Congress did nothing. The Indian Non-Intercourse Act—the federal law governing Indian land transfers—had been transformed by the Georgia Compact into a "rigged lottery" in favor of land speculators, settlers, and immigrants. Tribes in those states never stood a chance in state courts, and, when put to the test, the presumptive equal footing promised to them by Congress proved to be a canard. As southern landowners (meaning slaveowners) had hoped, Jefferson not only turned a blind eye to their provocations in Indian towns, he deliberately refused to enforce the Indian Commerce Clause, abrogated the 1791 Treaty of Holston with the Cherokee, and ignored the Non-Intercourse Act of 1790. Whether Jefferson was naive or a willing accomplice, or parts of both, Alexander Hamilton's assessment of the gardener of Monticello had earned its place in history books. Hamilton was not taken in by the rosy allure of Jefferson's sophistication and charm. What he saw instead was pompous pretensions to profound knowledge in a man who was "ignorant of the most useful of all sciences—the science of human nature." The day would come, warned Hamilton, when Jefferson would be revealed for what he was, "a voluptuary and an intriguing incendiary."

Unable to stop the lawlessness on the frontier until a case was brought before him, the new chief justice, John Marshall, watched the pattern of atrocities unfold from the distant vantage point of the high bench. Even Jefferson's good friend James Madison felt the president had made an "egregious miscalculation" with the southern Indians and told James Monroe that Jefferson was not only guilty of violating the Constitution to advance the cause of states' rights but, worse yet, had also committed a grave moral crime by exaggerating his "claims of civilized over un-civilized men."

Madison and Monroe, Jefferson's successors, would allow the nation's slowly emerging removal policy to move forward at a pace dictated by the tribes. Madison thought the government's case for removal was thin, at best, but after the War of 1812, the state government of Georgia, goaded by a fierce hotspur of ill-tempered impatience by the name of George McIntosh Troup, accelerated depredations against Indians. Then, when Troup was elected governor, he rallied the state court judges around him and dared the federal government to step in and stop it. Predictably, the Georgia legislature turned a deaf ear to Indian complaints of butchery and murder. Bloody provocations by whites became so constant in Cherokee towns that the Indians finally sought relief from Congress. This, at last, was the showdown that Troup and a later governor, Wilson Lumpkin, along with their judicial satraps, had pined for. Legal historian Joseph Burke, author of a comprehensive study of the Cherokee-Georgia conflict, "The Cherokee Cases: A Study in Law, Politics, and Morality," wrote: "The Governor, legislators, and judges of Georgia had publicly dared the Supreme Court to interfere; and the President of the United States, who had encouraged—or at least winked at—this outrage, now seemed prepared to stand by and watch the State defy the Constitution, laws, and treaties of the United States."

As George Washington had feared, the problem of Indian sovereignty had brought the young nation to its first violent constitutional crisis. Like the calamity it foreshadowed, the Civil War, this one was bullied onto the national stage by the "fatal schism" of states' rights. At the peak of the crisis, John Quincy Adams declared: "The Union is in the most imminent danger of dissolution. . . . The ship is about to founder." When *Cherokee Nation v. Georgia* reached the Supreme Court in 1831, John Marshall was shrewd enough to realize that the problem with that ship lay not with the states, but with the Constitution itself. The states were acting in a manner that was entirely predictable—promoting their self-interests to the exclusion of all others. To expect anything different from state legislatures was to invite the scorpion to become a butterfly. The problem to be fixed was in the incomplete framework of federalism. The thirteen states had ratified a founding document, the Constitution, without mentioning the dozens of sovereign nations that lived as independent governments in their midst. The tribes' preexisting sovereign status was not a whim of the state. It was long settled law. Marshall asked, how can we use existing law as a fulcrum to retrofit the Constitution with the architecture necessary to promote peaceful coexistence between whites and Indians?

Marshall crafted his solution by placing the federal government and the tribes, the two parties to treaties, into a legally binding partnership. This partnership would be the foundation for the "doctrine of trust" between the republic and the independent sovereigns on the frontier. But the southerners, including President Andrew Jackson, were hearing none of it. They wanted the Indians' land, not their trust and friendship. By 1830, southern legislatures were determined to remove Indian tribes from their midst, and they were ready to use whatever means were necessary to accomplish the task. As historian Morgan Gibson has pointed out, nineteenth-century America was a sociopolitical environment controlled by fiercely ethnocentric leaders and followers who, despite all rhetoric to the contrary, regarded all other races and peoples as subhuman.

When Andrew Jackson was elected president in 1828, the South's high-handed defiance of the Constitution, begun with sly deftness and calculated effect by Thomas Jefferson, was formally ushered into the light of day. Jackson, likely the first national political figure not considered "a gentleman" by eighteenth-century standards, was swept into office by the very rabble that Jefferson had most feared. In fact, Jackson was very much a fragment of that rabble, and as many men on the frontier could attest, Old Hickory was a man you crossed at your peril. He had killed three men in duels and he carried two bullets in his body when he took the oath of office. And, like Jefferson, he could not imagine a place in America's future for the savage. The Indians "have neither the intelligence, the industry, the moral habits, nor the desire of improvement which are essential to any favorable change in their condition," Jackson told Congress in December 1833. "They must necessarily yield to the force of circumstances and ere long disappear," he continued—though even Jackson could not deny that his matchless reputation as a battlefield general owed much to the Creek and the Choctaw tribes, whose alliance had been indispensable to the American cause in the War of 1812. "There is not a friendly Chief of distinction on our extensive frontier who does not wear a meddle, or a sword, presented by our government as a reward for his valor and fidelity in those conflicts during the late war with Great Britain," he wrote to President Madison. But these debts of honor would not be a cloud on the nation's future. Once Jackson was commissioned by Congress to make treaties with the southern tribes, all former loyalties were quickly disclaimed. After he negotiated a treaty with the Chickasaw nation in 1816, word filtered back to Congress from an anonymous source (someone no doubt worried about reprisals from the general) warning lawmakers that

Jackson's tactics were anything but honorable, and would likely cause the government considerable grief in future dealings with the tribes. Jackson's well-known "appeal to fear and avarice," using both intimidation and bribery, was so much a part of his negotiating tactics that the Indians themselves began taking it for granted.

Jackson personally negotiated half a dozen major treaties that succeeded in coercing land cessions from the "five civilized tribes." In time, courts would find each one to be a model of "deceit and dishonor," either in whole or in part. Old Hickory was a man of the frontier. His sensibilities and personal habits were as rough as the country that shaped him. When it came to treating with the Indians, the scruple had yet to be encountered that Jackson couldn't subdue with a lie, a threat, or a bribe. In treaty making, many Indians and government officials who witnessed Jackson's tactics firsthand would later report that no tool of deception—whether fraud, calumny, or outright swindle—was beneath him. Behind the Treaty of Doak's Stand, in 1820, was "the same old story of perjured faith." With a tone of bemused astonishment, historian Annie Heloise Abel later wrote, "Thus ended another futile attempt [by Andrew Jackson] to dispose of southern Indians without their consent."

But Jackson had the will of a despot and was not easily thwarted. Hoping to rid the western Mississippi forests of the last Choctaw Indian, he returned once more and offered the mingos—Choctaw elders—a much larger tract of land, this time in the Arkansas territory. The talks were nearly concluded with Major David Haley, Jackson's hand-picked agent, when the mingos were secretly informed by a friendly missionary that the Arkansas land had already been claimed by white citizens—citizens who, two years previously, had stolen it from the Quapaw Indians. This nixed the deal, but not before a mingo, Colonel Folsom, had said his piece: "The red people are of the opinion, that, in a few years the Americans will also wish to possess the land west of the Mississippi. Should we remove, we should again soon be removed by white men. We have no wish to sell our country. . . . [H]ere is our home, our dwelling places, our fields, and our schools, and all of our friends; and under us are the dust and the bones of our forefathers."

Jackson was infuriated by the mingo's audacious rebuff. He had heard these same appeals and laments from savages a hundred times before. That was all very well, he told them, but if they wished to be happy and to live in quiet and peace and to preserve their nation, he advised that they remove themselves beyond the Mississippi.

Out on the frontier, Jackson's final word was the only word that mattered. The laws of the land meant nothing to Old Hickory, except the ones he made up as he went along—to achieve a purpose or secure a goal. In his first message to Congress, on December 8, 1829, the hero of Horseshoe Bend and the Battle of New Orleans revealed his presidential objectives regarding the Indians and the unsettled question of states' rights. His administration would not interfere with the sovereign authority of a state inside its own borders. If the Indians still living in southern states wanted a home, they must go west. In his address to Congress a year later, on December 6, 1830, Jackson predicted the looming extinction of the Indian race. "What good man," he asked, "would prefer a country covered with forests and ranged by a few thousand savages to our extensive Republic, studded with cities, towns, and prosperous farms, embellished with all the improvements which art can devise or industry execute, occupied by more than twelve million happy people, and filled with the blessings of liberty, civilization, and religion?" With this coded message, the ethnic cleansing of the southern forests officially commenced, and while Jackson promised not to use force to achieve his administration's Indian policy goals, the whole country knew that his history in treating with Indians gave his words the lie.

A few years later, Congress answered Jackson's rhetorical question by sending four thousand Cherokees to their deaths on what is remembered as the Trail of Tears, a forced march of twenty thousand Indians to the new Indian Territory of Oklahoma in the dead of winter. The genocidal removal policies relentlessly advanced by the promoters of states' rights were a calculated assault on the Constitution and the law of nations. John Marshall's landmark opinions, which secured the legal status of Indians as sovereign "domestic dependent nations" in a realigned federalism, were summarily ignored by Congress and by the new president. When gold was discovered on Cherokee lands in Georgia, the state legislature sent white men to take it, boldly challenging the chief justice by defying active treaties and ignoring the Indian Commerce Clause. As his thirty-four-year career as chief justice was drawing to a close, Marshall saw the specter of a Civil War looming in the brazen actions of Congress. "The union has been preserved thus far by miracles," said Marshall, "and that cannot continue." He also saw dissolution in Jackson's brash disregard for the Constitution and in the banality of what Hamilton had once anointed "the great beast," the common man, of whom there were far too many at the highest levels of government, in Marshall's opinion, for the experiment in republican democracy to succeed. Forty years of evidence had shown that "those have truth on their side who say that man is incapable of governing himself."

No doubt James Madison, who in his dotage continued to reflect on those most troublesome and vexing of questions, *Once freed from the manacles of despots and monarchs, who are we? What is our nature?* now had his answer. It seemed the wise old fox from Market Street in Philadelphia had it right all along.

On that historic October morning in 1945, Felix Cohen certainly knew that his statement about Congress never condemning trust lands was technically incorrect, a neatly constructed falsehood. A renegade Congress and a complicit president had done just that, in Georgia and Alabama, in the 1830s, but in principle Cohen was on solid ground. If his omission was a calculated gambit to throw lawmakers into turmoil over the question of trust lands, it worked well enough to buy the Three Affiliated Tribes time to mount a defense. But their defense, however well grounded in law and Supreme Court precedent, would not be enough; nor would the searing criticism of a long-awaited report from the Hoover Commission, a seven-member panel of governors and agency heads convened at the request of Congress with a singular mission of investigating the inner workings of the Army Corps of Engineers and the Bureau of Reclamation.

Writing for the panel, Leslie A. Miller, a former governor of Wyoming, opened by explaining, "I went into this job with my eyes open . . . [but] my seven committee colleagues and I were amazed and dismayed to learn how bad the situation really is. . . . The two agencies are so violently jealous of each other that an extravagant and wholly senseless competition has sprung up." Under the most casual scrutiny, wrote Miller, the Pick-Sloan Plan had been turned into "a conscienceless bit of political compromising" whose centerpiece, the Garrison Dam, was regarded by anyone who knew the river as an extravagant waste of money that would create more problems than it would solve. At conception, the entire Pick-Sloan Plan was a fiasco that attempted to fuse two "bitterly contradictory" plans. The Corps of Engineers, downstream, would be dredging a channel to serve the needs of unnecessary river traffic, while upstream the Bureau of Reclamation would be building a storage dam for irrigation that would deprive the channel of water needed for navigation. Overall, the commission concluded that the Corps of Engineers "seems to have gone hog wild" with projects that were textbook examples of "rotten planning and wasteful execution." The commission concluded by urging Congress to disband the Department of the Interior entirely and, in its place, recommended the creation of a new Department of Natural Resources that would oversee both agencies. To that end, the commission also urged Congress to establish an oversight committee "to make certain that boondoggles, frills, and duplicating activities [of both agencies] are chopped off before they sprout."

Once the Hoover Commission's "shocking findings" were officially presented to Congress, its far-reaching recommendations were discussed in committee. Then, as they had so often in the past, lawmakers did nothing. The Hoover Commission's recommendations joined those of John Wesley Powell and General Lytle Brown on a dusty shelf in a dim corridor on Capitol Hill. The search for replacement lands for the Three Affiliated Tribes continued far and wide until the summer of 1947, scouring the country but finding nothing, and three years of committee logrolling by Republican congressmen reduced the compensation package for the Three Affiliated Tribes from $35 million to $12.5 million. On May 20, 1948, Louise Holding Eagle's father, George Gillette, the newly elected tribal chairman, covered his eyes to hide his tears as Secretary of the Interior Julius Krug took his seat at a desk on Capitol Hill to "touch the pen." The lawmakers and dignitaries gathered around the desk seemed to take one last look at the enigma of their trust obligations to the tribes. Then, as flashbulbs popped, they quickly swallowed the legal paradox in its entirety. With twenty more tribes awaiting a similar fate, and the nation's largest-ever public works project hanging in the balance, Congress once again turned its back on the Supreme Court and Article VI of the Constitution.

When the final details and valuations of the compensation package had been collected by the Bureau of Indian Affairs, the official "taking act," Public Law 437, was signed into law by President Harry Truman on October 29, 1949. What tribes learned that day, wrote Raymond Cross, Martin's youngest son, forty years later, was that "the inertia of history had the effect of foreclosing judicial scrutiny of 'good faith' federal takings of Indian lands in a veiled violation of the just compensation demands of the Constitution." Alexis de Tocqueville, that great student of social paradox and the American people's will to empire, noticed a similar phenomenon during his travels through the land: "The European is to other races of men what man in general is to animate nature," he observed with vivid insight. "When he cannot bend them to his use or make them serve his self-interests, he destroys them and makes them vanish little by little before him."

Chairman Gillette caught the next train home. "The future doesn't look good to us," he told the press. But all the meaningful words had already been spoken. There was nothing left to say. The tribes' exhausting four-year battle to save their homelands, one that had drained their coffers and their spirits and had "worn out the rails" to Washington, had come to grief. With a heavy heart, Gillette bravely tipped his hat to friends who had come to see him off at Union Station, then boarded the train. While he was speeding into the night across Minnesota en route to Minot, back home his daughter Louise was packing a small valise to elope into a new life with Matthew Holding Eagle.

For the next three years, life in Elbowoods, Nishu, Shell Creek, and Charging Eagle seemed largely unaffected by "the taking." For most, life went on just as it always had. Babies were born and people died. Crops were planted and harvested. Cattle were castrated and branded. While the men hunted deer in the fall, the women canned jellies and vegetables. Except for the streaks of red dust that hung high in the southern sky above the town of Garrison, there were few visible indications that a dam was being built, or that "the flood" was imminent.

In 1951, during "the starving time," the tribes' cheerful face of denial began to crack when the evacuation from the bottoms began in earnest. By late summer of 1954, the floodgates were closed, and the fast-rising lake lapped at the outskirts of Elbowoods. Martin Cross, the reelected tribal chairman, set out to salvage what he could from the taking, such as mineral rights and grazing lands, but the going was tough. In the intervening years, Congress had moved on to fight new battles with the Sioux, the Assiniboin, and the Crow people. Lawmakers were reluctant to revisit old business. The country was looking forward. At the dam's dedication, on June 11, 1953, President Dwight D. Eisenhower was seated on the reviewing stand between Chairman Cross and General Pick. When the president took the podium, he spoke for ten minutes from a carefully scripted speech that extolled the many wonders of Pick-Sloan, and not once mentioned the sacrifice made by the tribes.

Day by day, familiar landmarks disappeared. Many people in waning denial about the inevitable flood woke up one morning to realize they had waited too long to arrange for their homes to be relocated "on top." It was too late. Every Sunday morning for a year, Father Reinhart and Reverend Case had led their congregations in singing "Plant Your Feet on Higher Ground," but when the floodwaters reached Elbowoods, the disbelief turned to panic and a mad scramble during the final evacuation. Dozens of homes were left sitting on their foundations where the two-hundred-mile lake that formed behind the dam slowly swallowed them up. In the final dash to high ground, someone realized that all of the Elbowoods Warriors' athletic trophies had been left behind in the high school. Armed with flashlights, a group of former basketball players climbed into rowboats and returned to the school on a moonlit night and rescued them.

When the spring runoff began in late April, as it had since time immemorial, one by one the towns disappeared. The Four Bears Bridge was removed from its abutments and reassembled fifty miles upstream, at a new crossing near New Town. But the granite obelisk, that permanent fixture of the American landscape that was raised to honor the chiefs who made the journey in 1851 to the Fort Laramie Peace Council, was the final vestige of their old world to be vanquished by the waves.

THREE

White Men in Paradise

When the Eightieth Congress found itself wrestling with the legal ambiguity of Indian trust lands on the Upper Missouri River, men like Felix Cohen and Joseph O'Mahoney understood implicitly that they were modern hostages to a history shrouded in the mists of antiquity. This particular legal paradox could trace its origins to the royal courts of Elizabethan England. The parent of that sixteenth-century precept in turn followed its pedigree back through the legal luminaries of discovery-era Spain, and from there through the scholastic codifications of natural law by Thomas Aquinas in thirteenth-century Paris, and ultimately to Pope Urban II's Council of Clermont, in 1095. By surviving the social upheavals of the Middle Ages, the Renaissance, and the Reformation, the reconstituted Elizabethan law, after being pruned and grafted onto the Fifth Amendment by the First Congress in 1790, became the "takings" mechanism known as eminent domain, a well-oiled legal tool still favored by American legislators in the twenty-first century.

So although it was true that James Madison and his ideological allies had succeeded in building a new model of secular governance, one whose refreshing countenance was energized, thanks to the English philosopher John Locke, by something entirely new in the annals of human affairs—civil laws deriving their power from "the consent of the governed"—nevertheless, to hold its many loose-fitting parts together, the Founders were obliged to draw on the intellectual equity amassed across twenty-five centuries of western civilization. The administrative laws of Caesar Augustus and the Greek Ecclesia, the common law that grew out of Pope Innocent III's quarrels with King John of the Anglo-Saxons, the humanism of Thomas Aquinas in thirteenth-century Paris, and property law of the Normans each exerted an influence in shaping the foundational laws of the new republic. Of these many traditions, none had a greater extra-legal impact on the republic's expansion from the Atlantic seaboard to the Pacific Ocean, or on its original inhabitants, the American Indians, than laws borrowed from the papacy of the Middle Ages. But it isn't the exotic lineage of these laws, per se, that commands attention these many centuries later, as much as the personalities and storied events they manage to stitch together on their way to becoming the warp and woof of who we are.

On the final day of meetings at the Council of Clermont, in 1095, Pope Urban II's closing speech ignited a blaze of crusading fervor that burned in the hearts of European Christians for three centuries. Urban's appeal owed its force to his horrific portrayal of Muslim oppression of Christians in the Levant and the desecration of holy places sacred to all Christendom. This call to the First Crusade was a volatile interweaving of the secular and the religious, the political and the theocratic, an alchemy that sounds remarkably consonant with contemporary political thought nine centuries later.

On that day in 1095, the pope's immediate audience was made up of princes and their knights, but due to the social disarray that was then Europe—caused by chronic drought-related crop failures and pandemic diseases—the word of new opportunities to achieve heavenly redemption from earthly toils spread quickly among the peasantry. The First Crusade evolved from a parting supplication to noblemen into a mass movement of righteous peasants. Poor farmers, weighed down by wives, children, and their meager possessions, answered the call to extract tribute from the Saracens in the Holy Lands. In January 1099, an army of Europe's hardscrabble masses advanced on Jerusalem under the command of a French nobleman, Raymond of Toulouse, and laid siege to the city. When the Muslim defenses broke a month later, there followed "a dreadful scene of carnage" that went unchecked for days. The Vatican's army of saints massacred Muslims and Jews alike, chanting, *Deus lo volt!* —God wills it!—as the flow of blood turned streets into rivers. An army of Egyptians sent to break the siege was itself routed and mutilated by the victorious Christians at Ashkelon, in August 1099. This sanctimonious orgy of death thus commenced centuries of holy bloodletting under the auspices of the Petrine authority of the Vatican.

Out of the flames that engulfed Jerusalem would rise, a century later, an ascetic by the name of Lothario dei Conti di Segni, a cheerless blade-faced monk with dark, narrow eyes, a long Roman nose, and a ruthless and brilliant mind. On the day he was elected pope, at thirty-seven years old, Lothario had to be rushed into ordination. The monk who woke up a mere deacon, albeit a highly trained one, went to bed as the leader of Christ's earthly flock of believers. Consecrated Innocent III, he had one professional ambition—to rule the world by transforming secular monarchs into liegemen of the church. As heir to the papal revolution begun by Gregory VII, in which the church shook free from bondage to secular princes, Innocent III believed his duty was to elevate the papacy to the position of supreme monarch on earth. He accomplished this feat in eighteen short years, not because he was a shrewd politician but because he, like other despots before and since, had a talent for managing details. "His ideal was power; of love he knew nothing," wrote one of his biographers. By the time he died in 1216, Pope Innocent III had stirred Europe from its feudal night. The last words to cross his lips were a call to a new Crusade.

In eighteen short years Innocent III systematically transformed both the European monarchy and the papacy. He assumed Peter's mantle at a time when Christ's flock in Europe had descended into a decrepit state of squalor, hunger, disease, and not infrequent cannibalism. Innocent's principal instrument for consolidating power amid the social chaos of his day was the Crusade. But the bloodletting was the easy part, and it led to a more troubling question whose ultimate reckoning would have far-reaching effects: under what circumstances, he asked, might the church legitimately claim for its own the property and estate of pagans, savages, and infidels?

For Innocent III the issue was plain: The Crusades were justified because Christ's life and death had consecrated the Holy Land in Christian blood. Christ's followers, not those itinerant desert-dwelling disciples of Muhammad, had the divine right to dwell in the Levant. Infidels belonged to Christ's flock, certainly, but they did not belong to the sheepfold of the church. Consequently, as Christ's representative on earth, the pope not only had jurisdiction over the wandering infidels, he was also duty-bound to intervene in situations where those infidels were found to be in violation of natural and divine laws. In explaining his policies, Innocent III told heathens and savages that their refusal to admit Christian missionaries into their countries made him responsible as the leader of Christ's earthly flock to remedy their ignorance. In other words, it fell to a Christian prelate to protect Muslims from themselves. "There is only one right way of life for mankind," he reasoned, "and the Papal monopoly of this knowledge makes obedience to the Pope the only means of salvation."

Innocent III's legacy achieved full flower several decades later, through the work of Innocent IV. By the end of the thirteenth century, Innocent IV, also known as the Lawyer Pope, had given his successors the legal tools with which to secure and enforce the papacy's authority to uphold ecclesiastical law across secular boundaries, by means of an encyclical known as *Quod super his*. As Europe stirred out of its medieval coma, the notion of a supreme jurisdictional authority ruling over all secular powers, including the stragglers of Christ's far-flung flock, became the central lodestone of the Holy Roman Empire. The pope was empowered by a universal right, one recognized in natural law, to enforce the union of Christian civilization with that of the infidel races and religions who wandered aimlessly in the desert. Once voyaging explorers began "discovering" Africa in the fifteenth century, only the pope, declared the Vatican, could legitimize conquests made and claimed by secular rulers. Once codified, *Quod super his* assigned to future popes the ecclesiastical right and responsibility for enslaving non-Christian people who refused to submit to baptism under the cross of Christ.

After lying semi-dormant for 150 years, Innocentian discourses on the rights of infidels were revisited during the deliberations at the Council of Constance in 1414, in which papal theorists reasserted the pope's duty to deny that infidels had any valid legal right to own property and rule over their own lands. The timing of this edict could not have been more crucial, as the kings of Portugal and Spain were about to spend much of the fifteenth century bickering over the spoils of conquest in Africa. For two centuries, Saint Peter's apologists had been arguing that Rome had an unequivocal right, *ne*, responsibility, to authorize conquests of pagan territories through his agents, the kings and queens of the Holy Roman Empire. At Constance, the pope's lawyers declared that pagan people who happened to live in those newly discovered territories had no legal title to the land on which they lived. Citing the Crusade-era claims of his predecessors, Pope Eugenius IV (1431–1447) decreed that the pope could intervene in the internal affairs of foreign lands as the guardian of wayward souls who lived there. Pope Alexander VI (1492–1503) accordingly praised Isabella and Ferdinand of Spain for subduing the native inhabitants of the Caribbean, and subsequently he issued a bull to invest them with "full, free, and integral power, authority, and jurisdiction . . . over newly discovered lands and peoples" of the Indies. Here, then, was theocratic justification for the colonization and domination of native peoples in the New World that eventually morphed into laws that are still with us in the twenty-first century.

The theocratic assertion that spiritual grace legitimated the lordship of Christian rulers over the lives of pagans now pervaded the rationale of legal theory underlying the nascent law of nations as it emerged among the community of European states during the turbulent period known as the discovery era. In the Spanish universities of Salamanca and Valladolid, the best and brightest scholastic thinkers of the waning medieval era began to lay the foundation for monarchical claims to European dominion over American Indians and their lands. Innocent IV's claim that he could invoke secular power (a private army) to suppress ecclesiastically defined evil (Muslims in the Holy Lands) meant that the Papal See not only held sway over the kings of Christendom, but in his new role as supreme commander of Christendom's armies, the pope also could bring divine justice to heathens in order to coerce them into obedience to a universal church. To the natives of Central and South America, that justice would be expressed in a simple proposition: submit to the sacrament of baptism or perish. Millions resisted, settling for the latter. This approach to conquest and conversion worked for the Spanish and the Portuguese for nearly a century, until a gap of credibility opened up between the genocidal practices of the conquerors, raising serious questions about the efficacy of the salvatory doctrines of the Vatican. From the pope's vantage point, a lot of people were dying but not many were being saved. This was an unexpected development, one that raised for scholastic thinkers of sixteenth-century Spain another troubling question: *What, if any, are the natural-law rights and privileges that adhere to native peoples in distant lands?*

The most significant challenge to the legacy of the Crusades was mounted in the mid-1500s by a brilliant Spanish theologian named Francisco de Vitoria, a reclusive theoretician often cited as presaging Hugo Grotius and Emmerich de Vattel as the founder of international law. In a series of three lectures at the University of Salamanca titled "On the Indians Lately Discovered," de Vitoria became the first legal scholar to establish a natural-law connection between all nations by arguing that sovereignty of native people existed as a condition that preceded their discovery by agents of European monarchs, and the Vatican. But in order to make such a radical departure from established norms, de

Vitoria developed three dramatically new ideas, and each of these was eventually grafted onto enlightenment-era legal doctrines of Grotius and Vattel. A few centuries later, the legal foundations of these doctrines reemerged in the theories of governance that dominated the high ground in the thinking and ideas of colonial leaders in prerevolutionary America.

In a bold challenge to Innocentian claims, Francisco de Vitoria asserted that Indians did possess natural legal rights as free and rational people. And because they were free and rational, their sovereignty was inherent in the natural-law conditions that existed prior to their discovery by European adventurers and conquistadors. However, if native people transgressed universally binding norms of conduct, such as those stipulated in the law of nations, they did so at the risk of violating natural law. And if they violated the precepts of natural law, they risked forfeiting their rights as sovereign peoples.

Professor de Vitoria thereby set aside the papacy's thirteenth-century claims of supremacy over savages and infidels and modernized them for the discovery era in the sixteenth. Nevertheless, his first assertion regarding the Indians established the equality of rights of all people, a notion that was to become de Vitoria's most enduring contribution to the rights of native peoples. His second argument contested the Spanish monarch's natural-law claims to "title to the New World" by virtue of discovery. However, his third contention created the rationale by which civilized nations could subdue more primitive ones, by arguing that a rejection of universally binding norms by native people is a violation of natural law—a violation sufficiently momentous to justify their conquest and the taking of their lands.

On close reading, discovery-era advisers to European monarchs quickly recognized that Vitoria's final assertion closed the legal circle with Innocent IV's *Quod super his*. This is the same thread of medieval legal reasoning that would be picked up and reinvigorated two and a half centuries later by the Founders of the American republic. By arguing that savages could be conquered and colonized if they failed to observe the rational norms of the law of nations, Thomas Jefferson and Andrew Jackson staked their right to dispossess Indians of their lands on a legal principle that was first used by a Catholic pope to justify and to launch the Crusades six centuries earlier.

Around the turn of the seventeenth century, however, in a big stone castle on the other side of the English Channel from Vitoria and the popes, Elizabeth I noted the finer points of the deliberations in Salamanca, but because her father's numerous marriages and indiscretions had the desired effect of emancipating the English monarch from papal authority, the queen and her lawyers could do whatever they pleased, authorizing conquests of foreign lands without having to answer to God or the pope. This notion was forcefully underscored by the crown's advocate, Robert Johnson, when English ships set sail from Portsmouth to establish their colony at Jamestown.

In 1609, Johnson's widely distributed speech "Nova Britannia" caused a sensation by arguing that England's "just quest by the sword" of savage pagans in foreign lands was the solemn duty of civilized people. To anyone familiar with theological rationales for the Crusades, this logic was well known. Forest gypsies who resisted conquest, said Johnson, should be punished as enemies of civilized men. Popular clerics such as Robert Gray could not let the secular thinkers have all the fun, so the bloviating clergyman anticipated presidents Andrew Jackson and Theodore Roosevelt by centuries when he argued that civilized men committed a sin whenever they permitted blasphemous idolaters and brutish savages to lay claim to God's great creation, the earth. That a Christian king may lawfully make war upon a barbarous and savage people to save them from their wickedness was seen as more a duty than a right. Where the English were concerned, justifying the conquest of foreign lands was a simple matter of replacing hieratic authority with the secular crown. Lord Coke bundled all of these arguments into one by telling King James I that his foremost responsibility as king was to subjugate the savages to civilized laws of natural justice and equity, or suffer the consequences.

Coke's assertion was a skeleton dressed in new clothes, an extension of feudal common law over the rights of native people. Agents for King James abandoned their strategy of "silence and suppression" when the savages in Virginia resisted their civilizing influence. They had hoped the Indians would recognize the clear superiority of the encroaching civilization and embrace both ideology and practitioner. But Chief Powhatan, the father of Pocahontas, rejected this bargain, a challenge to the monarch's authority that left the Jamestown Company with no choice but to get tough. Here, papal logic succeeded in insinuating itself into the realm of the secular. For the English, the prospect of war drew its legitimacy from the church's mandate to remove the challenge to its "will to empire by normatively divergent non-Christian peoples and their opposed vision of truth."

This idea, centuries in gestation, formed the nucleus of the doctrine of discovery in the law of nations—a precept with many prickly corollaries that recognized the discoverer of new lands as having superior rights to those held by all others, including land occupied by native inhabitants. By the mid-seventeenth century, European powers abandoned the doctrine of discovery in favor of Francisco de Vitoria's humanistic recognition of the Indians' inherent and sovereign ownership of their homelands. However, as a matter of compelling self-interest, in pre-revolutionary America, members of the burgeoning plantocracy like George Washington and speculators like Benjamin Franklin were only too happy to abandon it as well. These aristocratic members of colonial land syndicates—whose foremost interest was the acquisition of Indian lands west of the Appalachians—wanted the right to negotiate directly with the tribes. This set up a three-way disagreement among the crown, colonial aristocrats, and the Indian tribes, a legal contest that would take seventy-five years and a small river of blood to resolve. But early in this dispute, the English king held the trump cards. As far as George III was concerned, Washington's claim that western lands were free and open to settlement was an unacceptable encroachment on the crown's preemptive rights. In the Proclamation of 1763, the edict that marked the end of the Seven Years' War with France, King George asserted his unitary dominion over the "discovered lands" west of the Appalachian mountains, thereby serving an imposing array of business interests, including his own and those of his friends on the privy council. In the short term, the proclamation prevented colonial land speculators from striking their own deals with Indian tribes. Also, for the foreseeable future it made the colonists dependent on London merchants for manufactured goods. In 1763, the English merchants' greatest fear was that their lucrative stranglehold on the colonies would eventually be frayed and severed by the Appalachian ridgeline.

For Washington, Franklin, and their various financial partners in proliferating land syndicates, this was more than a theoretical affront to their presumptions of limited autonomy. Washington viewed the king's claims as a mean-spirited joke, one meant to clip the horns of the crown's more rambunctious subjects in the southern plantocracy. "I can never look upon that Proclamation in any other light than as a temporary expedient to quiet the minds of the Indian," quipped the stymied future president. The king and his privy council were loath to relinquish any power to the colonists. As far as Washington and his business partners were concerned, if the king intended to make the idea stick, then his royal preemption would put them out of business and crush their dreams of accumulating wealth.

He made it stick. Accordingly, for Washington and the other land magnates of the tidewater region and beyond, the Proclamation of 1763 marks the initial phase of the buildup to war. In fact, there was no going back from that point. The king's declaration of preemptive rights on the western frontier left the colonial aristocracy with few realistic options. George III was openly challenging the colonists' semi-autonomous presumptions and their rights of life, liberty, and estate under natural law.

The crown and its advisers showed themselves determined to keep the colonial aristocracy's restive ambitions in check. For the landed gentry of Virginia, where, famously, "all the geese were swans" and wealth was measured by the acre, John Adams wrote five decades later, the revolution "was effected before the war commenced."

In fact, the king's claim to preemptive rights obliged men like Washington and Franklin to confront a new political reality: In victory over the French, George III cited the feudal doctrine of conquest based in Norman law to assert his prerogative power over lands occupied by "savages and infidels." This accomplished several important goals for the crown: it kept the land-hungry colonists from ranging over the mountains and establishing new centers of commerce, and it fostered peace with powerful Indian tribes on the frontier. In the end, King George's policymakers succeeded in imposing "the superior rights of Christian Europeans in lands held by . . . non-Christian people and asserted the feudally derived prerogative of conquest over North America."

As it had for the Spanish monarchs centuries before, the doctrine of discovery now bestowed upon the Mad King of England the right of ownership to all lands occupied by native people in the territories not yet divided up among the colonists. The Indians' aboriginal right of occupancy was tacitly recognized, but as to ownership of those lands, Indian title was a diminished claim. Indians could no longer make land deals without the approval of the crown. This meant that the land syndicates led by Franklin, Washington, and other colonial speculators were henceforth frozen out of the land trade beyond the mountains.

To the good fortune of the colonial syndicates, the king compounded this insult by levying a series of pernicious taxes that pinched the pocketbooks of his common subjects. Even though the hated Stamp Act was quickly repealed by Parliament, the damage was done, and talk of the colonists' independence from George III became the domestic currency of exchange throughout the colonies, while the contentious business about land being placed off-limits to speculators would turn about just as soon as the colonies won their independence. Or would it? Certainly, treaties between the monarch and the Indian tribes were transferred intact to the new government. But as for the management and disposition of western lands lying just beyond the blue-ridged horizons, the tables of fortune would now turn in the most unexpected of ways.

As a keen student of human behavior, Benjamin Franklin knew that out there on the frontier, where the law of the land evaporated into whimsy and rumor, individual self-interest would work diligently to divest the new government of its presumed authority. To prevent that from happening, the First Congress passed the Indian Non-Intercourse Act in 1790. This was a bold attempt to prevent unnecessary wars with Indian tribes and to foreclose on the frontier anarchy that would inevitably result from speculators freelancing land deals with tribes. (This law was subsequently revised a number of times and came to be known as the Indian Trade and Intercourse Acts.) Surrounded as it was by foreign powers—Spanish to the south, French to the west, British to the north, with only deep water to the east—the republic's first order of business was to secure the Ohio River valley as a buffer between itself and potential enemies. In the nation's first decade, the dangers from without dwarfed those that lurked within, which, by themselves, were potentially fatal. In these years, the historian Bernard De Voto remarked, the challenge faced by the young American government was "elementary: how to survive." The known world was a powder keg on fire. French peasants were in revolt, and the king had lost his head. The new first consul, Napoleon Bonaparte, marched his troops into Egypt to break the back of the British empire. In America, intrigues, plots, and conspiracies (including those hatched and nurtured by Jefferson) abounded on all sides. War looked inevitable on every front. The best-laid plans of the Founders were going awry before the people even had a government.

The most explosive domestic tensions were those building on the republic's western border. Every year since the War of Independence, thirty thousand pioneers crossed the mountains into the Old North-west territories in search of free land. The Miami, Wyandot, and Shaw-nee people soon lost faith in the new government's ability to keep the promises it had inherited from George III. White depredations were answered in kind by the Indians. In 1790, a divided Congress, fear-ful that the tribes might strike new alliances with King George III, sent General Josiah Harmar with a thousand men to subdue Shaw-nee renegades along the Scioto River. Harmar failed so miserably that ownership of the West now seemed beyond reach, just as Washington had feared. A year later, Miami warriors led by Chief Little Turtle shattered the forces of General Arthur St. Clair, leaving six hundred dead on the battlefield while the rest fled in panic. White men on the frontier demanded revenge. Thus commenced the cycle of violence that became so bloody and familiar over the next hundred years. "Alas for the inconsistency of human nature!" historian Annie Heloise Abel has written. "When white men fight for home and country they are lauded as the noblest of patriots. Indians, doing the same, are stigmatized as savages. What a fortunate and convenient excuse the doctrine of Mani-fest Destiny has proved!"

This, in fact, was a precise reflection of George Washington's closely held sentiments when he was elected president. By making the welfare of the western Indians a hallmark of his presidency, the Emperor of the Potomac wanted to use his influence to make certain the fate of the Indi-ans did not "end on a tragic note." During Washington's first term of of-fice he and his secretary of war, Henry Knox, expended more of their en-ergies achieving this objective than on managing diplomatic affairs with European allies. Washington, after all, had come away from the French and Indian War with great respect for the Indians, and unlike many of his countrymen he viewed them not as savages but as "familiar and formidable adversaries fighting for their own independence"—the very thing he would have done had their circumstances been reversed.

Washington and Knox were old and good friends. They had spent many years sharing close quarters and enduring trying circumstances during the Revolutionary War. Together they formed a seamless front on the Indian question. Both men agreed that the tribes should be regarded as foreign nations fully capable of keeping peace, making war, and managing their own governmental affairs. Accordingly, Indian treaties should be regarded as the supreme laws of the land, a status sanctioned by the authority and jurisdiction of the federal government that could in no way be abridged by the petty jealousies of states. In language that still sounds revolutionary two centuries later, Knox summarized their joint position by telling Congress: "Indians being the prior occupants [of the continent] possess the right of the Soil. . . . To dispossess them . . . would be a gross violation of the fundamental Laws of Nature and of that distributive Justice which is the glory of a nation." Washington took Knox's thinking a step further by arguing that forcibly removing the Indians from their homelands would be a permanent stain on the character of the nation. Determined to preclude that possibility, the president and first citizen underscored the terms of several treaties by issuing a proclamation of his own, in 1790, that forbade private or state encroachment on all Indian lands under the protection of treaties with the federal government.

After two terms in office, the young republic's exalted father bid adieu to public life with two lingering regrets and stern words of warning—in the form of his famous Farewell Address—to his many ill-mannered children and the generations they would spawn. "All the parts of our country will find in their union strength. And what is more valuable, an exemption from those broils and wars between the parts if disunited which, then, our rivalships, fomented by foreign intrigue or the opposite alliances with foreign nations engendered [by] their mutual jealousies, would inevitably produce. . . . The very idea of the power and right of the People to establish Government presupposes the duty of every Individual to obey the established government."

Deciphered these many generations later from the familiar rhetorical code of his day, Washington was warning Jefferson and his band of states' rights scoundrels that their determination to suborn the sovereignty of the nation to the sovereignty of its many fathers, the states, was a certain path to ruination. If you don't get beyond this pettiness, he was saying, our nation will be shredded and all of our efforts will have been for naught. The parts that survive such a calamity will be left to fend for themselves and face even bigger wars. As Joseph Ellis has noted, Washington "was going out as he came in: dignified, defiant, and decisive; clear about what was primary, what peripheral, confident about where history was headed."

Washington's two lingering regrets emanated from his failure to eliminate the nation's twin cancers: slavery and the Indian question. On the first, he was reconciled that a solution to this incendiary problem must be left to another generation; despite his own profound misgivings about slavery, Virginia's politically muscular plantocracy had made it clear that any attempt to tamper with it would be a call to disunion. But the Indians were a different matter. Washington marshaled his waning energies to write a farewell letter to his friends the Cherokee people, expressing his vision for mutual coexistence that even today underlines the man's revolutionary boldness. "I have thought much on this subject," he told them, "and anxiously wished that these various Indian tribes, as well as their neighbors, the White People, might enjoy in abundance all the good things which make life comfortable and happy." He told the Cherokee leaders that they were the best hope for transforming his vision of sovereign Indian nations prospering within the boundaries of the United States into a living reality. If they would continue to do their part and hold up their end of their solemn treaty agreements, he promised that the federal government would defend their honor and their rights to survival, both as a people and as independent nations. The Cherokee leaders responded to Washington's personal farewell with a gracious letter of thanks, acknowledging and accepting the president's promise as the sacred vow of a departing father.

But Washington's vision was not to be. He had no sooner departed Philadelphia for his long-awaited retirement at Mount Vernon, "beneath the vines and the figs," than his and Knox's assurances to the Indians were brushed aside and as quickly forgotten by the next Congress and President John Adams. Nevertheless, somewhere between coincidence and irony—and by means of the Indian Trade and Intercourse Acts—leaders of the new government had reclaimed the same legal argument about Indian lands that King George III had pressed upon the colonial land syndicates thirty years earlier. The once-radical pre-independence land speculators, now installed as officers of the new republic, had dramatically rejiggered their thinking so they might forestall chaos on the frontier. In hopes of maintaining social order and a steady flow of cash from future land sales to offset the new nation's $77-million debt to foreign creditors, they now disavowed Francisco de Vitoria's humanistic "natural law" theory of Indian land ownership in favor of the Innocentian-inspired doctrine of discovery preferred by the Mad King. Henceforth, land speculators in Indian country would have to answer to Congress, and no tribe could make a deal without the imprimatur of the federal government.

In its first hours, the republic's many fathers had demonstrated that they would gladly abandon the very principles of personal autonomy that twenty years before had lit the fuse to the War of Independence. Though often masquerading in other guises, time and again they abandoned their revolutionary ideals to secure the material object of their desires, as long as the price for that sacrifice could be levied on the black man or the Indian. Washington's motivations were imbued with sincere altruism, but his altruism, however lofty and noble, could not counterbalance the many others whose motivations were driven by greed. In consequence, the eastern tribes were the first to learn that the values of liberty and equality in America were contingent on the question of whose liberty and equality were at stake. Robert Williams, in *The American Indian in Western Legal Thought*, notes that the doctrine of discovery's evolution from its feudal beginnings came ashore in the New World to assert a fictitious discourse of conquest through laws that made it "available to legitimate, energize, and constrain as needed white society's will to empire over the North American continent," while its underlying ideology, "that normatively divergent savage peoples could be denied rights and status equal to those accorded to the civilized nations of Europe" had become "an integral part of the fabric of United States federal Indian law . . . whose discourse of conquest ensured that all future acts of genocide would proceed on a rationalized, legal basis."

In due time, these same precepts would be alchemized—by the elected leaders and lawmakers of the removal era—into the doctrines of Manifest Destiny and its lesser sibling, eminent domain. Like the enervating questions of slavery and states' rights, here was yet another deep fault line running through the foundation of the republic's charter that would demand its day of reckoning.

If a single cause can be pinpointed by studying its many effects, the removal of the American Indian from the eastern forests began in the summer of 1802 on the Caribbean island of Haiti. There, Napoleon's efforts to expand his hold on commercial sea routes ran afoul of unexpected difficulties. After putting down a slave revolt led by a charismatic black man, Toussaint L'Ouverture, French troops were gradually decimated by ceaseless guerrilla warfare and then laid waste by its virulent companion, yellow fever. Within months, fifty thousand French corpses lay rotting in the Caribbean sun. When he was imprisoned on the island of St. Helena many years later, Napoleon remembered the campaign in Santo Domingo as the greatest folly of his life.

The biggest mistake Napoleon made soon became a windfall for the new republic across the ocean. Having in 1800 reclaimed its Louisiana territories from Spain through the secret Treaty of San Ildefonso (Spain had been holding Louisiana for safe keeping since the end of the Seven Years' War), the French were set to once again raise their flag over

Governor's Square in New Orleans. Though the tricolor would flutter for only minutes when the final exchange took place in April 1804, there can be no question, says Bernard De Voto, that the Treaty of San Ildefonso would "change the face of the world."

In far-off Washington, the newly elected American president, Thomas Jefferson, had been trying to secure commercial rights to the port of New Orleans from the Spanish ever since he won office. American farmers cultivating lands right up to the eastern banks of the Mississippi needed a seaport to reach distant markets. Then, when Jefferson learned by chance that Louisiana had reverted back to its former owner, France, he was astonished and alarmed. While negotiating in good faith with the Spanish envoy to Washington to secure rights to the port, clandestine intrigues in Europe had made him the dupe of the French emperor.

Jefferson now confided his darkest fears to his neighbor, James Monroe. If France took possession of New Orleans, Bonaparte could forever deny Americans access to the Mississippi River. Under those circumstances, American enterprise would founder in the West for want of riverine highways to reach ports and distant markets. This was intolerable. Americans might know little about the western boundary that separated their country from Spanish lands, but they knew it was a river called the Mississippi, and that beyond that river lay unmapped lands that ran to the Pacific. Jefferson sent a secret message to Congress, saying only that the eastern bank of the Mississippi must somehow be wrested from the tribes by treaty, in order to secure the country's westernmost boundary. He then sent Monroe to Paris to support his plenipotentiary, Robert L. Livingston, and entrusted him to deliver a letter that underscored the president's apprehensions about Napoleon's plans for the future. "There is on the globe one single spot, the possessor of which is our natural and habitual enemy," Jefferson wrote. "The day that France takes possession of New Orleans fixes the sentence which is to restrain her forever within her low water mark." If France repossessed New Orleans, the president informed Livingston, it would leave the United States no choice but to "marry ourselves to the British fleet and nation," and prepare for war.

Napoleon's adversary in this trilateral intrigue was not the United States but the British crown. His strategy for humbling England was to damage its commerce by controlling sea routes through the Caribbean, and connecting the port of New Orleans to the St. Lawrence River. With those pieces on the game board of empire returned to French hands, France would own the keys to maritime commerce in North America. In Napoleon's mind, New Orleans sat at the south end of the road to Quebec. But when news of the death of his commander in Haiti reached Paris in January 1803, the great geopolitical mastermind of the era was dissuaded from pursuing any more costly adventures across the Atlantic. Henceforth, the consolidation of Europe would keep him busy, in Victor Hugo's phrase, "until God grew bored with him." Furthermore, Napoleon had nothing to gain by antagonizing the Americans. He had arranged the repossession of Louisiana as an attack on the colonial influence of France's perpetual nemesis, England, not as an affront to the Americans. "To emancipate nations from the commercial tyranny of England, it is necessary to balance her influence by a maritime power that may one day become her rival," wrote Napoleon. "That power is the United States."

As tensions in Washington propelled the president and Congress toward an international crisis, Jefferson became the target of the very criticisms he had leveled against his predecessor, John Adams. The editor of the *New York Evening Post*, William Coleman, chastised him for playing Napoleon's whipping boy when Spain denied the United States the right of deposit at New Orleans. Expressing a sentiment that soon became commonplace, Coleman wrote that "the destiny of North America" now belonged to the United States. "Ours is the right to the rivers and to all the sources of future opulence, power and happiness, which lay scattered at our feet; and we shall be the scorn and derision of the world if we suffer them to be wrested from us by the intrigues of France."

Jefferson, like Adams before him, was willing to wait out Napoleon. Jefferson had been the first and loudest to clamor for war when Adams was president, but now that the cock was crowing in his own ear he was willing to suffer any pains to avoid a military confrontation. Jefferson instructed his emissary, Robert Livingston, to be moderate and cautious with his persistent offers to purchase New Orleans outright. For months, Napoleon's foreign minister, the redoubtable Talleyrand, scoffed at Livingston's entreaties in a diplomatic game of cat and mouse. The idea was so preposterous, said Talleyrand, that he refused to broach the subject with the emperor. But the cogs that were turning in Napoleon's own mind, independent of his foreign minister, had already produced a vision of the world that was well beyond what either Talleyrand or Jefferson could have imagined. "I renounce Louisiana!" he informed a thunderstruck Talleyrand one morning in the spring of 1803. "Obstinacy in trying to preserve it would be madness. . . . This accession of territory consolidates the power of the United States forever, and I have given England a maritime rival who sooner or later will humble her pride."

On April 11, 1803, Robert Livingston arrived early for his regularly scheduled session of diplomatic charades with Talleyrand. As he had so many times before, the plenipotentiary planned to open the morning's pleasantries with an offer to purchase the port of New Orleans. Failing that, the Americans would consider purchasing right of access to the wharves and anchorage. The two men had no sooner exchanged personal greetings when the French minister preempted the American with a dramatic proposal. What, wondered Talleyrand, would the United States be willing to pay for all of Louisiana?

Although Jefferson can be credited with sitting beneath the tree that dropped the golden apple into his lap, he cannot be esteemed for simultaneously shaking the branch from which it fell. That was a later conceit, one whose legal underpinning and real-world meanings were finessed as it became a standard fiction of American history. The moment, ever since, has been mythologized as the defining and signature accomplishment of the Jefferson presidency, yet the fictive retelling of it effectively laid the groundwork for the great social migrations of the nineteenth century. As Felix Cohen explained more than a century later:

> The historic fact is that practically all of the real estate acquired by the United States since 1776 was purchased not from Napoleon or any other emperor or czar but from its original Indian owners. What we acquired from Napoleon in the Louisiana Purchase was not real estate, for practically all of the ceded territory that was not privately owned by Spanish and French settlers was still owned by the Indians, and the property rights of all the inhabitants were safeguarded by the terms of the treaty of cession. What we did acquire from Napoleon was not the land, which was not his to sell, but simply the power to govern and to tax, the same sort of power that we gained with the acquisition of Puerto Rico or the Virgin Islands, a century later.
>
> It may help us to appreciate the distinction between a sale of land and the transfer of governmental power if we note that after paying Napoleon 15 million dollars for the cession of political authority over the Louisiana Territory we proceeded to pay the Indian tribes of the ceded territory more than twenty times this sum for such lands in their possession as they were willing to sell. . . . While nobody has ever calculated the total sum paid by the United States to Indian tribes as consideration for more than two million square miles of land purchased from them, . . . a conservative estimate would put the total price of Indian lands sold to the United States at a figure somewhat in excess of 800 million dollars.

The treaty of cession was signed in Paris on April 30, 1803, and was ratified by the U.S. Senate on October 20. France's cession of governmental power over the 909,130 square miles of Louisiana more than doubled the size of the republic. The boundaries in the final accord were those claimed by the Sieur de La Salle in 1682 and formally documented on the map drawn by the famed Delisle in 1718. The annexation of Louisiana was an expansion of the nation's psyche as momentous as it was to its geographical boundaries, if not more so. With the scratch of a pen, all other meanings, said one historian, were reduced to nonentities. Among those nonentities was the fact that the sale was not only fictive, it was illegal. Napoleon sold Louisiana before the "retrocession" from Spain had actually taken place. Moreover, Napoleon ignored provisions in the Treaty of San Ildefonso that barred the French government from selling Louisiana to anyone other than the Spanish monarch. But, as time would tell, that condition was also trounced to mootness, as Napoleon kept news of the deal from his own government until the agreement was made with the Americans. Taken together, these nonentities measure the emperor's determination to drive a wedge between the Americans and the British. And while the deal merged "the implicit significance of the American political experiment to the implicit logic of continental geography," the United States and Great Britain would forthwith renew old antagonisms, just as Napoleon had hoped, and rush back to war in 1812.

But in 1803, those distant possibilities were of little concern to the ebullient third president. Whatever else Louisiana might represent, Jefferson told Congress that the republic's new territories were "the solution to the everlasting Indian problem." The nation now had a back door, one that opened on a vast, wide-open continent beyond the Mississippi, and that inexorable event, the removal of Indians from the eastern forests, could now commence in earnest.

As a child of the Enlightenment, Thomas Jefferson's dynamic curiosity lured his facile mind toward a dozen dissimilar mysteries simultaneously. Not least among those was a burning desire to see, through the eyes of his ambassadors, beyond all known geographical boundaries—a desire that produced a geopolitical wizard who never traveled fifty miles west of his home in Albemarle County, Virginia.

In his father's day, the frontier of the English colonial experience was the ridgeline of the Appalachians. By 1790, that frontier had reached the Mississippi. With the acquisition of Louisiana, it leaped across the Great Plains to the foot of the Rocky Mountains, encompassing nearly a million square miles of the great unknown. In Jefferson's mind, Louisiana was a geographic trust fund, a land bank of unknown riches that would be held in reserve for generations of Americans that were centuries from being born. He assumed another fifty years would pass before white settlements, following in the path of voluntary removals of Indian tribes, would subdue the wilderness between the Appalachians and the Mississippi.

Now that the great deed was done, the American republic could settle down to the civilized business of conquering that wilderness, one tree stump at a time. Jefferson was in no rush. For the time being he was more than content to see expansion follow an orderly pace, one that adhered to civil laws and moral requirements of human decency. After all, he spent Sundays in his garden or in his study, not in a house of worship. Jefferson had little use for organized religion as such, and less still for the lessons of Adam and Eve's fall in the mythical garden of Genesis. He had staked his political fortune on the common man's goodness outside of church—a readiness to abide by the laws of the land—so long as those laws remained within reason. "Not a foot of land shall be taken from the Indian without his consent," was his only cautionary caveat on the subject of expansion, one that was less presidential largesse than military prudence. As his predecessors had learned, Indian tribes west of the mountains were much too powerful in Jefferson's day to be removed by force, so he advised his countrymen to be patient. Indian wars in the Northwest had heaped an unnecessary burden on a bankrupt treasury, one that could have been avoided with diplomacy and forbearance. In time, the Indians would see that moving to the new lands in Louisiana, far removed from the whites, was in their own best interests. When that time came, they could be transplanted with little trouble, for they were wanderers by nature, and soon they would be wandering toward Louisiana.

In July 1803, the Louisiana Territory was so inextricably linked to Indian removal in Jefferson's thinking that he composed an "Indian Amendment" that he hoped Congress would append to the Constitution. Like most of his white constituents, friends, and neighbors, Jefferson was afraid that Northwest tribes could easily become a formidable barrier to white settlement beyond the mountains, just as they now were below the Mason-Dixon line. With the annexation of Louisiana, the tribes of both regions had a place "to remove" where they would be protected from the well-known ravages of white society. "The right of occupancy in the soil, and of self-government, are confirmed to the Indian inhabitants, as they now exist," the amendment began. "The United States shall have full rights for lands possessed by Indians within the United States on the East side of the Mississippi; to exchange lands on the East side of the river for those of the white inhabitants on the West side thereof, and above the latitude of 31 degrees." Below the thirty-first parallel (sixty or so miles north of New Orleans), Jefferson was reserving for settlement by whites. The United States would continue "to regulate trade and Intercourse between the Indian inhabitants and all other persons . . . and the legislature shall have no authority to dispose of the lands of the province otherwise than as hereinbefore permitted, until a new Amendment of the constitution shall give that authority."

"In at least one respect Jefferson was, contrary to his custom, consistent," says Abel, the foremost authority on removal-era legal history. "The greater part of the proposed amendment was taken up with . . . the removal of the eastern tribes to the upper Louisiana. Removal, as the term is technically used in American history, was apparently not only spontaneous, but absolutely original with Jefferson." Historian Anthony Wallace, in his exhaustive work *Jefferson and the Indians*, reduces Abel's conclusions to polite understatements. Jefferson peers down at us, he writes, "from a cliff in the Black Hills . . . , our own

version of the universal Trickster, that morally ambiguous mythic being who steals fire from gods and brings the arts, sciences, and social
institutions to the world." Just as Alexander Hamilton had predicted,
Jefferson's own record of deeds, as president, eventually betrayed his
record of words. As the foremost champion of individual liberty, Jefferson was the first to trample on the civil liberties of those who disagreed with him. Moreover, he was always quick to justify his actions
by declarations of virtuous and benevolent intentions. And while he
believed that "the tree of liberty must be refreshed from time to time
with the blood of patriots and tyrants," Jefferson often played the role of
the latter. Despite his many protests to the contrary, "Jefferson sought
power and exercised it forcefully, always of course in the name of the
liberty of 'the people'"—so long as "the people" did not include political
apostates or people of color. He was utterly intolerant and dismissive of
his political enemies, and those who disagreed with him were banished,
wherever possible, from government. As the historian Leonard Levy
has noted, no founder was more prepared to cast off the Bill of Rights,
to shed the blood of his countrymen, or to eliminate from the earth
anyone who did not bind himself to Jefferson's morally ambiguous and
paradoxical vision of liberty. In the end, says Wallace, this capacity
for accommodating political and moral contradictions "placed him on
the side of Indian-hating, riotous, even secessionist western frontiersmen rather than orderly, centralist eastern governments." Removal of
the Indians from their aboriginal homelands was completed as national
policy in the 1830s, but it was the champion of liberty from Monticello
who had been the original "planner of cultural genocide, the architect
of removal policy, the surveyor of the Trail of Tears."

Many public figures of Jefferson's day were clones of their constituents. Early Americans, particularly in the southern states, were fiercely
ethnocentric xenophobes. The new democratic philosophy was egalitarian in theory, though nowhere did egalitarian ideals translate into equality in the forest, on the plantation, in the government, or, for that matter,

on the wharf. Conversely, the autocracy the Founders had rejected so violently a generation before was known for embracing men and women of diverse backgrounds and nationalities. All the king's subjects were subjected (more or less) equally to the king's authority. The monarchical empire model was hierarchical, authoritarian, and ethnically inclusive, whereas the republican model was democratic, federalized, and ethnically monochromatic and exclusive. Although Jefferson was himself an unapologetic autocrat while he occupied the White House, his followers persisted in seeing the confederated community of towns and townships, cities and states, as a homogeneous mass of equals in which "no religion, party, faction, region, economic class, trade, or profession, or lineage could establish a tyrannical dominance over others." Yet that was precisely what was being done to anyone not belonging in the picture. Modern social concepts of diversity and pluralism would have been heresy in early America—even a cause for tarring and feathering on the white frontier. The homogeneous mass expected presidents and congressmen to perform two essential tasks: keep the intrigues of foreign states at bay and construct practical policies that promoted the expansion of democracy and opened up the public domain to settlement by whites. Only after those policies were in place was any thought given to providing legal and moral justifications for the methods used to achieve them. Therefore, after much consideration, Jefferson took the advice of Robert Smith, his secretary of the navy, and shelved his "Indian amendment." Smith warned Jefferson that guaranteeing the Indians possession of western land might, at some future time, act to impede settlement in the West and become an embarrassment to the government. The amendment, he argued, gave away too much in the absence of a compelling need. With remarkable prescience, Smith intuitively prefigured the emergence of a powerful expansionary social movement, Manifest Destiny, by four decades.

Between July 1803 and the passage of the Louisiana Territorial Act in 1804, Jefferson pursued alternative methods of removal with single-minded vigor. A scant ten years earlier, Secretary Knox had conceived an Indian policy for the Washington administration on the widely accepted notion that "the independent nations and tribes of Indians ought to be considered as foreign nations, not as the subjects of any particular state." If the federal government wasn't up to the task of enforcing its treaties, wrote Knox, contempt shown for federal authority by lawless white legislators and frontiersmen would quickly tell the more powerful Indian leaders that the agreements were "imbecile promises" made by a government that placed no honor in its word. In the intervening years, Indian wars on every frontier had borne Knox out. Neither President Jefferson nor the state legislatures had any intention of honoring the terms of the treaties. In Jefferson's mind, the only alternative to more wars was a vigorous removal policy.

Jefferson worked on his Indian removal plan through the fall and winter without ever consulting a tribal leader. The language of the Louisiana Territorial Act simply empowered the president to effect Indian emigration as events and circumstances warranted. This amounted to a blank check of unrestricted powers to commence and enforce ethnic cleansing in the eastern wilderness. The language was straightforward, unambiguous, and much to the liking of southern landowners. In their view, Indian removal was a fait accompli. Jefferson had already exempted them from contriving moral and legal justifications for removal when he signed the Georgia Compact of 1802. Now, it was just a question of how to best get on with the business of filling up all of those little squares in Indian territory with white people of democratic ideals and Christian faith.

In spite of his reputation for originality and strength of intellect, Jefferson's inordinate fear of monarchy prompted him to rule, particularly in times of crisis, with the fist of a tyrant, and his penchant for autocracy blinded him to the plots against the republic by jealous states whose cause he actively advanced toward a distant and violent reckoning with the federal government, half a century later. In the end, as his opponents had warned in the campaign of 1800, this myopic capitulation to the states' chronic perversions of the Constitution eventually led by a winding path to Civil War. But even if those things could be swept aside, he stands alone among the Founders for being "the originator of cultural genocide" of the American Indian. When played out to conclusion by his successors, Jefferson's policies and patterns of governance accounted for unprecedented misery for native people in the nineteenth century. It is one of America's great and unreconciled ironies that this seminal champion of "individual liberty" did more to limit "self-evident" and "inalienable" rights than any other founder, while his nemesis and cousin, John Marshall, did more as chief justice to protect individual liberty and enshrine those freedoms than perhaps any American before or since.

Over the next thirty years, Indian removal would expand and advance across the wilderness by fits and starts that were sometimes bloody, sometimes peaceful, always irrevocable. The official record of removal-era debates in Congress would eventually fill six volumes, each three inches thick. No other issue, including slavery, so thoroughly dominated the national agenda in the first half of the nineteenth century. Removal began with the voluntary migrations of small bands of Cherokee and Chickasaw people, then the Creek and the Choctaw, who were the first to relocate to the Missouri Territory during the Madison and Monroe administrations. In the north, the Kickapoo and the Pottawatomi, like the Sac and Fox, were torn between forming an alliance with the British and making peace with the Americans. They chose neither. Instead, they followed their friends the Delaware to the new Indian territory, in Missouri. Having signed their first pact with the Americans in 1778, the Delaware decided that they were finished with the business of treaty making. The preferred method for swindling tribes out of their land—make a treaty that recognized Indian lands and sovereignty, provoke a conflict with that tribe that could be contained and subdued by a larger military force, then revisit the earlier treaty and exchange promises of peace for new land cessions and removal—had been perfected on the Delaware. During the first thirty years of the nineteenth century, agents of Congress would use these same methods to acquire one hundred million acres of land between the Appalachians and the Mississippi River. Before Lewis and Clark set out with the Corps of Discovery in 1804, the treaty-making process had become the expedient of choice for sanctioning land grabs under the guise of diplomacy.

Once the tribes reached the Missouri Territory in the 1820s, it fell to the government's venerable superintendent of Indian affairs, William Clark, to carve out a piece of the map and help them adjust to their new surroundings. When Clark accepted his appointment from Congress in 1806 as Indian superintendent for the western tribes, the affable and mild-mannered adventurer was thirty-six years old. His new home, St. Louis, was little more than a river outpost of several hundred trappers, traders, whores, gamblers, and adventurers, that resilient breed of men and women who thrive on the seam between the rectangular order of civilization and the borderless wilds of the unknown. Before he died in 1838, Clark's career spanned a period that roughly paralleled the removal era in the East. A city of thirty-eight thousand had since grown up on the broad shoulders of frontier optimism and lucrative river trade. With its busy wharf and waterfront, St. Louis was a burgeoning inland port that connected trading posts on the Yellowstone with European seaports.

Even by 1820, that tiny American outpost had vanquished the British competition to the north and become the undisputed capital of the fur trade at the confluence of the Mississippi and Missouri rivers. St. Louis was home to fifteen physicians, twenty-three lawyers, forty-nine grocers and tavernkeepers, two printing offices, and enough prostitutes to relieve returning fur trappers of their wages in the city's one hotel. There was little order to the streets, which turned into bogs with the slightest rainfall, and the citizens, who lived mostly in widely scattered "mean little abodes" that were as likely to burn down as fall down, showed no interest whatever in public hygiene or cleanliness. Boatmen from New Orleans and the Ohio River mixed on the waterfront with trappers, Indians, slaves, missionaries, and entrepreneurs. Politics was the city's first blood sport, and differences of opinion, in a town where whites were outnumbered two to one by half-breed Frenchmen, Spanish Indians, and black mulattos, were settled with fists and weapons. Murders were common and often went unsolved, and after dancing and card playing, brawls were the city's favorite pastime. Women of all ranks, from slaves to rich dowagers, intermingled in the shops and on the streets and communicated across cultural boundaries in a rich patois of English, French, and Spanish. Father Pierre De Smet, a Belgian Jesuit missionary, wrote that from its earliest days St. Louis was unabashedly, incorrigibly American and "glittered in the morning sun like a Mexican fire opal. Boats lined the wharves where busy stevedores rolled cargo up and down the piers, and everything blazed with color." It epitomized the nation that the city was destined to help build, and Janus-faced, like the nation, St. Louis faced both the rising and setting suns.

Throughout his career, William Clark mediated these many tensions with the profiteering despotism of a benevolent warlord. Congress entrusted him with powers that came up just short of dictatorial. No expedition, whether for the exploration of new lands or to establish a commercial enterprise, could venture up the Missouri or down the Santa Fe Trail without obtaining his signature and his blessings. His home, a handsome two-story brick structure at the corner of Vine and Market streets, was, for Indians and whites alike, the western White House, the seat of the only authority that mattered on the frontier. Until his death, Plains Indians with business in St. Louis would say they were traveling to Clark's Town to visit the "red headed chief," and no one in government had greater knowledge of the land, of the rivers, and of the ethnography of the western tribes than the superintendent in St. Louis. While removal was getting under way in the Appalachians, Clark was uniquely familiar with the unofficial removal that commenced in the mid-eighteenth century from the northern forests of Minnesota onto the vast open grassland. In fact, he could practically see its effects from his back porch.

It was on those grasslands, while British colonists were preparing for war with the French in 1754, that the first of several waves of Indian migrations, including thirty or more tribes, was reaching the Great Plains from three different directions. From the northern woods came the Sioux and Cheyenne farmers who were pushed across Wisconsin and Minnesota by the powerful Chippewa and northern Cree tribes. Once on the plains, the Sioux and the Cheyenne migrated south along the Missouri River and spent time with the Mandan, who told them they might find a welcome homeland in the nearby Black Hills. About the time King George III was issuing his famous proclamation, the Sioux settled in the pine forests that overlooked the plains they were to dominate for the next hundred years.

From the northwest, Blackfeet agrarians, whose traditional homelands ranged from the Yellowstone River into modern-day Alberta along the eastern front of the Rocky Mountains, met up with the Crow and Shoshone, and finally with the Kiowa hunter-gatherers who migrated out of the central Rockies. The Kiowa, along with the Arapaho, had traveled east off the high plateau and then drifted south to the rich buffalo grounds of the Platte River country. And from the southeastern woodlands, the Osage, Ponca, Oto, Missouri, Kansas, and other Siouian-speaking people, advancing west ahead of the vanguard of white settlements, had met the long established Pawnee and Arikara, far out on the open plains of Kansas, Iowa, and Nebraska.

From north to south, the new homelands of the Plains tribes extended from the great wheat prairies of modern-day Canada to the Rio Grande on the border with Mexico. Not coincidentally, this ocean of short grass was also home to a humpbacked hairy beast, the American bison, which ranged freely across two million square miles in herds that were so large, wrote De Smet, that they turned the landscape black. The singular event that accelerated the nomadic colonization of the plains was the arrival of the horse, brought by the sixteenth-century Spanish expeditions of discovery into the desert southwest. This beast, first acquired by the Comanche from Spanish missions and trading posts, was a descendant of the animal that once revolutionized cultures on the Asian steppes and Arabian deserts. Now, it brought the same kind of roaming culture, and the same barter economy, to the nomadic Indian tribes that had recently migrated onto the vast American plains.

It was here that the horse and the bison—transportation and a plentiful source of sustenance—transformed the once semi-sedentary woodland agrarians into societies that were entirely new to the North American continent. With them, the Indians possessed the ingredients essential to economic success in an otherwise forbidding and hostile environment. During the latter half of the eighteenth century, the Comanche, Crow, Sioux, Cheyenne, Blackfeet, Arapaho, and Shoshone would flourish on the Great Plains. William Clark himself described them as the freest people ever to roam the earth. It was these voluntary migrations —seen firsthand by a few intrepid Hudson Bay fur traders—that formed the last obstacle on the plains to white migration across the continent to the Pacific Ocean.

By the end of James Madison's administration in 1816, the expansionist fever was spreading like a virus through frontier outposts across the eastern wilderness. The best efforts of Congress to coordinate orderly migrations of white settlers had collapsed into disorderly land grabs. Extinguishing Indian titles in what was then the Northwest (Ohio, Indiana, and lower Michigan) had become a mania with lawmakers in Washington. Madison's Indian commissioner, William Crawford, did his best to restrain these impulses, but even heroic labors could only retard the inexorable. For his contentious efforts, Crawford earned the eternal enmity of his nemesis in the South, General Andrew Jackson, who had shown himself ready and willing to use any means necessary to obtain the prize of Indian lands. Until this point, only one small faction of the four large southern tribes had actually taken up arms against the government, but the northwestern tribes were universally hostile. Having suffered depredations at the hands of whites since the days of William Penn, the Kickapoo, Pottawatomi, Sac and Fox, Delaware, and Miami tribes had no intention of accommodating the settlers.

Undaunted by the tribes' intransigence, Michigan's territorial governor Lewis Cass was not above using ruthless tactics of his own. The Indians, who had become well familiar with Cass and his methods of persuasion, decided the better part of valor was to remove while they could still obtain favorable terms for new homelands to the west. One by one, the northern tribes set out for the Missouri Territory in the first years of the Monroe administration, but they were living their prophecies. They were no sooner settled in Missouri than whites were again violating their boundaries and encroaching on their new treaty-protected homelands. James C. Calhoun, Monroe's secretary of war, was facing a problem that could not have been anticipated ten years before. After Missouri's petition for statehood was approved by Congress in the Compromise of 1820, it entered the union as a slave state. The subsequent relocation of the tribes into Missouri blocked free-state expansion north of the thirty-ninth parallel. It seemed that every solution that Congress contrived to solve its "Indian problem" only succeeded in spawning a new set of troubles elsewhere.

In the South, the last obstacles standing between whites and the Mississippi River were the formidable Creek and Cherokee tribes. If deep ambivalence characterized Madison's views on removal, no such doubts clouded the conscience of President Monroe, who, like his mentor Jefferson, was a staunch advocate of states' rights to the exclusion of all else. Monroe resisted pressures from southern legislatures to use coercive measures against the southern tribes in their midst, but the fox was already inside the henhouse. Monroe's friend and favorite treaty commissioner, Andrew Jackson, was not above using bullying tactics on congressmen from the North when they dared to question his treaty-making tactics, and President Monroe's good intentions were not well enough anchored in either personal character or the U.S. Constitution to overcome Jackson's relentless lobbying. By the end of Monroe's first administration, in 1822, Jackson was secretly encouraging the state of Georgia to provoke the tribes into war. What had worked with Florida's savages, the Creek and Seminole people, should work just as well in Georgia. In Jackson's view, something had to be done to dislodge the tribes and finish the business started by Jefferson. The tiny land cessions granted by the Creek and the Cherokee since 1812 were making a mockery of the Georgia Compact of 1802.

Land acquired from the Indians in the Northwest became part of the public domain, but not in Georgia. Due to the unique terms of the 1802 compact—terms that violated both the commerce and the supremacy clauses of the Constitution, as well as the Indian Non-Intercourse Act of 1790—Indian land cessions immediately became the property of the state. In Georgia's view, the federal government's policy of humoring the savages was effectively denying the state its birthright. Monroe was inclined to agree, but Georgia's well-documented treachery and murderous blackmail in earlier treaties, particularly the Treaty of Indian Springs with the Creek nation, had left such a humiliating diplomatic stain on his administration that even he was losing his enthusiasm for treaty making. What Monroe wanted most of all was an end to indignities. To achieve that, Congress needed to finance new talks with the tribes in order to get the state of Georgia off his administration's back.

For Georgians, talks could not begin soon enough. The discovery of gold on Cherokee lands during the late 1820s renewed the state's appeals for coercive measures against the intransigent savages. The finding of gold tripled the value of Indian lands in a matter of months. With encouragement from Georgia's political leaders, including former governor Troup and the new governor, George Gilmer, white prospectors flocked across Indian country borders from every direction. With deliberate provocation and defiance, Governor Gilmer thumbed his nose at the U.S. Congress and the Indian Trade and Intercourse Acts. Until that act was modified in 1834, whites could not legally travel across Indian land without passports, so Georgia toyed with those laws in an effort to goad the federal government into reacting. Miners took up their stations in Indian country, and the governor dared the U.S. government to evict them, promising war if federal troops violated Georgia's sovereignty. The president avoided that trap, but what followed was a period of lawlessness that stripped the War Department of its dignity and pretense to ultimate authority. To provoke the Indians (and the federal government) further, Georgians accused them of stealing the miners' personal property. After a flurry of inquiries, government investigators reported back to Congress that "hogs missed and no bones found in the woods" did not prove that Indians were the thieves. The entire episode had been carefully choreographed by Troup and Gilmer to provoke war.

Even after the Cherokee people had been surrounded on all sides by hostile whites, they remained steadfast in their refusal to move. When talks began in October 1823, the government's commissioners argued that the Great Father of the Universe had intended the earth "equally to be the inheritance of his white and red children." The Indians had heard this argument dozens of times. The people of Georgia must be speaking to a different god, they said, because that was clearly not the case. No amount of cessions would satisfy these whites, who wanted it all. And where was the incentive to move, the Cherokee leaders asked. Tales of horrific atrocities were already filtering back from their friends who had left for the western territory beyond the Mississippi. It was well known to them that whites, who became enraged when the government allowed Indians to select the best lands in Missouri and Arkansas, formed vigilante posses and went on a rampage. Rather than attack the government, the vigilantes burned Indian towns, slaughtered their livestock, incinerated their crops, and murdered their tribal members, all while the White Fathers stood by and watched from the distance, helpless (or unwilling) to stop the mayhem. The treaty makers had lied to the Creek, the Choctaw, and the Chickasaw. All had suffered great hardships, and they missed their homelands. The Cherokee, who had been put in this place by the Creator when time began, intended to remain until time ended. They had no intention of removing to the West, or to agreeing to make a new treaty.

The government commissioners had little leverage against this intransigence. The Cherokee claims were true. White men living on the frontier were proving to be reluctant followers of Jefferson's long cherished assumptions about human nature. Most of the whites encountered by the Cherokee were anything but "law abiding." For their part, the Choctaw and Sac and Fox people had no sooner arrived in Missouri than they were once again petitioning William Clark to move them— this time, as far from whites as possible. In fact, white settlers already occupied the new Choctaw homeland. It seemed that little about the nature of the frontiersmen had changed since 1790, when Caleb Swan told Congress that Indian country had become the last refuge for white rogues, villains, and rascals.

After hearing the Georgia Cherokee's complaints, Secretary Calhoun explained that President Jefferson's compact with the state placed insoluble burdens on the Great White Fathers. Despite their well-founded protests, in his view the only solution to this predicament was to find the Indians a new home. Through their legal counsel, William Wirt, the former attorney general for President Monroe, the Cherokee replied that they knew the compact word for word. They had studied it carefully. Full compliance with its terms required the government to secure the consent of the tribes, and they were unwilling to give that consent. They were not moving.

Calhoun relayed the Cherokee's position to the president and to the newly elected governor of Georgia, George McIntosh Troup. Troup responded by promising violent retaliation unless the federal government fulfilled its obligations to the state under the terms of the 1802 compact. Troup also claimed that William Wirt was bringing the two parties, Georgia and the federal government, to the point of spilling blood. Southern congressmen joined in, declaring on the floor in Congress that the diplomatic courtesy shown the savages by the Monroe administration was a scandal. The tribes must be removed at once.

The Cherokee were aware that Georgia's strongest argument for their removal was their adherence to primitive customs. The tribe hoped to preempt those charges by inventing its own alphabet, adopting a constitution, and building churches and schools. Their constitution, which was formally recognized by the federal government, declared the Cherokee to be absolutely sovereign. "We have a perfect and original right to remain without interruption or molestation," it read. "The treaties with us and the laws of the United States made in pursuance of treaties, guaranty our residence and privileges, and secures us against intruders. Our only request is, that these treaties may be fulfilled, and these laws executed."

In a counterintuitive twist, the Cherokee's preemptive measures proved to be their undoing. Georgia now exploited a flaw in federalism to press its point by ignoring the supremacy clause in Article VI of the Constitution and passing laws that abolished the Cherokee government. The state also claimed the right to distribute Cherokee lands among its citizens. Governor Troup asked the state courts to declare all Cherokee laws and land claims null and void. The state courts complied immediately. The state then argued that Georgia's actions were legal because the Cherokee, by declaring themselves a sovereign nation within the state boundaries, were in violation of Article IV of the Constitution.

This flaw in the Constitution's language, one prohibiting the creation of a state within a state without excluding Indian tribes from this proscription, now became the focal point for Cherokee removal. The incoming president, John Quincy Adams, took the Indians' view that their preexisting sovereignty exempted them from the state's claims, but that was the constitutional rub that had yet to be resolved. Despite the clear language in the Indian Commerce Clause of the Constitution, southern courts and legislators refused to recognize any special conditions governing tribal relations with the federal government. To them, the word *sovereignty* as it applied to Indians was an empty term of art, a meaningless confection that carried no legal weight. Georgia believed it now had the means to force a constitutional crisis. James Barbour, the secretary of war under Adams, took a courageous stand against the "southern tyrants" by laying the problems created by existing policies at the feet of the national government. He told lawmakers:

> Missionaries are sent among them to enlighten their minds by imbuing them with religious impressions. Schools have been established by the aid of private, as well as public, donations, for the instruction of their youths. They have been persuaded to abandon the chase—to locate themselves and become cultivators of the soil—implements of husbandry and domestic animals have been presented them, and all these things have been done, accompanied with professions of a disinterested solicitude for their happiness. ... And when they have so done *you* send your Agents to tell them that they must surrender their country to the white man, and re-commit themselves to some new desert, and substitute as the means of their subsistence the precarious chase for the certainty of cultivation. The love of our native land is implanted in every human bosom, whether he roams the wilderness, or is found in the highest state of civilization. ... Can it be matter of surprise that they hear, with unmixed indignation of what seems to them our ruthless purpose of expelling them from their country, thus endeared? They see that our professions are insincere—that our promises have been broken; that the happiness of the Indian is a

cheap sacrifice to the acquisition of new lands; and when attempted
to be soothed by an assurance that the country to which we propose to send them is desirable, they emphatically ask us, what new
pledges can you give us that we shall not again be exiled when it
is your wish to possess these lands? It is easier to state, than to
answer this question. A regard to consistency, apart from every
other consideration, requires a change of measures. Either let him
retain and enjoy his home, or, if he is to be driven from it, abstain
from cherishing illusions we mean to disappoint, and thereby make
him feel more sensibly the extent of his loss.

As Washington had warned in his Farewell Address a generation
earlier, the federal government, by refusing to resolve the states' rights
problem embedded in federalism, was now pitted squarely against itself.
Federalism, whose most salient flaws were waiting to be corrected at
Gettysburg, was now in a dangerous state of limbo. Every time Congress sought to enact a policy, one or more states would simply ignore
the central government's will with impunity. John Quincy Adams left
office with the Cherokee problem unresolved. When Andrew Jackson
replaced him, there could be no illusions about the eventual outcome.
Just as Jefferson had before him, President Jackson emasculated the
U.S. Constitution by refusing to intervene on the Indians' behalf if it
meant interfering with a state's authority inside its own limits.

Once again, the frontiersman was making up law to suit his ambitions, but Jackson had fierce allies who were eager to put his resolve
to the test. Governor George Gilmer, like his predecessors in Georgia,
echoed Jackson in his justification of removal when he stated: "Treaties
were expedients which ignorant, intractable, and savage people were
induced without bloodshed to yield up what civilized peoples had a right
to possess by virtue of that command the Creator delivered to man
upon his formation—be fruitful, multiply, and to replenish the Earth,
and subdue it."

Nevertheless, while Secretary of War Barbour had his admirers in Congress, many more agreed with the former president, John Quincy Adams, that humanitarian considerations demanded that Congress remove the Indian for his own protection. "In appropriating to ourselves their hunting grounds," he declared in his final message to Congress in 1828, "we have brought upon ourselves the obligation of providing them with subsistence. . . . This state of things requires that a remedy should be provided."

Northerners, as a bloc, were sympathetic to the Indians' "plight" and refused to endorse Jackson's harsh methods. In a speech from the floor that became the basis for dozens of future Supreme Court cases involving tribal sovereignty, Representative Henry R. Storrs of New York attacked Jackson for embarrassing Congress by attempting to render the intercourse laws "a dead letter on the statute books and virtually annulling Indian treaties, some of which he personally negotiated." Jackson, declared Storrs, had arrogated to himself powers that had never been conceded to the executive, said Storrs, for once a treaty is fixed as the supreme law of the land, he has no power to "supercede it by giving to his own proclamation the force of law."

Jackson's first message to Congress was an open invitation to southern lawmakers to send him a bill that would formally adopt removal as national policy. The Indians could either move west, beyond the Mississippi, or suffer the wrath of hostile state governments. His speech was no sooner printed in newspapers than petitions demanding that the government honor its obligations to the Indians began flooding congressional mailboxes. The Senate's Committee on Indian Affairs, made up entirely of southerners—including former governor Troup, now a senator from Georgia—ignored these appeals and pressed ahead. In 1830, following a debate that went on for weeks, Congress passed a removal bill with 102 ayes and 97 nays. When it was sent to the Senate for consideration, Senator Theodore Frelinghuysen of New Jersey attached an amendment requesting protection for the Indians from states until removal could be effected. It lost. He then asked that treaty rights be respected until removal began and lost again. Senator Peleg Sprague, of Maine, insisted that treaties, as the supreme law of the land, could not be undone at the whim of the executive, but that, too, was voted down. The bill, thus unamended, was sent to the president for his signature.

To the average citizen, nothing about this law, the Indian Removal Act, suggested anything out of the ordinary. It simply gave the chief executive the authority to offer an exchange of lands to any of the tribes "now residing within the limits of the states or territories." Though the law itself said nothing about compulsory removal, its purpose was clear to the Indians. Within weeks, the Chickasaw signed a provisional treaty of removal, and three weeks later, the remaining Choctaw signed a removal treaty at Dancing Rabbit Creek, on September 27, 1830. Land that had belonged to the Indians in perpetuity, guaranteed by the "supreme law of the land," was now on the auction block in the white man's marketplace. While northern lawmakers continued to press Jackson for an accounting of his enforcement of the Indian Trade and Intercourse Acts in his dealings with the state of Georgia, the president snubbed them by withdrawing federal troops from Cherokee lands. He then turned a blind eye as Georgia sought to extend its own laws over the Cherokee lands and people.

Until *Johnson v. McIntosh* reached the U.S. Supreme Court in 1823 and forced the question of just who controlled title to Indian-occupied lands, the high court had very limited experience with issues pertaining to Indian's civil liberties under United States law. As Chief Justice Marshall would point out in a later opinion, disputes between Indians and whites were typically settled by appeals to Congress—or by resorting to bloodshed. More often than not, Indian attacks on white settlers were the result of the white man's failure to abide by the terms he himself had dictated. *Johnson,* the first of the three Marshall trilogy cases that form the basis for modern-day federal trust relations with Indian tribes, spawned cottage industries within the legal profession. Over the next 180 years, its legal freight would be parsed, weighed, and analyzed through myriad lenses and scales. Apart from these well-reasoned explications and extrapolations, *Johnson*'s lasting importance for federal Indian law would be borne not only by the high points of its ruling but also by the questions it seemed purposely to defer to later cases.

The question to be answered in *Johnson* was whether parcels of land sold by the Illinois and Piankeshaw nations to a land syndicate in the Ohio Valley in 1775 carried with them a title that could be recognized in a court of law. Writing for the majority—as was his long-standing custom—Marshall took a middle road by first explaining that the legal relationship between Indians and the discovering nations of Europe was one forged by "necessity." Rather than aligning himself with the sixteenth-century Spanish philosopher Francisco de Vitoria and his humanistic application of natural law—which would allow the Indians to sell their land to whomever they pleased—Marshall recognized instead the aboriginal "right of occupancy," a condition that restricted the sale of their land to the "discovering" sovereign. In this case, Marshall dismissed Vitoria's conclusions in "On the Indians Lately Discovered" by saying that natural law did not apply to contests involving persons whose "character and habits" were so at odds with whites. In other words, the doctrine of discovery controlled the origin and disposition of titles to the Indian lands. The title acquired by the land syndicate directly from the Indians was therefore null and void.

Marshall was threading a legal needle in *Johnson*. As the editors of *Cases and Materials on Federal Indian Law* have noted, this decision, rendered in the narrowest of legal senses, had enormous downstream implications. Nevertheless, it also succeeded in raising far more questions than it could answer in such a limited dispute. How, for example, would colonization of Indian lands define the federal-tribal relationship beyond the simple question of land rights? What was the significance of the treaties? What would balance and define the legal relationship between the Indians and the states in future contests over resources?

Felix Cohen argued a century later that, rather than being a clever balancing act, Marshall invented a solution that reflected his sense of remorse over the way Indian rights had been treated under the European law of nations. Marshall could not know it yet, but before his career ended he would get the opportunity to address that remorse. A letter the chief justice wrote to his friend and fellow judge Joseph Story, shortly before the Cherokees filed suit against Georgia in 1831, supports Cohen's reading of Marshall's veiled nuance.

Story, who was deeply concerned about the fate of Indians, had recently delivered a speech in which he observed that native people were owned by "ferocious passions, . . . independent spirit, [and] their wandering life," qualities that prevented them from assimilating successfully into the white society. This dissimilarity between the cultures, said Story, would pose serious problems as white settlement moved west. The big question in his mind was "whether the country itself shall be abandoned by civilized man, or maintained by his sword as the right of the strongest." Characteristically, Marshall's response was thoughtful and penetrating: "It was not until the adoption of our present government that respect for our own safety permitted us to give full indulgence to those principles of humanity and justice which ought always to govern our conduct towards the aborigines when this course can be pursued without exposing ourselves to the most afflicting calamities. That time, however, is unquestionably arrived, and . . . I often think with indignation on our disreputable conduct in the affairs of the Cherokees in Georgia."

The Georgia Cherokee demanded an audience with the president, but Jackson declined. He also refused to uphold their treaty rights against Georgia's incursions on their sovereignty. Not ones to be intimidated by the blustering Jackson and Gilmer, the Cherokee decided to take the only path left to them. At the urging of Daniel Webster, they asked William Wirt to take their case to the U.S. Supreme Court. Wirt agreed and was immediately excoriated in the southern press. Anyone who doubted that the problem of states' rights would one day lead to war had only to read the *Knoxville Register* of Tennessee on July 21, 1830, where the editors wrote: "We are thus convinced that Mr. Wirt and his employers can have but one object in view—and that is to increase the excitement that has been got up on the Indian Question. They may hope to enlist the Supreme Court in their behalf, and to procure a decision adverse to the sovereignty of Georgia and to effect thereby, in the sequel, a severance of the Union . . . , [and] should they [Georgians] be forced to resist a decree of the federal judiciary, they would not stand alone in the conflict. Thus, under pretense of sustaining the pretensions of the Cherokees to sovereignty and independence, the opposition are obviously striving to overthrow the State governments or to dissolve the Union. The treason of [Benedict] Arnold, though more palpable, was not more reprehensible or base."

With the passage of the Removal Act, the legislature of the young American republic had conceived and promulgated its own direct descendant of Pope Innocent IV's *Quod super his*. A claim of superior rights over heathens and infidels made by a medieval pope, a Spanish king, an English queen, seven southern legislatures, and three American presidents was now on its way to a reckoning with Chief Justice John Marshall and the U.S. Supreme Court.

John Locke, the leading seven-
teenth-
century British empiricist of the
Enlightenment whose original ideas
and writings on liberal political
theory, including "government
with the consent of the governed"
and the inalienable rights of life, liberty, and property, found their most
influential expression in the Americans' Declaration of Independence.
(Portrait by H. Garnier de Fon-
rough/Library of Congress)

Chief Justice John Marshall, probably the most important of all the
Founders of the nation, and certainly the most underappreciated.
Appointed to the Supreme Court
in the final days of John Adams's
turbulent presidency, Marshall
spent the next thirty-five years
using the court to turn the theories
proposed by the makers of the
U.S. Constitution into the workable
machinery of republican government. Much of that machinery was
dismantled or ignored by subsequent Congresses and presidents.
(William E. Barton Collection,
Special Collections Research
Center, University of Chicago
Library)

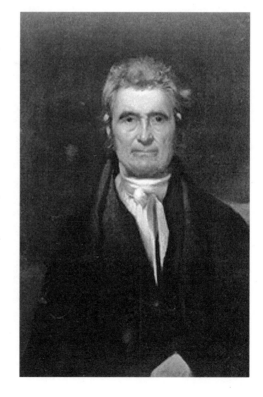

Above: Riverfront view of
St. Louis in 1836, at the time
Thomas Fitzpatrick was leading
the first wagon trains across
the Oregon Trail. (T. Moore
lithograph of a painting by
E. W. Playter; courtesy of
the Missouri History Museum,
St. Louis)

Right: An Arikara woman
gathering bullrushes at Fort
Berthold, on the Upper Missouri
River, in the modern-day
state of North Dakota. (Photo
by Edward Curtis)

Irish immigrant Thomas Fitzpatrick played a singularly important and unheralded role in the settlement of the American West by Europeans. He arrived in the frontier town of St. Louis in 1822, and a few months later joined the famed Ashley expedition to the Rocky Mountains. A natural leader of men, Fitzpatrick soon teamed up with the legendary mountain man and guide Jim Bridger to own and run the Rocky Mountain Fur Company. In March 1824, Fitzpatrick discovered South Pass in the Wyoming country, the geographic landmark on the continental divide that made it possible for him to lead the first expeditions of settlers and missionaries over the Oregon Trail in 1836. Later he guided the expeditions of John C. Frémont and General Stephen Watts Kearny to California and the Oregon and New Mexico territories. Other than his friend Father Pierre De Smet, no white man enjoyed greater respect among the tribes of the high plains and the Mountain West than Fitzpatrick. He became the Indian agent for the Platte River region in 1846, and was named co-commissioner, with David D. Mitchell, for the unprecedented gathering of western tribes at the Horse Creek treaty council in 1851. (Used with permission, State Historical Society of Missouri, Columbia)

Albert Bierstadt's painting of a wagon train entering the Oregon Territory on the Oregon Trail, the ultimate destination for hundreds of thousands of nineteenth-century settlers.

Legendary mountain man Jim Bridger was peerless in his knowledge of the American West, and indispensable to the Fort Laramie Peace Council in 1851. After he and Thomas Fitzpatrick disbanded their fur company, Bridger built an eponymous trading post and fort on the Oregon Trail, at Black's Fork of the Green River in the Wyoming territory. Highly regarded by all the western tribes and fluent in most of their languages, Bridger married the daughter of the Shoshone chief Washakie, and acted as the Shoshone's translator to the Horse Creek council. (Courtesy of the Fort Laramie National Historic Site/ Meyers Collection)

David D. Mitchell, treaty commissioner at Horse Creek, and the superintendent of Indian affairs in 1841–1844 and 1849–1853. Mitchell was an early advocate of native rights and, along with Thomas Fitzpatrick, a chief proponent of a treaty council with western tribes to forestall open conflict between white settlers and Indians on the Oregon Trail. (Courtesy of the Missouri History Museum, St. Louis)

Born in Belgium in 1801, Pierre De Smet helped establish the Jesuit mission in St. Louis in the 1820s, and went on to become the most peripatetic Roman Catholic missionary in the American West, traveling many thousands of miles by foot across unmapped territory. Known as Black Robe, De Smet became a trusted and valued friend to dozens of tribes, and his counsel would eventually be sought by the nation's leading generals and explorers. Like Mitchell and Bridger, De Smet was a fierce and unwavering advocate for native rights. (Used with permission, State Historical Society of Missouri, Columbia)

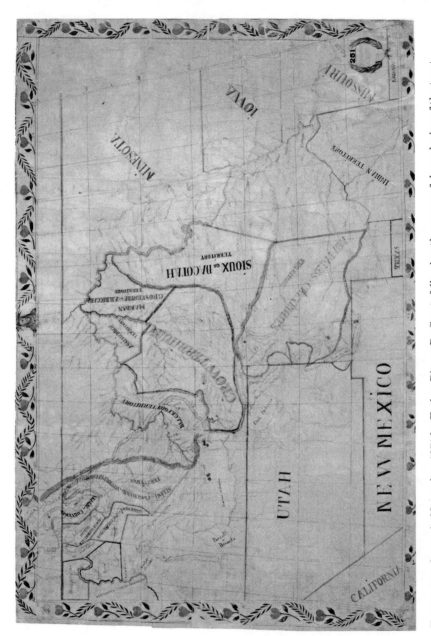

Treaty map drawn in November 1851 by Father Pierre De Smet, following the successful conclusion of the treaty council at Horse Creek. (Courtesy of Geography and Map Division/Library of Congress)

Originally called Henry's Fort when it was first built by fur traders in 1832, Fort Laramie was eventually purchased by Congress in 1848 and turned into a military outpost. (Painting by Rex A. Norman/Fort Laramie National Historic Site)

A *Harper's Weekly* illustration of Custer's Seventh Cavalry attacking Black Kettle's village on the Washita River, near Cheyenne, Oklahoma, at daylight on November 27, 1868. This unprovoked attack, coming four years after the massacre of the Cheyenne at Sand Creek, caused a new generation of Indian leaders to repudiate treaties and declare open warfare on the whites.

Left: Martin Cross as a young rodeo cowboy in the 1920s. He was among the first modern-day Native American leaders to use the law and the U.S. Constitution to protect his tribes' treaty rights when he became tribal chairman of the Mandan, Hidatsa, and Arikara nations in 1944. (Photo courtesy of Martin Cross family)

Below: Overcome by grief, tribal chairman George Gillette fights back his emotions at a signing ceremony held in Congress on May 20, 1948, as Secretary of the Interior Julius Krug signs the formal takings act that allowed Congress to "condemn" 156,000 acres of the tribes' ancestral homelands, to make way for the building of Garrison Dam on the Upper Missouri River. (AP Images/William Chaplis)

FOUR
Pioneers of the World

William Wirt was a reluctant but conscientious conscript into the Cherokee's war with Georgia. In many respects, he was the intellectual and moral mentor to Felix Cohen, who freely quoted Wirt's principled arguments in his *Handbook of Federal Indian Law*. Throughout his career Wirt was a tireless defender of native rights, but that did not prevent his brother-in-law, Governor Gilmer of Georgia, from scoffing with contempt at Wirt's latest gamble. Wirt was worried that the governor, for all the wrong reasons, might have a narrow point on which to grind the ax of states' rights. Among the Constitution's many problematic omissions was its failure to explain how Indian tribes could bring lawsuits against states in federal courts. Since Article IV prohibited the tribe from being a state, the Cherokee's only recourse was to file for an injunction against Georgia as a foreign government.

With Daniel Webster acting as his neutral messenger, Wirt attempted to determine from Marshall whether the Cherokee's status as a foreign nation would raise a jurisdiction issue for the court. In his encouraging reply, Marshall expressed his mounting despondency over the passage of the Removal Act and commented that "Humanity must bewail the course which is pursued" by Jackson and Congress. The chief justice then added, as if in afterthought, that to comment before the hearing on the underlying question of jurisdiction would be an improper use of his authority.

Wirt's apprehensions about Article IV were well founded. The court heard his motion for an injunction against the state of Georgia on March 5, 1831. As usual, his arguments were both moving and persuasive. He told the court that Indian sovereignty was a sacred legal principle that predated the formation of the national government, and this principle had been affirmed in international law by the governments of all 'civilized' nations. "So long as a tribe exists and remains in possession of its lands," he said, "its title and possession are sovereign and exclusive, and there exists no authority to enter upon their lands for any purpose whatever, without their consent. . . . They do not hold under the States, nor under the United States; their title is original, sovereign, and exclusive. We treat them as separate sovereignties, and while an Indian nation continues to exist within its acknowledged limits, we have no more right to enter upon their territory without their consent than we have to enter upon the territory of a foreign prince."

While the justices were weighing the case's merits, the Georgia state legislature was presented with a propitious opportunity to convey to Mr. Marshall what it thought of his court's jurisdiction. A Cherokee named Corn Tassel was arraigned before the state court for murdering a fellow tribesman in a dispute that took place on Cherokee land. The tribe appealed to the U.S. Supreme Court for a writ of habeas corpus, arguing that the Treaty of Holston recognized the tribal court's jurisdiction in deciding disputes between its own citizens in its own territory. While the high court's decision was pending in *Cherokee Nation v. Georgia*, Marshall issued the writ supporting the tribe's claim. The Georgia legislature responded by passing a motion that condemned the chief justice for meddling in state affairs. The legislature then ordered the state court to carry out the sentence. Corn Tassel was hanged five days later by a state executioner.

At the same time that *Cherokee Nation v. Georgia* was the talk of the Atlantic seaboard, a twenty-six-year-old aristocratic Frenchman named Alexis de Tocqueville happened to be traveling across America with his companion, Gustave de Beaumont. The young Parisian lawyer had applied for a visa to study the American penitentiary system. This was a pretext only, as the real object of his yearlong journey was to observe the machinery of democracy at work in various regions of the new republic. Like Felix Cohen a century later, Tocqueville seemed to understand intuitively that the Indian was the "miner's canary" in this grand experiment in representative democracy. Events the Frenchman witnessed firsthand, such as the forced removal of the Creek people in 1831, did not bode particularly well for either the Indians or the whites. "[President] Washington said in one of his messages to Congress, 'We are . . . bound in honor to treat them [the Indians] with kindness and even with generosity,'" wrote Tocqueville, but "this virtuous and high-minded policy has not been followed." In fact, he observed, the rapacity of the settlers for land was usually supported by "the tyrannical measures" of state governments." With his trademark precision of insight, Tocqueville went on to explain: "The Union treats the Indians with less cupidity and rigor than the policy of the several States, but the two governments are alike destitute of good faith. The States extend what they are pleased to term the benefits of their laws to the Indians, knowing the tribes will recede rather than submit, while the central government, which promises a permanent refuge to these unhappy beings does so knowing it lacks the will and the resolve to secure it to them. Thus, the tyranny of the states oblige the savage to retire; the Union, by its promises and resources, facilitates their retreat; and these measures tend to precisely the same end."

To the resounding joy of southerners, Wirt's request for an injunction was dismissed by the Marshall court for "want of jurisdiction." The case was anything but clear cut. With justices Story and Thompson dissenting, the court split 2–2–2, with one justice absent. Marshall dismissed the request in a straightforward manner, explaining that the Cherokee tribe did not constitute a foreign state within the meaning of Article III, section 2, of the Constitution. Therefore, the Indians lacked standing to bring the challenge as it was presented to the court.

But Marshall could not pass up the opportunity to address questions left over from *Johnson v. McIntosh*. He was feeling his years, and though his mind was as sharp as ever, it was impossible to know if, or when, another Indian case might come before the court and offer the opportunity to resolve the ever-mounting problems with federalism—problems that were becoming more pronounced and contentious with each passing year. His "obiter dictum" commentary transformed *Cherokee Nation v. Georgia* from an obscure dead-letter legal footnote into one of the most important Indian law cases ever decided by the high court. "If courts were permitted to indulge their sympathies," Marshall wrote, "a case better calculated to excite them can scarcely be imagined." But before he addressed the merits of the case, Marshall explained that the court was obliged to address first a preliminary inquiry. "Has this court jurisdiction of the cause?"

Since the tribes resided within the acknowledged boundaries of the United States, they could not, "with strict accuracy, be denominated foreign nations." Rather, said Marshall, they were "more correctly domestic dependent nations" that were separated from others, and fully capable of managing their own affairs, just like any foreign nation. The relationship between the federal government and the Indian tribes "is perhaps unlike that of any other two people in existence . . . marked by peculiar and cardinal distinctions which exist no where else." Marshall also noted—with his irritations in clear view—that the Founders had failed to either explain or account for how tribes and states were to address their grievances against each other in federal courts. In a tone that invited the opportunity to correct this oversight, he added that this was an issue that fell outside the conceptual parameters of this case.

Even if the court had jurisdiction, which justices Story and Thompson claimed it did, *Cherokee Nation* would not have given Marshall access to the issues he wished to tackle. The didactic tone of his opinion belied a tension between the legal question at hand that pertained to federalism, and those that fell just out of reach. Unbeknownst to either the court or the Indians, the wheel of fate was already turning and grinding toward a momentous confrontation.

Encouraged by President Jackson and the passage of the Removal Act, the Georgia legislature overstepped its authority by declaring the Cherokee government a non-entity. It compounded the illegal effect of this calumny by passing a simple resolution extending state sovereignty over Indian lands. This brazen usurpation of federal power was a first. Nor had any state government ever made such an affront against the sovereign immunity of an Indian nation. Without realizing the possible consequences of its actions, Georgia had already obliged Marshall and the Indians by engaging them in a new dispute that would encompass a much broader range of issues than either *Johnson* or *Cherokee*. When a group of white missionaries visited their Cherokee friends and held a meeting in the Indian town of New Echota without first obtaining a license to travel in Indian country from the governor of Georgia, the state sent its marshals to arrest the missionaries for violating state law. This was a new day and a new law, said the state, and the Georgia legislature was determined to show that it had the upper hand in Indian country by enforcing it to the last letter.

The missionaries, of whom Samuel A. Worcester was a principal, were arrested, found guilty, and sentenced to four years of hard labor at a state-owned rock quarry. The arrests were made "without a warrant from any magistrate, or any civil precept whatever," and "the proceedings were entirely of a military character." The state of Georgia, with unabashed contempt for due process of law, had summarily suspended the missionaries' civil liberties. The *Missionary Herald* newspaper reported that the missionaries were arrested for "having exerted on the Cherokees an influence unfavorable to their removal" and for failing to obtain "a license from the governor of Georgia."

While *Cherokee Nation v. Georgia* was being deliberated by the U.S. Supreme Court, Worcester, who also happened to be the United States postmaster at the Cherokee town of New Echota, and eight of his fellow missionaries were immediately shackled in leg irons and put to work making small rocks out of big ones. As word of the arrests spread to

Washington—that nine men of God had been sent to state prison for taking religion to the Indians—the Worcester affair very quickly degenerated into a public relations nightmare. Governor Gilmer, realizing that no good could possibly come of it—that the state had picked the wrong people to test its authority over Indian country—attempted to reverse the state's course by offering to set the missionaries free with a full pardon. Of the nine inmates, Worcester and Dr. Elizur Butler were not mollified by the governor's belated attempts to save face. Worcester declined the offer in a long letter to Governor Gilmer that stated, in part:

> Your excellency is pleased to intimate that I have been guilty of a criminal opposition to the humane policy of the general government. I cannot suppose that your Excellency refers to those efforts for the advancement of the Indians in knowledge, and in the arts of civilized life, which the general government has pursued ever since the days of Washington, because I am sure that no person can have so entirely misrepresented the course which I have pursued during my residence with the Cherokee people. . . . [Y]our excellency is pleased further to intimate that I have excited the Indians to oppose the jurisdiction of the state. In relation to this subject, also, permit me to say, your excellency has been misinformed. Neither in this particular am I conscious of having influenced, or attempted to influence the Indians among whom I reside. At the same time, I am far from wishing to conceal the fact, that, in my apprehension, the circumstances in which providence has placed me, have rendered it my duty to inquire whose is the rightful jurisdiction over the territory in which I reside; and that this inquiry has led me to a conclusion adverse to the claims of the state of Georgia. This opinion, also, has been expressed—to white men with the greatest freedom; and to Indians, when circumstances elicited my sentiments.
>
> I need not, however, enlarge upon these topics. I thought it

proper to notice them in a few words, because I understood your excellency to intimate that, in these respects, I had been guilty of a criminal course of conduct. If for these things I were arraigned before a court of justice, I believe I might safely challenge my accusers to adduce proof of anything beyond that freedom in the expression of opinions, against which, under the constitution of our country, there is no law. . . . Your excellency will accept the assurance of my sincere respect.

After reading the prisoners' response to the charges, Governor Gilmer again extended Worcester and Butler the offer of a pardon if they would drop the suit and quietly go away. Though evidence is lacking to put the proof beyond doubt, his proposal suggests that the governor was beginning to appreciate the legal perils the case posed for the state, which had been temporarily obscured by zealots acting in haste. The legislature's irrational exuberance over finally ridding itself of its Indian problem had, as an unintended effect, swept the state government into dangerous legal waters. Although seven of the missionaries had accepted the governor's pardon, Worcester and Butler persisted in declining. Hoping to defuse the situation, Gilmer asked governor-elect Wilson Lumpkin to pay the recalcitrant inmates a visit. Ruefully, Lumpkin reported back to the legislature that the two missionaries, though they were visited in prison "by a number of highly respectable gentlemen who urged them not to appeal to the Supreme Court of the United States, but to accept of a pardon from the governor of the state and promise not to return to the Cherokee nation," were nevertheless unlikely to do so.

Worcester and Butler's response to the highly respectable gentlemen was, in a word, astonishing. It was also reminiscent of, if not inspired by, that of Sir Thomas More, three centuries before, when he challenged the authority of King Henry VIII. *"What are we to gain by the further prosecution of this case?"* the prisoners asked. *"Our personal liberty?*

There is much more prospect of gaining it by yielding than by perseverance. And if not, it is not worthy of account in comparison with the interests of our country. *Freedom from the stigma of being pardoned criminals?* That also is a consideration of personal feeling not to be balanced against the public good," they replied. *"The arresting of the hand of oppression?* It is already decided that such a course cannot arrest it. *The prevention of the violation of the public faith?* That faith, it appears to us, is already violated; and, as far as we can see, our perseverance has no tendency to restore it. *The privilege of preaching the gospel to the Cherokees?* That privilege is at least as likely to be restored by our yielding as by our perseverance. *The reputation of being firm and consistent men?* Firmness degenerates into obstinacy if it continues when the prospect of good ceases; and the reputation of doing right is dearly purchased by doing wrong."

The prisoners' resolve was not to be dislodged by appeals from the state, or by offers of clemency. In their opinion, what the state was doing to the Cherokee nation was also making a moral and legal mockery of the Bill of Rights, a challenge that demanded the attention of a higher court. Until the case came to trial they were content to continue smashing rocks in the Georgia sun. Accordingly, Worcester and Butler asked William Wirt to appeal to the high court on their behalf. The petition for relief must complain that the state had overstepped its constitutional authority by trespassing on Cherokee lands. Additionally, it must allege that the state had violated Worcester's and Butler's civil liberties by arresting them. Coincident to this growing litany of transgressions, the suit argued that the state of Georgia unlawfully abrogated the Cherokee's Treaty of Holston, an audacious action for which it had no authority. Former attorney general Wirt filed the suit. Rather than marvel at the resolute fortitude and principled sacrifice of the two plaintiffs, the governor and the legislature were instead enraged by their bold presumptions.

Johnson v. McIntosh, all ramifications aside, raised a narrow question whose answer had far-reaching implications for native ownership of aboriginal lands. The second case of the Marshall trilogy, *Cherokee Nation v. Georgia*, stumbled on the issue of jurisdiction. Nevertheless, it was not dismissed before Marshall reformulated federalism by re-aligning the trust relationship between the federal government and the tribes. *Worcester v. Georgia* pitted the sovereignty of Indian nations and the sanctity of treaties against the jurisdictional presumptions of the southern states. For the Cherokee, this was the last game of the season in the last season of the world. Here, too, was the case that gave the aging Marshall the opportunity to render definitive answers to questions that had been so carefully avoided by the Founders: How does a state's sovereignty match up against the sovereignty of an Indian nation, and, given that Article VI of the Constitution protects the tribal compacts as "the supreme law of the land," which trumps which? But time, more than ever, was of the essence. Worcester and Butler were hard at work in the stone quarry, and President Jackson was pressing Congress and the states to commence implementing the Removal Act as soon as possible. With these things in mind, Marshall spent just two weeks composing the court's majority opinion.

The restrictions inherent in the previous two cases were no longer constraining factors in *Worcester*. "Necessity" and "jurisdiction" had fallen away as defining issues. In the court's decision, delivered on March 3, 1832—almost a year to the day after the court heard *Cherokee Nation*—Marshall at last redressed his long-standing discomfort with the "necessity" of relying on the doctrine of discovery as the principle of genesis for federal Indian law. *Worcester* allowed him instead to return to Francisco de Vitoria's assertion based on natural law—that the Indi-ans were inherently sovereign—as a starting place. The governmental mechanisms brought to the American shore by European discoverers, or imposed on the Indians by force subsequent to that discovery, in no manner diminished the inherent natural law rights of the Indian inhabi-tants. Furthermore, the state of Georgia had no authority to violate Worcester's and Butler's civil liberties, nor any expressed or implied right to extend its jurisdiction onto the lands of a sovereign people. Accordingly, the state had no authority to unilaterally abrogate the tribe's Treaty of Holston, a solemn Washington-era compact in which the federal government had assumed a constitutional obligation to protect and defend the Cherokee tribal government and its citizens and resources. In summary, wrote Marshall, the state of Georgia's actions were extensions of authority it never possessed in the first place. "The acts of Georgia are repugnant to the Constitution, laws, and treaties of the United States. They interfere forcibly with the relations established between the United States and the Cherokee nation, the regulation of which, according to the settled principles of our constitution, are committed exclusively to the government of the union." For its part, the federal government had long been on the record as formally recognizing "the pre-existing power of the [Cherokee] nation to govern itself." It was also the high court's opinion that the state's judgment condemning Samuel Worcester and Elizur Butler to hard labor "is void, as being repugnant to the Constitution, treaties, and laws of the United States, and ought, therefore, to be reversed and annulled."

To this day, the high court's opinion in *Worcester* reverberates in aftershocks that periodically rattle and rumble through the bedrock of federalism. When the state of Washington sought to deny Indians access to ancestral shellfish harvests, in 1998, the U.S. Supreme Court cited *Worcester* in finding for the tribes. After the Mille Lacs band of Chippewa demanded their usufructuary right to fish on their ancestral lakes in Minnesota, Justice Sandra Day O'Connor in 1999 reminded an indignant Antonin Scalia and William Rehnquist that the federal government had an unimpeachable trust relationship with the tribes that was secured in perpetuity by *Worcester*. When the Salish-Kootenai tribes of Montana imposed water quality standards on non-Indian residents living on their reservation, including a white-owned town, in 1996, *Worcester* applied. When the Yaqui and Pequot and Santa Rosa Pueblo went to court to open tribal casinos, Marshall's opinion in *Worcester* was the argument that controlled the outcomes. The principles established by *Worcester* have since been invoked in hundreds of Indian law cases where jealous state governments have sought with tenacious persistence to encroach on tribal resources or to restrict tribal sovereignty.

But in 1832, the court's opinion was viewed by the state of Georgia, and the president of the United States, as an egregious abridgment of states' rights and an unconscionable perversion of the republic's Constitution, one they were duty-bound to denounce and ignore. Which they did. President Jackson was well aware that the court had no mechanism for enforcing its will, and no army or police it could call upon to impose its mandate. So Jackson dismissed Marshall's ruling with casual indignation and advised the southern states to do the same. Meanwhile, through the magic of legal logrolling and political trickery, Georgia contrived a means for releasing the two missionaries without ever acknowledging their victory. A proclamation issued on January 14, 1833, by Governor Lumpkin directed the keeper of the state penitentiary to release the missionaries from the state's custody.

In anticipation of the *Worcester* verdict, governors Gilmer and Lumpkin, and President Jackson, conspired to press ahead with compulsory removal measures aimed at the Cherokee. The tribes pushed back with administrative counterattacks that bought them some more time, and the ensuing tug of war with Georgia and Congress ran on into the presidencies of Martin Van Buren and William Henry Harrison. Despite these delays, President Jackson's refusal to enforce Marshall's opinion in *Worcester* achieved its ultimate purpose. The Cherokee's fate was sealed. When one of their chiefs, John Ross, was asked what the Indians had learned from all of this wrangling in the courts, he answered: "In America, the perpetrator of a wrong never forgives his victim."

One hundred and seventy years later, the impact of the republic's early-nineteenth-century Indian policy on tribes east of the Mississippi is still symbolized by the Cherokee's final removal from their homelands in Georgia and Tennessee. The Cherokee, however, were only one among dozens of tribes compelled by the government's removal policies to endure a similar fate. Unfortunately, the "Indian state" that secretaries Calhoun and Barbour had lobbied for—out of humanitarian concern for the tribes—was never created. "Doubtless, they [the tribes] would have gone readily if just that had of been done," wrote Abel, "but it never was." The disencumbering of southern states was the prize all along, and any other distractions—though they involved the decimation of a race, not to mention the flagrant and repeated violations of the Constitution and federal statutes—were pushed aside, or simply ignored. For more than fifty years, ever since George Washington and Henry Knox came to their defense in 1787, the Cherokee had been waging a battle to save their homelands, but this was a contest destined to end in desperation and defeat at the hands of a much different kind of president.

In one of his last messages to Congress, Andrew Jackson boasted of his administration's successful "Indian consolidation" west of the Mississippi River. For southern lawmakers and aristocrats, the long-awaited removal of the Cherokee, Chickasaw, Creek, and Seminole people from the forests in their midst was the final solution to a persistent problem, a solution that could now be celebrated as the promised fulfillment of Jefferson's compact with Georgia in 1802. For many others, particularly in the North, Indian removal was viewed as a national disgrace, one that foreshadowed, as Marshall predicted with brooding prescience, dark days ahead. The chief justice knew that his detractors in the South were animated by a burning desire to undo his work. Furthermore, he knew that burning desire was certain to outlive him.

Andrew Jackson, for one, was fain to declare his ambition to own the judiciary, either in life or posthumously, which he did, in both. Before his presidency ended in 1836, Old Hickory appointed five new justices, four of whom were staunch states' rights activists, thereby commencing an ideological metamorphosis of the nation's highest court that would have delighted his aristocratic predecessor Thomas Jefferson. Appropriately enough, it was the posthumous legacy of Jackson's court, led by Chief

Justice Roger B. Taney, that completed the work begun by Jefferson's states' rights policies by rendering the fateful Dred Scott decision on the eve of the Civil War. As Marshall had lamented decades earlier, it was now plain to see that the road to the bloody reckonings at Manassas, Shiloh, and Gettysburg had been surveyed half a century earlier— by the master of Monticello—through Georgia and Indian country. Despite the laurels of liberty that crowned his cousin's sainted head, it is said that when John Marshall died in Philadelphia, on July 6, 1835, he was the last person for whom the Liberty Bell would ever toll.

The Cherokee's forced march to the Oklahoma Territory was conducted under the command of "Old Fuss and Feathers," General Winfield Scott. Thousands perished on the road. The stories of mothers burying their children, husbands burying wives, and children burying parents are too numerous to recount. As one eyewitness later reported, the removal of the Cherokee represented "the most cold-blooded . . . , cynical disregard for human suffering and destruction of human life" the human mind is capable of imagining. Reports of the cruelties soon found their way back to Congress, and because the rumors were so horrific, appalled lawmakers asked Ethan Allen Hitchcock, the esteemed namesake of his illustrious grandfather, a man widely known for his unimpeachable honor, to conduct an independent investigation of these stories and report back on what he found.

Hitchcock pursued the investigation with cool fervor and determination. For a time he had worked for the Indian Department in St. Louis, so he was already well acquainted with many of the tribes and their removals. They had begun with the Choctaw and Creek in the early 1830s and were followed by the Chickasaw in 1837 and the Cherokee the following year. The last to be removed were the Seminole, who arrived in Oklahoma in 1840. Contrary to the general perception, most of these campaigns were managed by private contractors under the auspices of the War Department. Civilian handlers were expected to feed the emigrants en route and be responsible for their well-being until they reached their destinations. Some contracts were honestly performed, but most ran afoul—from the shoddy to the deplorable. Hitchcock soon uncovered widespread profiteering and fraud, enough, before he was finished, to fill nine notebooks with detailed evidence. Bribery, perjury, and forgery were the procedures that governed contracts for Indian removal. Incredibly, the cost for these extravagant adventures would be levied against the Indians themselves. Private contractors billed Congress for food never delivered, for spoiled meat and rotten grains, for phantom employees, and, noted Hitchcock, for "every other conceivable subterfuge."

Hitchcock's final report, which he filed with President John Tyler's secretary of war, John C. Spencer, contained more than one hundred exhibits. The chairman of the House Committee on Indian Affairs asked that the report be immediately delivered to him for review. When his request was denied by the White House and Secretary Spencer, congressmen were astonished by the president's arrogance. A violent debate broke out on the floor of the House on June 4, 1842, to decide what should be done about the administration's insolence. Said one witness to the fight, "Of this much we are certain—too many friends of the administration are involved in the plundering to permit the report to become public." When Hitchcock himself intervened in the quarrel and asked Secretary Spencer to send a copy of his report to Congress, Spencer replied to Hitchcock with curt opprobrium: the House should not have the report "without my heart's blood." Secretary Spencer's copy of Ethan Allen Hitchcock's report on Indian removals mysteriously vanished from the War Department's files, and no trace of its contents has ever been found.

With the final removals now complete, the legal and moral battle first begun by the Cherokee tribes fifty years earlier was now decided. Willy-nilly, the robust pioneers of the young republic managed to reach the Mississippi River without invoking God or the gilded words of biblical prophets. They marched across the wilderness toward Canaan behind the vague line of receding savages, clearing the wilderness as they went. Removing the forest gypsies was a relatively antiseptic and straightforward matter of ignoring civil laws, undoing official proclamations, rewriting executive orders, abrogating treaties, defying courts, tearing up congressional compacts (the Northwest Ordinance and the Indian Trade and Intercourse Acts), flouting the Constitution, and failing those, the government could fall back on the all too familiar bloodletting of last resort. In any case, Ethan Allen Hitchcock's report would not have been the final word. The first wave of removals had been accomplished with the machinery of a secular government, cogs and spindles that had proven cumbersome, even tedious, and unable to keep pace with the vanguard of westward-looking settlers. Appropriately enough, the task of planning and executing the second removal era would be passed to an American with extensive knowledge of the West and its original inhabitants, William Clark, the intrepid explorer and co-leader of Thomas Jefferson's Corps of Discovery.

Clark, who was now the Indian superintendent for all western lands, would enlist a handful of fearless agents to begin writing the opening chapters of America's grand adventure in the West. Over the next twenty years, a small group of licensed fur traders, trappers, missionaries, and enterprising mountain men blazed a trail through Indian country that would eventually lead hundreds of thousands of Euro-American immigrants across the continent to the mythical Eden of California and the Oregon territories. To the Indians, it seemed that the first removal era had no sooner ended than the second—a drama that would require the energizing authority of much different nature—was set to begin.

When William Clark accepted the invitation of Congress to become the first superintendent of Indian affairs of the West in 1806, the village of St. Louis was the new republic's westernmost outpost. Jefferson assumed that it would take settlers fifty years to clear and subdue the wilderness between the Appalachians and the Mississippi River, but as Tocqueville observed, no one in government anticipated the social force that was building, in the first decades of the nineteenth century, behind the idea of national "expansionism." Yet by 1832 it was already clear to the astute Frenchman that "the continuous progress of the European toward the Rocky Mountains . . . is like a deluge of men rising unabatedly, and daily driven onward by the hand of God."

Just a decade earlier, political leaders were bandying about a prosaic secular "doctrine" known as "national completeness." This popular euphemism advanced the idea that the nation's domain would soon extend from the Atlantic seaboard to the western border of Missouri. As late as this—the beginning of the Monroe administration—national leaders could not conceive of a republic of states that might heave itself across the Mississippi River. By the end of Monroe's administration, an event that Thomas Jefferson had imagined taking place centuries in the future—settlers reaching the Rocky Mountains—was now only years, if not months, away.

While lamenting the impoverished state of the eastern tribes he was helping to relocate, Clark warned Congress that the oncoming tide of humanity was not going to halt at the great river. Whites were his biggest worry, for everything west of that river was filling up with refugees. Like the beaver before it, the buffalo was constantly receding, observed Clark, and where these wild beasts were once common on the prairie in Illinois, they had been pushed across the Mississippi seeking refuge from the bells of the settlers' domesticated cows. He also reminded lawmakers that just because the eastern tribes had migrated over the western horizon, that did not mean the "Indian problem" was magically solved. In fact, the relocated tribes were now confronted with an additional burden. They not only had to adjust to a radically different way of life in new and strange environs, but they now found themselves on a frontier where other Indians resented them for encroaching on their own reduced territory.

Many years had passed since Clark last visited the tribes of the western plains. During that time he had developed his own network of traders, *coureur de bois*, and mountain men—a ragtag band of high-spirited ruffians and lawless vagabonds—who continually brought him valuable intelligence when they returned to St. Louis to sell their pelts and buy provisions. None would become more important to maintaining Clark's slender reed of communication between St. Louis and the wild tribes than Thomas Fitzpatrick and his good friend Jim Bridger. These two adventurers had joined the great Ashley expedition in 1822 as young men of twenty-three and eighteen, respectively, and they went on to defy the long odds against them by living to tell their tales as old men.

General William Henry Ashley and his partner, Andrew Henry, had correctly perceived that great fortunes were to be made by trapping a furry-cheeked tree-felling rodent in the Yellowstone country. That fabled region of the Far West had already acquired an ominous nickname, the Blackfeet Wall, in honor of its ferociously belligerent first citizens, and was renowned in Europe for producing prized albino plews. The bleacher's art had made the beaver's fur more valuable than ever to European hatters, so the two entrepreneurs obtained a license from William Clark and formed the Rocky Mountain Fur Company. They solicited trappers in the *Missouri Gazette and Public Advertiser* on February 13, 1822, letting it be known that "the subscriber wishes to engage One Hundred Men to ascend the river Missouri to its source, there to be employed for one, two, or three years," at two hundred dollars per year. The trappers who answered the ad would henceforth be known as "Ashley's Hundred."

Among the first two groups to reach the Rocky Mountains with Ashley were Fitzpatrick and Bridger, along with Jedediah Smith, Hugh Glass, William and Milton Sublette, Robert Campbell, Etienne Provost, Louis Vasquez, and Thomas Eddie. In time, each of these men added raw material to the complex fusion of myth, fact, and legend that is unique to American lore west of the Missouri River. Of the few hundred men who ventured into the "territories unknown" to open the fur trade, less than half survived the first winter. Of those, many were eventually scalped, killed for their plews by competing beaver men, or fell victim to the Indian ambush and tomahawk. Though death from disease—the bane of city life in early America—was virtually unknown in the wilderness, a return to domesticated life was unthinkable. Of the handful of men who survived the first decade of the beaver trade, none were more resilient than Thomas Fitzpatrick, the taciturn Irish immigrant from County Cavan, or James Bridger, the gray-eyed, square-jawed son of tavern owners from Richmond, Virginia.

Thanks to skill, instinct, native intelligence, physical stamina, courage, and liberal rations of luck, by 1832, Fitzpatrick and Bridger had beaten odds that had already vanquished many of their associates. Ten years after setting off with the expedition, their faces were familiar to tribal leaders in trading camps that ranged across a million square miles of the mountain West. Both men had married Indian women, and in addition to the requisite fluency in Spanish and French, both spoke more than a dozen Indian tongues, including the universal sign language of the Plains tribes. In 1824, while Bridger was "discovering" the Great Salt Lake on a solo adventure in the Wasatch Mountains— one he would repeat (and greatly regret) for Brigham Young and the Mormons in 1847—Fitzpatrick discovered the famed South Pass that twelve years later became the vital link between east and west on the Oregon Trail, which he blazed open in 1836. Though his partner Bridger never received a day of formal education, he carried a mental map of the Rocky Mountain West that was far more detailed—with every spur range and mountain pass, canyon and river valley, Indian encampment and trading trail—than any map yet printed. With a pointed stick and a patch of bare ground, it was said that Bridger could draw an accurate map to any remote outpost or Indian camp a thousand miles away.

Both men were slender framed, "well knit and muscular," and both were endowed with keen eyesight and central nervous systems capable of tolerating acute pain for days, even weeks, without compromising their ability to reason with detachment in life-threatening situations. In ten seasons in the wild, Fitzpatrick and Bridger had become fearless in the face of danger and philosophical in misfortune. Both had survived dozens of fights with Indians, weathered ferocious winter storms, and were now thriving as founding partners in the new Rocky Mountain Fur Company. Their legendary status in the barrooms and parlors of St. Louis and Washington was utterly unknown to them, and the embroidered stories and tall tales of their exploits would not have impressed either man.

Fitzpatrick volunteered to return to St. Louis in the spring of 1831 to buy provisions for their new company. It was his first trip back to civilization in nine years, and he didn't know quite what to make of it, but he didn't have long to be dazzled by the sights and temptations. He reached the city a week later than planned and discovered the following day that his provisions had been sent on to markets in New Mexico. Wasting no time, Fitzpatrick chased the trading party all the way to Taos, across six hundred miles of treacherous Comanche country, only to find that everything had been sold in Santa Fe. He bought what he could from the traders there and picked up some new recruits, including a twenty-one-year-old runaway named Kit Carson, who had recently bolted from an apprenticeship to a saddlemaker in Franklin, Missouri. Having obtained about six thousand dollars worth of supplies, Fitzpatrick now turned north with a band of forty men to make his rendezvous with Bridger. After two minor skirmishes with horse-thieving Comanche and Shoshone—concluding a four-thousand-mile trek on foot and horseback through the most hostile Indian country on the continent—Fitzpatrick and Bridger were belatedly reunited with their men at the Willow Valley rendezvous, on the western flank of the Wasatch Range in modern-day Utah.

The annual rendezvous of beaver men and Indians was first initiated by General Ashley, in 1825. Ashley's idea was to organize a great trading fair each summer as an efficient means of collecting pelts and distributing provisions among the trappers for the following year. In its final years in the early 1840s, the annual rendezvous of trappers, traders, and Indians became an informal recruiting center for guides to lead the great migrations across the Oregon Trail and to the California goldfields. The month-long summer gathering soon became the signature spectacle of the lawless, unmapped West, weeks of drinking and gambling, prank playing, trading, whoring, and feasting that, for twenty years, until beaver felt gave way to silk, was the pan-cultural trading bazaar and gathering place for beaver men and friendly tribes. As a thousand people, half of which were Nez Perce and Flathead Indians, gathered at the appointed destination, the primal silence of the mountain West would give way to raucous celebrations. "But the horse-racing, fine riding, wrestling, and all the manlier sports, soon degenerated into the baser exhibitions of a crazy drunk condition," wrote Joe Meek, a mountain man who later helped settle the Oregon territory. "One of their number seized a kettle of alcohol and poured it over the head of a tall, lank, redheaded fellow, repeating as he did so the baptismal ceremony. No sooner had he concluded than another man with a lighted stick, touched him with the blaze, when in an instant he was enveloped in flames. Luckily, some of the company . . . began beating him with the pack-saddles to put out the blaze."

It was at Pierre's Hole, in July 1832, that Fitzpatrick and Bridger learned from lips loosened by aguardiente that men working for John Jacob Astor's American Fur Company had been instructed to stalk Bridger and Fitzpatrick to their trapping grounds when the rendezvous broke up. The exalted status of these two men was underscored in the minds of their competitors by their willingness to trap beaver in Blackfeet country. Like the Comanche in the south, Blackfeet warriors were the most belligerent and aggressive Indians on the northern plains, a tribe feared by all who had the misfortune of crossing their path. So after rendezvous broke up that fall, Bridger and Fitzpatrick, knowing they were being followed, made straight for the Blackfeet Wall. While camped by a stream north of the Judith River, they had just settled in for an evening beside the campfire when a band of Blackfeet attacked them from two directions.

Outmanned six to one, Fitzpatrick and Bridger leaped into the fray, hoping to neutralize the warriors' advantage in close combat. The Blackfeet leader, a fearsome young war chief who singled out Bridger, sprang from his horse, tackled the mountain man, and dragged him into the frigid stream. The two men, tangled up like a ball of angry wolves, wrangled in the creek in a furious embrace. Across the camp, Fitzpatrick was fighting off two more braves with knives. Realizing their chief was in trouble, warriors waiting in the shadows let go with a volley of arrows at the two men in the water. Bridger slashed his attacker's throat with a knife, then slew one of the two who pounced on him screaming for revenge. Having had enough, the surviving warriors mounted their horses and vanished into the night. Four Blackfeet braves lay dead in the firelight. Fitzpatrick and Bridger hastily packed up camp and made their escape, but not before the Irishman pulled five arrows out of Bridger's back—the sixth being too firmly lodged to be extracted. At rendezvous the following year, the partners learned from the Flathead Indians that the enraged Blackfeet had returned with more warriors the following day, looking for retribution. The two were long gone, but the Blackfeet mistook the men of the American Fur Company, who were camped nearby, for Bridger and Fitzpatrick, and killed them all. Such were the stakes of competition among freewheeling capitalists in the early American West.

For the next three years, Jim Bridger would travel thousands of miles on horseback and on foot with a barbed arrowhead buried in the muscle of his back. He seldom spoke of the incident, which was largely forgotten until he arrived at the Green River rendezvous in 1835, where the arrowhead became the first footnote to westward expansion, as this was to be the beaver men's first encounter with a group of missionaries traveling west to the Oregon country. One of them, William H. Gray, expressed his personal revulsion over the buying and selling of Indian wives by the white trappers, to say nothing of the trappers' dissolute antics and wild carousing. "No tongue can tell the extent that blasphemy is carried at this place," he noted in his journal. The immodest displays of human passions that Gray and his missionaries witnessed—with their own unshielded eyes—convinced them that they had been called to the right place.

Among their party were Dr. Marcus Whitman, the devout Calvinist who had organized the caravan, and his traveling companion, Reverend Samuel Parker, and they were already in camp when Jim Bridger rode onto the scene. "Dr. Whitman was called upon to perform some very important surgical operations," wrote Parker in his journal. "He extracted an iron arrowhead that was three inches long, from the back of Capt. Bridger, which was received three years before in a skirmish, with the Blackfeet Indians. It was a difficult operation, [because] the arrow head was hooked at the point by striking a large bone, and a cartilaginous substance had grown about it. . . . The Indians looked on meanwhile, with countenances indicating wonder, and in their own peculiar manner expressed great astonishment when the projectile was extracted."

It was that same year that Bridger, Fitzpatrick, and their new partner, Lucien Fontenelle, purchased Fort William (soon to be renamed Fort Laramie), on the Laramie River, from William Sublette and Robert Campbell. Bridger chose to pass the winter in a camp on the Snake that winter, so Fitzpatrick bundled up their company's pelts, and after selling them in St. Louis and buying provisions for the following summer's rendezvous, he agreed to guide the intrepid Dr. Whitman and his God-fearing reinforcements back to the Oregon country in the spring.

The previous summer, Whitman had located what he took to be an ideal spot for a mission, in the rolling hills of Cayuse country, where he and his wife hoped to begin "Christianizing the savages" and aiding white settlement of the distant West. Until then, life in the wilderness had been a stubbornly secular affair, as white men who ventured there had no reason to believe that God would protect them thousands of miles from a church. "We are really a moving village," wrote Whitman's indomitable wife, Narcissa, who happened to be an avid diarist. Once their expeditions had merged, the train included "nearly four hundred animals with ours, mostly mules, and seventy men. The fur company has seven wagons and one cart, drawn by six mules each. . . . [We] look way ahead and see first the pilot and the Captain Fitzpatrick, just before him." Six years before he guided Captain John C. Frémont's expedition over South Pass into the Great Basin, earning for Frémont the nickname of Pathfinder, Fitzpatrick guided six missionary women over the same track that would henceforth be known as the Oregon Trail. It was fast becoming clear to men like Fitzpatrick and Bridger that the world of the mountain man was being shaped by forces beyond their control, forces that had already launched Thomas Fitzpatrick on his next career. Over the next fifteen years, he would guide the now legendary migrations of settlers across the vast Indian country land bridge to the Pacific West. Intermingled with these nameless thousands were Frémont, John Sutter, Father Pierre De Smet, Brigham Young, and Stephen Watts Kearny. Bridger, too, was among the first to realize that the furry rodent's glory days of preeminence in European fashion was about to pass, while the epoch of the emigrant was just beginning. Bridger also knew that pioneers on the White Man's Medicine Road, the Indians' name for the Oregon Trail, would need to make repairs and refresh their supplies before pushing on to the Columbia River region, so in 1843 he settled down in the homeland of his Shoshone wife and built his eponymous fort at the confluence of Black's Fork and the Green River, in the Mexican-owned territory of western Wyoming.

With each passing year, the rendezvous of beaver men grew smaller and smaller until it finally passed into legend. The last, held at Green River in 1840, was reached by another caravan of missionaries in transit to the Oregon Territory, and it included the peripatetic Jesuit priest

Pierre De Smet, whose purposeful but wandering path crossed Fitzpatrick's many times in the following years. At the end of the final rendezvous, the veteran beaver man Robert Newell wrote a letter to his old friend Joe Meek, conveying rough sentiments that foreshadowed the epic story about to follow the one that was just then coming to a close: "Meek, We are done with this life in the mountains—done with wading in beaver dams and freezing or starving alternately—done with Indian trading and Indian fighting. The fur trade is dead in the Rocky Mountains . . . but we cannot or will not return to the States. Let us go down to the Wallamet and take farms. . . . What do you say? Shall we turn American settlers?"

For the next fifty years, Newell's whimsical proposition to Meek would be the catalyzing dream of hundreds of thousands of westbound pioneers who flung themselves, and their families, into the great river of humanity that was beginning to flow like a spring flood across the continent. In just two decades, Fitzpatrick and Bridger had seen an era open and close. Both were among the first white men to penetrate the Rocky Mountain wall, and to make the "discoveries" celebrated in the famed explorer John C. Frémont's widely published journals that set the stage for the nascent migration. No white man in the mountains had Fitzpatrick's unique combination of acquired skills, natural diplomatic abilities, and physical stamina, and no one held him in higher esteem than Frémont, who wrote of being guided by him: "Long residence and familiar acquaintance had given to Mr. Fitzpatrick great personal influence among them [the Indians], and a portion of them were disposed to let him pass quietly; but by far the greater number were inclined to hostile measures." Fitzpatrick's standing with them "at length prevailed, and obtained for us an unmolested passage. I have no doubt that the emigrants owe their lives to Mr. Fitzpatrick."

On May 10, 1841, Fitzpatrick led the famous Bidwell-Bartleson party, the first official wagon train of settlers, from Independence, Missouri, to the Oregon Territory. Frémont's journals, telling of the beautiful lands to be had in distant Oregon, had already ignited the imaginations of a new generation of westward-looking settlers. By the spring of 1843—known as the Year of the Great Emigration—the streets of Westport and Independence, Missouri's new frontier towns, teemed with emigrants eager to get on the trail. More than thirty thousand wagons and a quarter million head of livestock crossed the plains that year. Such was the extent of the destruction to Indian country in those first years of the Oregon Trail that Fitzpatrick dispatched an urgent letter to Thomas Harvey, the superintendent of Indian affairs at St. Louis, warning him that the flow of humanity across the buffalo plains had turned the Cheyenne and Sioux hostile. The caravans, which had grown in some instances to ten miles in length, were interrupting the migration patterns of the buffalo. The Great White Fathers in Washington needed to know that trouble was brewing on the Great Plains. The only way of preempting a catastrophe was to build a string of military garrisons to protect the trail and to compensate the Indians for permitting the whites to travel through their country.

Fitzpatrick's alarming missive anticipated a debate that had already begun in Washington: how to best protect the settlers. Like Fitzpatrick, Frémont advocated a string of forts along the entire Oregon Trail. Congress ordered Colonel Stephen Watts Kearny, led by Fitzpatrick himself, to conduct a survey of the trail and report back with his recommendations.

With pennons aflutter, Kearny, Fitzpatrick, and the 250 men of the First Dragoons, the mounted precursors to the cavalry, made the 1,700-mile round trip from Independence to South Pass in just seventy-two days. Of their legendary guide, Lieutenant J. W. Abert later noted: "The best years of his life have exposed him to the toils and vicissitudes of the mountain and the prairies, and he has acquired an intimate knowledge of the Indian character, which enabled him to conduct our little party safely and successfully through a country inhabited by numerous and powerful hordes of people, long notorious for their faithlessness and treachery."

Once back from his tour of Indian country, Kearny told Congress that establishing forts along the Oregon Trail would be expensive and impractical. An occasional show of force by a detachment of dragoons wearing bear hats and firing cannons would do more to discourage attacks by the large roaming tribes of savages than a string of small garrisons. It seemed to Kearny that such outposts, far apart and difficult to provision, would be militarily ineffective in such a vast country.

Fitzpatrick and Kearny's conflicting opinions about the Oregon Trail did not color their mutual admiration. Kearny's encomiums for his guide prompted Senator Thomas Hart Benton—the inimitable bombastic booster of expansionism from Missouri known as Old Thunderer—to recommend him to Indian Commissioner William Medill for a new post as Indian agent for the Upper Arkansas and Platte country. Fitzpatrick's life in the mountains had been a twenty-year apprenticeship for his new profession. The man the Indians called Broken Hand—after a fight with the Blackfeet crippled the fingers of his right hand—was to be the government's principal eyes, ears, and voice among the nomadic tribes of the central plains. No white man alive commanded more respect from tribal leaders of the West's "wild and savage Indians." The welfare of hundreds of thousands of emigrants and Indians was about to ride on Fitzpatrick's good name, and their fate would often depend on his best judgments. On September 11, 1846, an editorial in the *St. Louis Republican* declared: "This is one of the few appointments of the present Administration to which we can subscribe with pleasure." The *St. Louis Reveille* agreed, noting with xenophobic condescension that Mr. Fitzpatrick's "opinions on Indian matters are worth more than the combined expression of a dozen political theorists."

When the U.S. Senate approved his appointment, on August 3, 1846, Fitzpatrick had already departed St. Louis. He was riding in his customary place, at the head of a column of 1,600 men, 1,500 wagons, and 20,000 mules, oxen, and horses—the recently assembled Army of the West. On this second expedition with Kearny, their destination was the desert

Southwest, through the heart of Comanche country. The unspoken reason for this dramatic show of force in Indian country, and the march into Mexican territory—all on the orders of President James K. Polk—was to promote a bold new American doctrine called Manifest Destiny.

In the election of 1844, forty-nine-year-old James K. Polk was a dark-horse candidate who survived his own feeble campaign to become the unlikely eleventh president of the United States. Dubbed "Young Hickory" by his supporters who hoped to evoke a beneficial coattail effect with his ideological predecessor, Andrew Jackson, Polk was a phlegmatic martinet with long gray hair, a blocky forehead, and vivid gray eyes that conveyed no emotion. John Quincy Adams knew Polk as a man with "no wit, no literature, no gracefulness of delivery, no elegance of language, no philosophy, no pathos, no felicitous impromptus." The no-name former governor of Tennessee was nevertheless nominated on the ninth ballot, finally breaking a deadlock at the Democratic Party convention in Baltimore. The news of Polk's improbable candidacy was transmitted instantaneously to Washington by Samuel Morse's newfangled contraption, the telegraph.

Behind Polk's cheerless but firm jaw was a man of stubborn resoluteness, a quality that he would use to great effect against his many adversaries in Congress, the British government, and the Mexican army. He promised to seek only one term of office, a vow he kept after winning the White House amid rancorous and widespread claims of election fraud. When the dust of democracy had settled, no one could explain how such a small-time backwater politician had managed to defeat the undefeatable Whig, Henry Clay. But Polk, unimpressed by his own political success, had only four years in the White House with which to transform the world. And in that quest he succeeded—first by wresting Texas and California away from Mexico, then by rescuing the Oregon Territory from the clutches of England, and finally by increasing the territorial dominion of the American republic by half a billion acres.

Thus finished, he quietly crept back into obscurity in Tennessee and died three months later.

When Polk was sworn into office on March 4, 1845, what lay before him were two paths to "continentalism." Continentalism was the new political term of art that had superseded the previous expansionist creed, national completeness, a phrase that captured, in its day, a sea change of great account. Whereas politicians in the Monroe and Jackson administrations had viewed expansion across the Mississippi as a great threat to the original Union (John Quincy Adams notwithstanding), expansion across the continent was now viewed as an essential defense against the imperial designs of European interlopers. One path of that "continentalism" led to California (by way of Texas, whose citizens were clamoring for statehood), and the other led to the Oregon Territory. Both were fraught with confounding obstacles and challenges whose origins were to be found, and resolved, in civil and international law. Pursued in this manner, satisfactory resolutions were arduous contests and years in the making.

Thanks to a technical oversight in the Adams-Onís Treaty of 1819, the rightful ownership of the Oregon Territory, contested by the United States and Great Britain, had been in limbo for twenty-five years. As Americans poured west over the Oregon Trail and filled up the fabled verdure of the Willamette Valley, Englishmen and Americans glared suspiciously at each other from opposite banks of the great Columbia River. In Adams-Onís, the American republic acquired eastern and western Florida, and all of Spain's former claims in the Pacific Northwest north of the forty-second parallel, in exchange for relinquishing any and all future claims to Texas. This meant Bridger's Fort, therefore, was safely inside American territory. When Mexico won its independence from Spain two years later, the terms of this treaty were transferred to the new constitutional government in Mexico City. Just who controlled those terms was insignificant to President Polk, a man who could not be troubled by agreements made by other administrations or by the byzantine requirements of international law. As a dedicated expansionist, Polk pursued his political objectives with unwavering zeal, directing members of his cabinet to make up new laws, exploit circumstances, and rationalize pretexts for action as his ambitions for westward expansion dictated.

In 1845, the American republic was three generations removed from its founding. Few people alive had any memory of the republic's tumultuous and difficult birth. A series of financial crises, in 1837, 1839, and 1841, had crippled business and left the nation economically destitute. The price of cotton sank to an all-time low. Nine out of ten Americans lived in rural communities, where the market's price for corn, hogs, and beef had dropped to levels not seen since the Monroe administration. The ensuing depression fueled the flight of destitute farmers—to the promised land of Oregon and California—until the eve of the Civil War. Democracy, it seemed, was floundering. Americans began clamoring for reforms of every kind. Desperate for a new energizing philosophy, the *United States Journal* declared, in May 1845, that only youth could pull the country out of its terminal malaise: "Young America, awakened to a sense of her own intellectual greatness by her soaring spirit," wrote Theophilus Fisk, an ultra-expansionist Jacksonian Democrat, "demands the immediate annexation of Texas at any and every hazard. It will plant its right foot upon the northern verge of Oregon, and its left upon the Atlantic crag, and waving the stars and stripes in the face of the once proud Mistress of the Ocean, bid her, if she dare, 'Cry havoc, and let slip the dogs of war!'"

Polk was embraced by the electorate as the antidote to America's mounting litany of ills. In the end, faced with a choice of north or south, to Oregon or to California, President Polk, the ardent expansionist, invoked the name of God and chose both. His secretary of state, James Buchanan, expressed his doubt that God would help the Americans in a war for territory north of the forty-ninth parallel, but God need not have been troubled by Polk's palingenesis or legal quandaries. It was at this time, as Congress debated the merits of funding an illegal war that President Polk had stirred up with Mexico, that a small group of lay theologians came to the president's assistance.

Preeminent among this group was a visionary literary artist, publisher, and scholar named John L. O'Sullivan. As the co-founder and editor of the *Democratic Review* and the *New York Morning News*, O'Sullivan was described by his friend Julian Hawthorne as "one of the most charming companions in the world, . . . always full of grand and world-embracing schemes, which seemed to him, and which he made to appear to others, vastly practicable and alluring." In the final days of 1845, O'Sullivan exposed one of those schemes to a society anxiously awaiting a galvanizing force. In an essay called "The True Title," O'Sullivan captured the unsettled impulses and aspirations of the American republic by repeating an electrifying phrase he had already used in other essays published in the *Democratic Review*. "To state the truth at once in its neglected simplicity," O'Sullivan wrote, "our claim [to Oregon] is by the right of our manifest destiny to overspread and possess the whole of the continent which Providence has given us for the development of the great experiment of liberty and federated self-government entrusted to us."

O'Sullivan's jingoistic phrase was immediately picked up by expansionist politicians in Congress. "A free, confederated, self-governed republic on a continental scale—this is Manifest Destiny!" declared Senator Daniel Dickinson of New York. Within days, Polk was using the phrase in conversations with his cabinet. To the penny press of the day—which relied principally on sensationalism to hawk its product—it seemed that no news could generate more widespread interest than this new soul-stirring phrase, Manifest Destiny. It was a coupling of words that imbued "continentalism" with its missing ingredient, the hand of providence. Expanding on the religious theme, Polk's ventriloquist at the *Democratic Review* refined the idea of America's divine mission in the world in an essay titled "The Great Nation of Futurity."

Our national birth was the beginning of a new history, the formation and progress of an untried political system, which separates us from the past and connects us with the future only; and so far as regards the entire development of the natural rights of man, in moral, political, and national life, we may confidently assume that our country is destined to be the great nation of futurity. . . . We are entering on its untrodden space, with the truths of God in our minds, beneficent objects in our hearts, and with clear conscience unsullied by the past. We are the nation of human progress, and who will, what can, set limits to our onward march. Providence is with us, and no earthly power can. We point to the everlasting truth on the first page of our national declaration, and we proclaim to the millions of other lands, that "the gates of hell"—the powers of aristocracy and monarchy—"shall not prevail against it."

Yes, we are the nation of progress, of individual freedom, of universal enfranchisement. . . . The far-reaching, the boundless future will be the era of American greatness. In its magnificent domain of space and time, the nation of many nations is destined to manifest to mankind the excellence of divine principles; to establish on earth the noblest temple ever dedicated to the worship of the Most High—the Sacred and the True. Its floor shall be a hemisphere—its roof the firmament of the star-studded heavens, and its congregation an Union of many Republics, comprising hundreds of happy millions, calling, owning no man master, but governed by God's natural and moral law of equality, the law of brotherhood—of "peace and good will amongst men."

Overnight, "continentalism" was discarded and replaced by Manifest Destiny, a doctrine—when broken down into its simplest elements—claiming that American expansion to the Pacific was prearranged by heavenly authority. The principal boosters of O'Sullivan's vision were among the leading American figures of the day: Ralph Waldo Emerson,

Walt Whitman (editor of the *Brooklyn Eagle*), William Cullen Bryant, Alexander Everett. James Bennett, the editor of the *New York Herald*, hailed a new day for the angels of democracy: "The patriotic impulses of the United States have been awakened to fresh and greatly augmented vigor and enthusiasm of action. . . . The minds of men have been awakened to a clear conviction of the destiny of this great nation of freemen . . . [who] seek distant territories, stretching even to the shores of the Pacific; and the arms of the republic, it is clear to all that men of sober discernment, must soon embrace the whole hemisphere, from the icy wilderness of the North to the most prolific regions of the south."

O'Sullivan's ideas found their sharpest expression in his essay of December 27, 1845, in which he swept aside all potential claims of international law to have a modulating influence on this new expansionist doctrine. "Away, away with all these cobweb tissues of rights of discovery, exploration, settlement, and contiguity," he wrote, dismissing any legal obligations to the international society of nations. America's right to expand to the Pacific was "as that of the tree to the space of air and earth suitable for the full expansion of its principle and destiny of growth."

O'Sullivan's manifesto on westward expansion organized itself into parallel propositions—one pseudo-legal, the other providential. Of the former, he was claiming that the republic's legal title would outweigh the strongest legal title of a European monarch or emperor. Yet implicit in this assertion, suggests historian Frederick Merk, is the argument that the moral ideal of democracy was more relevant to the justice of the issue than any technical considerations raised by international law. In other words, for O'Sullivan, the providential moral source of right embodied in the doctrine of Manifest Destiny outweighed the secular legal ones that had sufficed for the Founders when they invented the republic and drafted a basic framework of laws in the Constitution.

Expansionist Congressmen were enthralled. Representative Ely Baker delivered a stemwinding speech on the floor of Congress declaring the providential end foreshadowed by history, for in Manifest Destiny the nation could claim "a higher and better title under the law of nature and of nations" to its rightful possession of Oregon and California. In other words, said the expansionists, the republic had secured a doctrine of preemptive rights over all other claims. These extra-legal justifications were grist for Polk's war-provoking intrigues on the Rio Grande, and though not all Americans were enamored of the president's appetite for far-flung adventures, it seemed by September 1845 that Polk was determined to have his war with Mexico regardless of the prevailing public opinion.

Texans were once again clamoring for annexation into the Union, and Mexico was once again refusing to accept their declaration of independence. After his envoy was rebuffed by the administration of President Mariano Paredes, Polk sent the army, under the command of Zachary Taylor, to the mouth of the Rio Grande. There, Taylor stirred up the Mexicans' nationalist ire by setting up his cannons to command the public square of Matamoros, across the river. A detachment of Mexican cavalry was dispatched upstream to reconnoiter the disputed territory north of the river and soon encountered a party of American dragoons. In the skirmish that ensued, three American dragoons were killed before their compatriots retreated back to General Taylor's encampment. When this news reached the White House on May 9, 1846, Polk knew that he had his pretext for war. He spent the evening and the next day writing his formal message to Congress. His request for a declaration of war claimed that Mexico "has invaded our territory and shed American blood upon American soil. War exists, notwithstanding all of our efforts to avoid it." The war had been brought on by Mexico itself.

Polk's précis for war was heralded with huzzahs from expansionists and with ridicule from Whigs and northern Democrats. They claimed that Polk had raised the American flag on ground the United States had no claim to. "Does history furnish an example of more abhorrent perfidy?" asked Representative Garrett Davis, a Kentucky Whig, who quickly added, "Was any government through its Chief Magistrate ever more vilely prostituted?" The president's former Tennessee neighbor, Senator Meredith P. Gentry, described Polk's arguments for war as an "artful perversion of the truth—a disingenuous statement of the facts—to make the people believe a lie." Senator John Dix of New York reported to former president Martin Van Buren that the war was "a violation of every just consideration of national dignity, duty, and policy."

Polk's strident justification for the war was soundly condemned by many, but rather than answer their countercharges directly, the president battled back with a well-worn canard. He accused his detractors of treason by giving "aid and comfort" to the nation's enemies. No charge could have been more absurd, but the caterwauling Whigs, in the end, capitulated and voted to go to war. They had unwittingly allowed themselves to be lured into Polk's trap. Toward the end of 1847, in the last year of his life, John Quincy Adams wrote to Albert Gallatin to complain that he was confounded by the contradictory actions of Congress. "The most remarkable circumstance of these transactions is, that the War, thus made, has been sanctioned by an overwhelming majority of both Houses of Congress," he explained, "and is now sustained by similar majorities, professing to disapprove its existence and pronouncing it unnecessary and unjust."

Once the war began and the Mexican army proved itself a formidable opponent on the battlefield, Congress found itself embroiled in a harsh dilemma of its own design: either endorse Polk's fictitious justification for war or reject it and suffer the political consequences of voting down appropriations supporting the troops. Democrat John C. Calhoun declared that he would find it "easier to plunge a dagger into his own heart than vote for the lie," and Senator Thomas Corwin of Ohio pronounced the conundrum "a flagrant . . . desolating . . . usurpation of authority," and a senseless quest for more land. Corwin also predicted that the war would precipitate a bloody sectional clash over slavery by plunging the sister states of the Union into the bottomless gulf of civil conflict. Although two-thirds of the country's newspapers denounced the war's instigation for "no adequate cause" by Polk and its "having been prompted on our side chiefly, if not solely, by personal ambition, by motives of territorial acquisition and aggrandizement, for party ends," the resounding verdict in the press did little to dislodge Manifest Destiny as the new energizing force behind expansionism. Just as editors at the *Hartford Times* had argued during the run-up to war with Mexico, the battle for Texas statehood was now seen by many Americans as the easiest method for towing California into an American port.

With the Treaty of Guadalupe Hidalgo in the offing, and the 1846 agreement with Great Britain dividing the Oregon Territory at the forty-ninth parallel safely in the president's hands, it was hard for anyone to claim that John L. O'Sullivan's masterwork had not generated miracles in four short years. In 1851, the commissioner of the government's General Land Office reported to Congress: "The great and fertile valley of the Mississippi, which a few years since was the out-post of civilization and the hunting ground of the savage, has now become the geographical and commercial center of our ocean bound republic. Villages, towns, and populous cities have sprung up as by magic." The sale of public lands the previous year approached two million acres, and since the last Congress adjourned, "the industrious land surveyor is now found, greeted by the adventurous expectants of advancing civilization in Oregon, between the Cascade mountains and the coast, stretching his chain along the fertile valleys of the Umpqua and the Willamette. . . . Amid the formidable hill ranges, extensive forests and mountains, which impart to the physical features of the country extraordinary grandeur, the surveyor is engaged in surmounting obstacles unprecedented in his professional experience."

In 1906, the Texas historian George P. Garrison finished an extensive survey of James K. Polk's letters and presidential papers. Garrison concluded that the Tennessean's mind was a "place of easy lodgment" for dogmas supporting his expansionist ambitions. Polk had never wavered in his righteous purpose or doubted his means of attaining it. "Such men as he," wrote Garrison, "rarely catch an historical perspective or see the whole truth that lies in any group of facts; and they are often involved in painful struggles by their own unconscious inconsistencies. No paralyzing scrupulosity or forecast of possible danger holds them back, and woe to the land if they be misguided, for they do things."

James K. Polk had done things that realized Madison's and Hamilton's most ominous forebodings half a century earlier. In a cascade of breathtaking events, O'Sullivan's poetic hyperbole had been elevated to the status of national policy. In a single decisive stroke, Polk, O'Sullivan, and their numerous disciples had desecularized the Founders' machinery of government and the republic's ambitions for empire and persuaded the American people to gather behind a banner of righteousness as they squarely faced their preordained destiny to lay claim to the entire continent. During Polk's final year in office, the stream of westbound settlers traversing Indian country became a river, and as one traveller noted, beneath the great clouds of dust that stretched from horizon to horizon it seemed as though all of humanity was heading westward. The people were answering Polk's call, and in doing so they were reconstituting on American soil the theocratic footing for the doctrine of conquest so energetically employed centuries earlier by their crusading ancestors. Wrapped in a veil of righteous nationalism, the young expansionist society was incapable of admitting that "it was doing violence to its moral instincts," particularly at a time when that violence and moral waywardness were being condemned by such political pharisees as John C. Calhoun and John Quincy Adams.

Like Polk and O'Sullivan, average Americans came to view themselves as a chosen people, the anointed ones, men and women who had been hand-picked by God to sweep across the land, to vanquish the savage and the infidel, and to prosper in the bosom of providence. This was the preordained pathway to the gates of Eden, and proof of this self-evident truth arrived at the White House from California in late

1848—in an oyster tin filled with gold dust. On September 9, 1850, California became part of the Union—gleaming with gold and dripping with blood. In the ensuing mania for "yellow dirt," the mostly peaceful native citizens of the thirty-first state were slaughtered like plague-infested vermin. Fewer than one in six Indians survived the state's first decade, although no white man was ever prosecuted for an atrocity committed against a native. Gold and God had been wedded in Washington under the banner of Manifest Destiny. The Constitution and the treaties, as well as the law of nations, could be easily sloughed aside when they became impediments to America's destiny. According to Robert Williams, "The Doctrine of Discovery, the primordial mythic icon of Europe's medieval, feudal past, had been preserved and brought to readability in a modern form that spoke with reassuring continuity to a nation that was about to embark on its own colonizing crusade" on the North American continent. In one guise or another, on the North Platte, the American River, or the Euphrates, so it has been ever since.

Among Thomas Fitzpatrick's first clients on the Oregon Trail was an indefatigable Swiss emigrant by the name of John Augustus Sutter. A man of restless grandiosity and incurable dreams, Sutter set out on foot for the Mexican territory of California in the spring of 1838. In less than ten years he owned an empire of fifty thousand acres of productive farmland, along with a trading post and fort on the Sacramento River, and employed hundreds of Mexicans to run his farms and trading enterprises. What he lacked at the end of 1847 was a sawmill to make lumber to build his ever expanding dreams. In January 1848, he sent a team of men to the south fork of the American River, forty-five miles upstream from Sacramento, to harness the stream's swift currents to mill dimensional lumber. On the morning of January 24, one of those men, James Marshall, was digging in the millrace to increase the flow of water at the paddlewheel, when "my eye was caught by something shining in the bottom of the ditch." Marshall, who never made a cent from his discovery, lifted from the clear Sierra snowmelt a gold nugget the size of a pea. With that glint of light, that dim flash from the argillaceous sediment, a new American narrative commenced, appropriately enough, on its namesake river.

The fusion of Manifest Destiny and the discovery of gold in California precipitated a social cataclysm that was greatly accelerated by a coincident explosion of technological marvels. The steam engine was collapsing time and space as never imagined, and electricity was annihilating frontiers through a single strand of copper. Newspaper editors in San Francisco could set the type of a president's speech before the inaugural balls had ended in Washington. For millennia, life at its swiftest had passed by at eight miles per hour. Now, the day when the East and West coasts would be connected by passenger trains was a looming certainty. But nothing revolutionized the American society's sense of its own mission more than the dissemination of information through the whirring gears and drums of high-speed presses. Hundreds of "penny presses" turned James Marshall's discovery of gold on the American River into the young republic's first large-scale media event.

As news from the goldfields swept through communities east of the Mississippi River, young men looking for a way out of the tedium of urban living or off the family farm, or emancipation from a life of poverty, were packing their rucksacks and heading out to take their chances with fate in California. By the spring of 1849, ninety thousand immigrants reached the goldfields. San Francisco exploded from a seaside village of a few hundred fishermen to a city of thirty thousand in less than a year. There were three ways to reach California from Savannah, Georgia, or Boston, Massachusetts: around Cape Horn on a clipper ship, across the Isthmus of Panama, or over the Oregon Trail. Of the hundreds of thousands of men who struck out for the goldfields in the 1850s, most chose the latter, what the Indians called the White Man's Medicine Road. The trail that Fitzpatrick had opened through the Rockies, thirty years before, was the most direct route to the fabled Pacific.

"Imagine thousands of all countries . . . deserters, sailors, robbers, murderers, the scum of the States . . . with some honest men among them, no doubt . . . all living lawless and unbridled lives," wrote Father Pierre De Smet, with notable prescience. "The news of the abundance of gold seems to have shaken the United States to the foundation, while the facts reveal clearly the melancholy future which at no very remote epoch awaits [the Indian] nations if efficient needs are not employed for preventing the woes with which they are threatened."

No one was more sensitive to those woes than Thomas Fitzpatrick and David Dawson Mitchell, the superintendent of Indian affairs in St. Louis. For the first half of the nineteenth century, an uneasy peace between the Great White Fathers in Washington and the "wild and savage tribes" of the West had held its own. But William Medill, James Polk's commissioner of Indian affairs at the newly established Department of the Interior, was beginning to hear alarming reports from Fitzpatrick and Mitchell of Conestoga wagons pouring westward by the tens of thousands through territory owned and controlled by hostile Indians. The opening of the overland trail and the discovery of gold in California had brought the Brulé and Ogallala Sioux, the Cheyenne and Comanche, the Pawnee and Crow and Shoshone, into close relations with a class of white people quite unlike any they had previously met. With the fur traders, these tribes had once shared common ground, but the settlers were a different breed altogether. Fearful of the wild tribes, these whites hurried along the Medicine Road in ever-growing numbers, a flood of humanity that left in its wake a path of devastation. Some wagon trains were twenty miles long and drawn by thousands of teams of oxen. In ten short years, the settlers' livestock had destroyed a broad swath of grasslands through the heart of Indian country, while pioneers themselves had shorn the land of its precious timber, fouled its water, and driven the country's principal commodity, the bison, far north into the land of the Crow and Blackfeet.

In the summer of 1849, both Fitzpatrick and Mitchell wrote to the new commissioner of Indian affairs, Orlando Brown, warning him that the Plains tribes were growing increasingly distraught over the invasion of their homelands. Congress could expect the Indians to go to war at any time unless the Great White Fathers could "conciliate these formidable tribes" by holding a treaty council, one that would secure a right of passage through their homelands for white immigrants and compensate them for the destruction of their resources. Unless they made these guarantees to the tribes, warned Fitzpatrick, the Manifest Destiny of the United States could not be realized without great bloodshed. What the emigrants want, wrote Fitzpatrick, "is a free and unmolested passage through to their destination . . . they ought to have it, cost what it may."

Mitchell underscored Fitzpatrick's sentiments with his own appeal to Washington. "It is only by some measure of this kind that we can ever establish friendly relations with these Indians," he told Brown, and warned him that "the bones of American citizens that now whiten the plains from the borders of the western states to the Rocky Mountains all admonish of the necessity for peace. We can never whip them into friendship; the prowess of our troops and the vast resources of the government would be wasted in long and toilsome marches over the plains in the pursuit of an *ignis fatuus*; they never see an enemy." To Mitchell, it seemed that "justice, as well as policy requires that we should make remuneration for the damages which the Indians sustain in consequence of the destruction of game, timber, etc., by the whites passing through their country." He closed by recommending that annuities be distributed to the western tribes as payment for depredations and a guarantee of their good behavior.

Brown, a humanitarian who fully supported Mitchell's proposal for a peace council, presented his agents' requests to the secretary of the interior, Thomas Ewing, urging him to do whatever was necessary to expedite funding for the treaty council. Brown's predecessor, Commissioner Medill, had given Congress fair warning the previous year when he urged lawmakers to determine the legal "nature and extent of [the tribes'] title to their lands." Once Congress realized that the western two-thirds of the continent was still legally owned by the Indians, Medill recommended that lawmakers make the Indians "some annual compensation for the right of way through their country." Lesser tributes would be exacted in settler's blood, cautioned Medill, and time was of the essence. If Congress let this opportunity be missed by inattention, it might never get a second chance to make peace with the warlike nomads of the American West.

With visions of white women's scalps dangling before their eyes, lawmakers were forced to delay a decision on the peace council while they struggled to prevent a war from breaking out over the unsettled question of slavery in Kansas and Nebraska territories. Brown acted on his own initiative during the delay and extended to Mitchell and Fitzpatrick a subsidy of five thousand dollars to begin purchasing gifts for the tribes. Unfortunately, Brown resigned after the untimely death of President Taylor, so the two agents had once again to educate a new commissioner, a very capable administrator and bureaucrat by the name of Luke Lea. Having just returned from a fact-finding mission among the Platte River tribes, Fitzpatrick took the opportunity to remind Lea: "Through these districts all the great leading thoroughfares pass; and the immense emigration traveling through that country for the past two years has desolated and impoverished that country to an enormous extent." Fitzpatrick pointed out for the new commissioner that the government had recently learned of the havoc that could be created by a few poorly armed wretches in the Southwest. In light of those problems, he asked both Lea and Congress to consider the bloodshed that would result from "twenty thousand well armed, well mounted, and the most warlike and expert in war of any Indians on the continent."

After Congress settled the territorial questions in Kansas—by compounding its earlier removal problems by opening up land for settlement that had already been awarded to tribes relocated from the East a generation earlier—lawmakers quickly passed the Deficiency Appropriations Act on February 27, 1851. This bill funded many of the programs and proposals that had been waylaid by the protracted debates on the Kansas Territory, and set aside $100,000, half of what Mitchell had requested, for the "expense of holding treaties of friendship with all the wild tribes and savages of the prairie." Commissioner Lea flashed a telegram of congratulations to his agents in St. Louis. After naming them co-commissioners, he instructed them to make all the necessary arrangements with as much haste as prudence made possible.

Mitchell and Fitzpatrick lost no time. After their first meeting at Mitchell's office in St. Louis they informed Lea that they were scheduling the council to begin on the first day of September at Fort Laramie—some eight hundred miles west of Mitchell's office in St. Louis. The two commissioners then sent runners, in early April, to distribute circulars to traders, interpreters, bourgeois, and dozens of tribes—now scattered in their spring hunting camps across a million and a half square miles of plains and mountains—inviting them to "A Great Smoke" at the end of their summer hunts. Tempering the commissioner's optimistic enthusiasm was a keen appreciation for the obstacles arrayed against them. Nevertheless, no two men in America brought more resources critical to the council's success than Mitchell and Fitzpatrick. Together, the veteran mountain men who had first met at the Green River rendezvous of 1835 had fifty years of experience among the roaming tribes of the western plains and mountains. Their circular, an invitation unique in the official records of the federal government's intercourse with Indians, announced that the "Great Smoke" was intended "for the permanent good of the Indians." The Great White Fathers in Washington wanted to "compensate the tribes for all the depredations of which they complain" resulting from the passage of emigrants, and to divide the country into geographical districts in a manner entirely satisfactory to the tribes concerned. Such territorial divisions would help "extinguish the bloody wars which had ravaged tribes since time immemorial." Tribes were invited to attend en masse, including all their women and children, and all who attended would receive gifts, the commissioners promised. The Indians were assured that a large military force would be on hand to keep the peace. Following ratification of the new treaty, Mitchell and Fitzpatrick told the Indian headmen, the tribes that participated would receive presents annually from the Great Father.

Fitzpatrick agreed to leave St. Louis in May to begin contacting and recruiting interpreters for Fort Laramie. Mitchell then sent word to his old friend Pierre De Smet, asking him to distribute the circular among the tribes of the Upper Missouri, and for his assistance in persuading the Mandan, Hidatsa, and Arikara tribes to attend the council. "Understanding that you will shortly start for the upper Missouri country on your missionary labors . . . you will do me a favor by informing such of the upper tribes as you may see of the intentions of the government. . . . Should your other engagements permit, I shall be rejoiced to see you at Fort Laramie. Any sketches that you can make and the outlines of maps of this prairie and mountain country will be of great importance and would be highly appreciated by the Government, as well as any information with regard to the habits, history or other interesting matters appertaining to the Indians."

De Smet accepted the mission with enthusiasm, but the yearlong congressional delay pushed the commissioners' organizing efforts into the midst of a new catastrophe that jeopardized the entire peacemaking enterprise. California-bound Forty-niners, crowding into the frontier towns of Westport and Independence, brought with them a cholera epidemic that threatened to spread across the plains. By mid-May, when his request was approved by Jean Elet, the father-provincial in St. Louis, De Smet wrote that cholera was "raging all around us." Two weeks later, the pestilence was ravaging the city, and even though "thousands have died of it already," wrote De Smet, "it appears still to be on the increase." Out on the Oregon Trail that spring, the water-borne bacteria swept through the wagon trains "with a fearful mortality." Dr.

Thaddeus McCollum, a westward traveler, reported: "The road from Independence to Fort Laramie is a graveyard."

On June 7, as De Smet was boarding the steamboat *St. Ange* for the two-thousand-mile passage up the Missouri to the Mandan Villages, Fitzpatrick's runners were scouring the far reaches of the plains to invite the Comanche, Kiowa, Apache, Arapaho, and Cheyenne people to Fort Laramie. Back in St. Louis, Mitchell had received the official go-ahead for the peace council from Washington at the end of May, but the bouts of indecision in Congress about its own demands, second-guessing of annuities, and last-minute backpedaling on the original appropriation left Mitchell in the lurch with his suppliers and interpreters. Even after his departure on July 24 aboard the steamboat *Cataract*—with his companions A. B. Chambers, the senior editor of the *Missouri Republican* newspaper, and Chambers's secretary, B. Gratz Brown—the fate of the entire adventure was mired in doubt. At Westport, Mitchell received word that President Millard Fillmore's secretary of war, Charles M. Conrad, had denied his request for a thousand troops. Worse yet, the twenty-seven wagonloads of gifts that he had purchased for the tribes were still sitting on the dock in crates when they should have been hundreds of miles ahead on the plains. Without gifts for the tribes, the entire treaty council was in peril before the principals had even convened.

The Great White Fathers in Washington could no better imagine the scale of the endeavor undertaken by Fitzpatrick and Mitchell than a Comanche chief could conceive of high society life in Boston. Despite the assurance of making a lasting peace with the Great Father, and despite his and Fitzpatrick's good names and their promises of gifts and annuities, Mitchell, a man given to periodic alcohol-induced bouts of depression, had no way of knowing which, if any, of the wide-ranging tribes had received and accepted his invitation to the "Great Smoke." As his five-mile-long wagon train snaked its way across the prairie throughout the month of August, stories reached him confirming Mitchell's worst fears. Cholera, transported by settlers on the Medicine Road, was now said to be racing ahead of them through Indian country like a prairie fire. Mitchell had witnessed firsthand the scourge of smallpox that devastated Plains tribes in 1837. No news could have plunged him into deeper despair, and the threat of this new scourge was only compounded by another quandary—the mysterious absence of buffalo. The roaming commissary that Mitchell had counted on to feed the Indians seemed to have vanished altogether from the plains.

The prospect of failure was now so probable that Mitchell was left to endure the monotony of the interminable grasslands in a state of deep and unshakable gloom. For weeks to come he would wake each day to face the same featureless horizon, the same inscrutable dome of sky, the same nauseating loneliness and ocean of grass. Just four years earlier, members of the Cayuse people had butchered Marcus and Narcissa Whitman and several of their adopted children, including Jim Bridger's daughter, after an outbreak of measles carried by immigrants killed dozens from that tribe, including the chief's beloved daughter. If this new rumor proved to be true—and the pestilence reached the Rocky Mountains—in all likelihood, he and Fitzpatrick had spent the previous six months on a foolish and expensive lark. Furthermore, no white man or woman between Independence, Missouri, and the Columbia River would be safe from tribes seeking retribution, and for all Mitchell knew, the Blackfeet, Crow, and Comanche, the Sioux, Shoshone, and Cheyenne, were already at war.

FIVE

The Great Smoke

When Thomas Fitzpatrick arrived at Fort Laramie in late July, he was bearing disappointing news of his own. On the road north from Bent's Fort on the Arkansas River—from which he had sent messengers to find the larger southwestern tribes—word reached him that the Comanche and the Apache would not be attending the Great Smoke at Fort Laramie. This was discouraging news, and although their rebuff of Fitzpatrick's personal invitation was not entirely unexpected, it deflated the commissioner's already tempered expectations for the peace council. The outnumbered Apache had receded into the relative safety of the southwestern mountains, but the Comanche, a fearless and wide-ranging band of expert horsemen, had grown in strength and boldness, and now dominated the southern plains. Making peace with the Comanche was seen as the key to protecting settlers and trading caravans on the Santa Fe Trail, just as the safety of settlers on the Oregon Trail depended on a meaningful peace with the Sioux. The Comanche informed Fitzpatrick that they would be in the middle of their fall hunt during the gathering at Fort Laramie, and a trek to the North Platte was deemed by the headmen to be too distant a journey. With their regrets came a caveat—they would be happy to meet with their good friend Broken Hand after the fall hunt, at a location of his choosing that was closer to their own council fires.

Of the two commissioners, Fitzpatrick had far greater firsthand experience with the tribes of the plains than his city-bound partner, but Mitchell was the accomplished statesman and diplomat. Mitchell was a stocky man with dark hair and large intelligent eyes, and he was known for a reserved but straightforward manner, qualities that complemented his reputation among businessmen and politicians as a man of high principle and honesty. His years as a bourgeois at Fort Union on the Upper Missouri, and later as a partner in the American Fur Company, put him in line to take over the post formerly held by William Clark, who had died in 1838. After serving with distinction under General Zachary Taylor in the Mexican War, he returned to St. Louis in 1847 and two years later was reappointed as the superintendent of Indian affairs, a post he had previously held in 1841–1844. His years in the fur business allowed him to speak knowledgeably about western tribes and their homelands, but it was Fitzpatrick—a careful and nuanced writer without peer among mountain men—that he depended on for current intelligence and insight into the diplomatic thicket of intertribal relations among the tribes of the Far West.

Fitzpatrick's own views of what might be gained by the peace council were closely tethered to his unique cast of mind—a bank of hard-edged realism annealed in a lawless environment by the best and worst of human nature. He was the first government official to urge Congress to compensate the western tribes for the devastation brought to their homelands by settlers on the Medicine Road, but his compassion was balanced by countless eyeball-to-eyeball dealings with nomadic warriors —or the bloody aftermath of their hostile passions. After burying a family of settlers that had been raped, butchered, and scalped by Comanche warriors on the Santa Fe Trail in 1847, he wrote to Superintendent Thomas Harvey that "the real character of the Indian can never be ascertained because it is altogether unnatural for a Christian man to comprehend how so much depravity, wickedness and folly can possibly belong to human beings." Fitzpatrick held many Indian leaders in the highest esteem, but he feared that these men were exceptional members of "a doomed race" that would soon fulfill its unhappy destiny. Nor were his instincts tricked by the romantic altruism of eastern politicians who believed the savages could be successfully assimilated into the larger culture. "I am not one of those who expect and look for the immediate improvement and civilization of the Indian tribes," he wrote to Harvey, "and I have yet to learn and decide whether the full-blooded Indian is capable of such a change." Despite his deep-seated ambivalence about the Indian's future, Fitzpatrick was first and foremost a man of justice. He lived fully in the moment, and the moment called for the protection of settlers on the Oregon Trail, a formal recognition by the government of tribal territories, and compensation by that government to the Indians whose homelands had been permanently damaged by the migrating hordes of its citizenry.

As he approached Fort Laramie, Fitzpatrick's gloomy outlook for the Great Smoke was dispelled by the unexpected appearance of many old friends. The Cheyenne and Arapaho and several bands of Sioux, including the Brulé and Ogallala, had already arrived and were camped around the fort. For old Broken Hand, returning to Fort Laramie was always a homecoming of sorts, since he and Jim Bridger had owned the fort before they sold out to the American Fur Company. He had spent many months here, both trading with the Indians and guiding settlers to the Oregon Territory.

William Sublette's men had built the fort beside the Laramie River in 1834, at an ancient intersection of Indian trade routes approximately eight hundred miles west of St. Louis. In the intervening years, the fort became an oasis for emigrant trains, a place to refresh both man and beast for the final push over the Rocky Mountains. With a view of the Black Hills to the north and west, the fort's palisaded quadrangular walls, one hundred and fifty feet on a side, were twenty feet high, with bastions anchoring the diagonal corners. Since Congress purchased the outpost for the U.S. Army in 1849, it was home to two hundred soldiers and dragoons, and the main entrance was guarded by cannons in a large blockhouse-like tower with a sweeping view of the plains.

For almost twenty years, Fort Laramie had been as familiar to fur traders as it was to the Indians who gathered here several times a year to trade in pelts and dry goods, tobacco, vermillion, brass, and alcohol. Fortunately, the first tribes to arrive in the summer of 1851 were all friendly with one another. But as he and his wife set up their camp a mile upstream on the Laramie, the unspoken question in Fitzpatrick's mind was whether the small force of dragoons would be enough to keep the peace when the mountain tribes arrived. All he could do was sit back and wait and hope that Mitchell arrived soon with his regiment of mounted troops.

Several days before departing from St. Louis, Mitchell wired a letter to Indian Commissioner Luke Lea to explain once more that he and Fitzpatrick were expecting to meet with as many as five thousand Indians at Fort Laramie. He had hoped, in vain, that this large a number might bolster his last-ditch appeal to the War Department for more troops. As his wagon train lumbered across the short-grass prairie toward the North Platte through the month of August, Mitchell also feared that his early optimism about the peace council might have filled Congress with unreasonable expectations. Anything less than five thousand attendees might now be viewed as a failure. But as his wagon train crested a rise at sunset on August 31, and gathered its first distant view of the fort, his flagging spirits were emancipated from doubt. Arrayed in a patchwork of encampments around the small fort were the teepees and cooking fires of twelve thousand Indians. Fifty thousand ponies and countless dogs ranged loose on the plains as far as the eye could see. From horizon to horizon, wrote the treaty secretary B. Gratz Brown, there was nary a blade of grass to be seen.

The last wagon trains of the year had passed this way months earlier. By August, settlers who had left Independence, Missouri, in April were approaching the Columbia River on the high desert, northwest of Fort Hall, but the evidence of their passing was still plainly visible on the mute and barren plain. As the widely scattered tribes converged on Fort Laramie at the end of August, many were seeing the Great Medicine Road for the first time. It was a vision, wrote Pierre De Smet, that filled the hearts of all the Indians seeing it for the first time with an unsettling mixture of fear and awe. For hundreds of miles in either direction from Fort Laramie, the trail was strewn with the detritus of civilization on the march, and lined by the hastily made graves of the many who had perished. Black flies buzzed in clouds above the rotting carcasses of oxen and cattle, mules and horses. Discarded hammers and axes, kettles and cooking utensils, furniture and clothing, lay everywhere amid the graves, hundreds of them, as if simple crosses and crude cairns had been used to mark the shortest path across the continent. When De Smet's entourage reached the trail in September, Four Bears, Raven Chief, and Gray Prairie Eagle, the chiefs of the Mandan, Hidatsa, and Arikara tribes, gazed in astonishment at the road "with disbelieving eyes." These men, accustomed to traveling hundreds of miles across open country on trails no wider than their moccasins, could not fathom the forces that could conspire to create the sight that now lay before them. Surely, they told De Smet, whom they called Black Robe, a road such as this was made by so many people that it left their homelands empty. To the contrary, De Smet told them, the trains of the settlers that passed this way would not be missed from the cities of the East.

Mitchell's spell of euphoria at seeing so many Indians and learning that the dreaded cholera was not among them was fleeting, for he was no sooner reunited with Fitzpatrick, on September 1, than the two commissioners took stock of their predicament. B. Gratz Brown, a twenty-two-year-old lawyer and future governor of Missouri, accompanied Mitchell to Fitzpatrick's camp on the afternoon that his wagon train arrived at the fort. "He [Fitzpatrick] is a real mountain man, and adapts himself completely to the habits and mode of life of the Indians," wrote Brown. "I have seen no man in the country who seems to have so entirely and implicitly the confidence of the various tribes. What he says passes for law with them, and even where they may not agree, they respect him and pay great deference to his opinion."

Fitzpatrick advised Mitchell that trouble was already brewing between enemy tribes, and if war broke out in their midst, Washington's refusal to provide troops would be paid for in barrels of blood. Also, word was in the air that the Shoshone, or Snake people, a tribe that had not been invited because they were blood enemies of the Cheyenne and Sioux, were en route, and Jim Bridger was traveling with them as their interpreter. If that wasn't portentous enough, buffalo were very scarce in the country surrounding the fort, and this late in the season there was not enough water in the Laramie River or enough pasturage in the surrounding hills to keep the thousands of Indian ponies alive for more than a few days. And even if "god water," rain, replenished the Laramie, all the horses and ponies traveling the plains had already made the country so desolate for miles in every direction that the prairie breezes, rather than bringing the usual evening relief, enveloped the entire encampment in clouds of choking dust and flying insects.

If these things alone were not reason enough to cancel the entire council, the absence of gifts for the headmen was an unforgivable blunder. This glaring diplomatic indiscretion could rupture the entire adventure unless the chiefs could be persuaded that wagons bearing gifts would soon arrive from Independence. The Plains Indians viewed thrift as a kind of cowardice, and the commissioners worried that if the Indians suspected that the promised gifts were being withheld in exchange for an agreement, they would consider the entire council an elaborate ruse of deceit and trickery. This prickly diplomatic challenge was made even more risky by the glaring absence of the Crow and the Blackfeet. Those tribes, like the Comanche and the Apache, were out on the chase and sent word that they would not be coming. This was discouraging, for like the Comanche in the south, the Crow were the key to keeping the peace on the northern plains. Yet it was the Cheyenne, according to Brown, that worried Mitchell the most. "The Cheyenne, who were formerly looked upon as the best Indians of the Plains," he wrote after the meeting on the first of September, "are now universally regarded as the worst. . . . They have great contempt for the white men and the power of the Government. . . . The Cheyenne and Comanche are much alike in character, and neither entertain any dread of the Government troops. . . . The great and leading occupation of these Indians of the plains is war, hunting, and stealing horses."

But the problem that needed to be solved immediately by the commissioners was how to procure enough food, out of thin air, to feed fourteen thousand people. Another group of Sioux had arrived early that morning, swelling the encampment's population by a thousand, and they brought with them the news that more were on their way. Feeding all of these guests was an obligation that rested squarely on the shoulders of the two commissioners.

In hopes of buying time for the wagon train, they decided first to postpone the introductory feast and distribution of gifts for the headmen. Whatever supplies the quartermaster held inside the fort would be commandeered by Mitchell and replaced with those that were soon to arrive from Independence. In the meantime, it was clear to both commissioners that the entire encampment had to be moved to a place better suited to hosting such a huge gathering, one, at the very least, with enough water and pasturage for the horses. All of this, they decided, needed to be explained at a council of the chiefs the following day. At that point, the council of headmen should be asked to decide on a new venue.

As Fitzpatrick and Mitchell were finishing their initial meeting, a great excitement suddenly raced through the encampment. Word spread faster than wind could carry it that the Snake people were approaching from the west, led by their revered chief, Washakie, who also happened to be Jim Bridger's good friend and father-in-law. The long line of dust that rose behind their column stretched to the horizon, and even though they had not been invited it was too late now to turn them back. Unfortunately, they had already encountered trouble when they met a band of Cheyenne on their march across the mountains from the Green River. Two of the Snake braves had been killed and scalped in an ambush. As they rode over the rise toward the fort, the air was electric with tension. More than ten thousand Indians turned to watch them approach. War cries went up from the camps of their enemies, but just as suddenly a troop of mounted dragoons rode through the camp and galloped off to meet them. A dragoon by the name of P. G. Lowe, stationed at the fort, described in his journal what he witnessed as the Snake warriors approached.

> Soon, a long line of Indians came moving slowly down in battle array, arms ready for use and every man apparently expectant, the women and children and baggage bringing up the rear, well guarded. It turned out that Major Bridger, the interpreter, had reported to headquarters the approach of the Snakes, and he had been directed to lead them down near to our camp. All the head men of the Sioux and Cheyenne had given assurance that they should not be molested, so down they came, moving very slowly and cautiously, the chief alone a short distance in advance. They were dressed in their best, riding fine war horses, and made a grandly savage appearance. . . . Just below us was a large Sioux camp, and the people were showing great interest and some excitement at the approach of their hereditary enemies, and a few squaws howled in anguish for lost friends who had died in battle with these same warriors. When the Snakes reached the brow of the hill overlooking the beautiful Laramie, less than a mile away, and the chief commenced the descent, a Sioux sprang upon his horse, bow and arrows in hand, and rushed towards him. A Frenchman, an interpreter, had been watching this Sioux, expecting trouble, and he, too, mounted his horse and was instantly in pursuit. The Snake column stopped and sent up a wild shout of defiance, the

chief moved a few steps farther and raised his gun ready to fire just as the intrepid Frenchman reached the reckless Sioux, pulled him from his horse, disarmed and stood over him.

The wild Sioux, who had sought to revenge himself on the Snake chief who had killed his father some time before, was led back to camp while the Snakes held their ground. Their position was a good one; every man had a good gun and plenty of ammunition, besides bows and arrows. Not one out of a hundred Sioux had guns, and the Snakes, though not one to five of the Sioux, would have defended themselves successfully, and the battle would have been the most bloody ever known amongst the wild tribes. The attitude of the Snakes, the cool, deliberate action of the chief, the staunch firmness of his warriors . . . was a lesson for soldiers who might never again see such a grand display of soldierly manhood, and the lesson was not lost. Every Dragoon felt an interest in that tribe.

The freelancing Frenchman had singlehandedly saved the peace council from degenerating into a bloody war before the tribes could even gather for the first smoke. But David Mitchell, too, had met his first diplomatic challenge with decisive intervention. By sending the small detachment of dragoons to escort the Snake tribe into the camp, the commissioner had telegraphed a bold message to the headmen among the Snake's enemies. Though they were few in number, the three hundred well-armed dragoons were more than capable of maintaining the peace. They could suppress any challenge to Mitchell's authority, and he would not hesitate to call on them to punish the wayward. Once the Sioux firebrand was returned to his camp and the Snake had ridden safely between the lodges of their enemies, tensions abated. Fitzpatrick directed the Snake people to set up their teepees near the tents of the dragoons, who for the duration of the council would maintain sentinel lines between the hostile tribes.

The rest of the afternoon and night passed without incident. Feasts and dancing broke out in the Cheyenne and Sioux camps, and the ceaseless drumming kept Mitchell awake late into the night. After reviewing troops with the inspector general, Colonel Cooper, on Sunday morning, the chiefs were all called to meet with Fitzpatrick and Mitchell under a temporary arbor at Mitchell's camp. Once the headmen had arranged themselves in a circle under the arbor, as was their custom, tobacco was handed around for general smoke from the traditional calumet, a redstone pipe from the northern homelands of the Chippewa. After the pipe was offered to the seven directions, east, west, north, south, above, below, and here, Mitchell rose to address his expectant audience. Assembled were the Cheyenne and Brulé, the Ogallala and the Two Kettles, the Yankton, the Arapaho, the Snake and the Assiniboin, whom he thanked for making the long journey. He would have much to tell them in the days to come, once the Blackfeet and Crow, Mandan, Gros Ventre, and Arikara arrived. "The only object today is to ask you among yourselves to fix upon a place for an encampment. I will not suggest a place, but if a place is selected below the fort, we will sooner meet the train, which has the provisions and gifts for you. I leave it to you to select that place."

The chiefs were clearly disappointed about the delayed gifts, but Fitzpatrick's reassurances seemed to mollify them. Each said he had complete faith in Broken Hand's word, and with that, the blunder was temporarily set aside. "I do not want your lands, your robes, your horses, or anything you have," Mitchell concluded. "I want to make peace between the tribes, and peace between the whites and the Indians. . . . I leave you to consult among yourselves, and when you have agreed upon a place, let me know."

The venerated Brulé leader Terra Blue suggested that the encampment be moved to Horse Creek, a two-day march to the east. There, where the North Platte and Horse Creek met beneath a swale of cottonwood trees, there was plenty of fresh grass and running water for all the horses. Also, it was far enough removed from the white man's fort for the hunters to have better luck at finding buffalo. Knowing this place, all the chiefs readily agreed, and Mitchell was advised that the Great Smoke would be moved to Horse Creek.

The chiefs then returned to their own camps, where most spent the rest of the day engaged in games and tournaments with their tribesmen. "In every direction over the plain, warriors are careering at the full speed of their horses, rushing to meet or see the various processions," wrote Brown. Of the Cheyenne parading past Mitchell's headquarters tent, he said: "During all the march the Indian shout and whoop was ringing over the plain, and the old men kept up a constant harangue to the young men, to behave themselves and make friends with the Cheyenne, to give them presents and treat them as brethren. The beauty of the morning, the wildness and novelty of the scene, gave it an exciting interest."

That night, thousands of fires flickered beneath the vast prairie firmament like a galaxy of stars that had fallen to Earth. Dancing and feasting carried on late into the night in all the camps. The singing and wild chants and cries of the dancers were answered by yips and howls from coyotes and wolves. As Mitchell looked out over the scene from his campfire, he could only wonder about the Crow and the Blackfeet, or the whereabouts of Father De Smet, who should have arrived at the fort weeks earlier. Exhausted from the events of the previous three months, Mitchell tumbled into bed and plunged into a bourbon-induced sleep. When he woke the following morning and stepped out of his tent, he gazed in wordless amazement at the apparition before him, a vast and silent plain. Without making a sound, the Indians had struck their teepees, packed up their lodges, and were now disappearing over the sun-baked hills toward the confluence at Horse Creek.

To circumvent the long-standing Jesuit prohibition against participating in the affairs of state, on June 7 Pierre De Smet and Father

Christian Hoecken had boarded the steamboat *St. Ange* in St. Louis under the pretext of performing "missionary business" among the tribes of the Upper Missouri. Once there, they would be free to take part in whatever events transpired. This was familiar country to De Smet and Hoecken, and both were well known among the country's semi-nomadic tribes. Hoecken had spent several years running a mission school among the Pottawatomi at Fort Pierre, while the silver-headed magus of the plains, De Smet, with his stocky broad-shouldered frame, piercing blue eyes, and trademark cross was a familiar and trusted face at every council fire between the Mandan Villages and the Pacific Ocean. Of all the vagabonds, interlopers, adventurers, and renegade curs that the Indians had come to know in the past thirty years, the widely told stories of De Smet's supernatural powers elevated him to a unique and exalted status among the Plains tribes. With the exception of Alexander Culbertson, a bourgeois at Fort Union who had married into the Blackfeet tribe, no other white man was so eagerly welcomed into the camps of the Blackfeet or allowed to pass unharmed through their country.

This was in part due to the fact that the Indians of the plains were a deeply religious people. They believed that the Great Spirit, the benevolent maker of all things, was a living force of goodness manifested in all the elements of the natural world. They prayed to the Great Spirit with the utmost faith and went into the hunt or battle certain that their efforts on this mortal plain would be rewarded in the afterlife—the Happy Hunting Grounds—a place abundant in buffalo and good water where the little children, the aged, and the squaws would never go hungry. So it was not beyond the realm of their believing when, two years earlier, after Father De Smet prayed for the return of an Ogallala chief's daughter who had been captured by the Crow, that the young woman—having escaped from her captors—dashed into camp just moments after the prayers were finished and leaped into her father's arms, prompting shrieks of astonishment and cries of joy. From that moment onward, De Smet held a place of esteem among the Dakota tribes that no other white man would ever enjoy. He wore a black robe, had pale skin, and spoke a strange tongue, but like them, he was in close and constant communion with the Great Spirit who had endowed him with special powers.

De Smet and Hoecken embarked on their new adventure with the fresh optimism of the season. But just three days after the St. Ange turned into the roily currents of the Missouri, a dark cloud seized Captain LaFarge's little ship. A brawny young employee of the American Fur Company, Lewis Wilcox, fell ill with cholera and was dead within hours. "A mournful silence took the place of the rude shouts and boisterous conversations," wrote De Smet, "and soon, the St. Ange resembled a floating hospital."

Of the roughly one hundred passengers and crew, dozens were stricken within twenty-four hours. The two priests worked tirelessly to comfort the sick and the dying, pausing only to commit the dead to the river's inscrutable currents in hasty ceremonies. Within three days, Father De Smet fell ill and took to his own bed, beseeching Hoecken to hear his final confession. By this time thirteen passengers had perished, but Hoecken assured him that he was not mortally ill. And then, just hours later, he put himself to bed. After making his final confession to Father De Smet in the wee hours of June 19, the forty-three-year-old Belgian priest, who had survived North Atlantic storms and years of rugged life among the wild tribes of the West, died in De Smet's arms from the virulent pestilence. De Smet, a hard-nosed pragmatist by nature, wrote in his journal that this brush with death had unhinged his nerve. Worse still, he feared the advancing plague would soon engulf all the tribes of the plains.

Unbeknownst to De Smet, Alexander Culbertson had briefly boarded the St. Ange at St. Joseph, Missouri, but he quickly jumped ship to avoid exposure to the disease. This, it turned out, was a fortuitous turn in several respects, as it was there that a messenger from Mitchell caught up with Culbertson and asked him to help Father De Smet persuade the tribes of the Upper Missouri to attend what he called "the Big Smoke" at Fort Laramie. By the time the two men were reunited at Fort Union, in mid-July, De Smet's good spirits and optimism had returned. Culbertson, he learned, had already extended Mitchell's invitation to the Mandan's revered winter chief, an old man named Cherry Necklace. As a young warrior it was Cherry Necklace who returned from a raid on the Western Shoshone with a Shoshone girl named Bird Woman, Sakakawea, and adopted her into his clan.

To Cherry Necklace, whose great-grandson Martin Cross would one day lead the tribe in the twentieth century, the risks of the journey seemed to outweigh the potential rewards. The Mandan had suffered greatly in their friendship with the whites, while their enemies, the Sioux, had grown stronger by remaining hostile. "When our men go off hunting, the women cannot work in the fields without being raped and murdered by the cowardly Sioux, who only attack us when our backs are turned," Cherry Necklace told Culbertson. "We ask for help from our friends, the white men, but they grow scarce when times are difficult." Despite their reservations, the chiefs promised to postpone a final decision until the arrival of their old friend Black Robe.

As De Smet listened to their complaints, he exhibited shrewd diplomatic skill in waiting for the right moment to present his argument. Like Fitzpatrick, De Smet knew the truth of things through the eyes of the Indians. For twenty years he had watched as policies dictated by politicians in Washington gradually but relentlessly destroyed their loyal allies on the Upper Missouri River. To hope that the Indians of the Great Plains and mountains would receive any better treatment than those of the middle country had received would be delusional. In De Smet's opinion, the moral to be learned from the drama unfolding all around them was simple to read: "The wicked and the strong always find plenty of pretexts to oppress the innocent and the weak, and when they lack good reasons they always have recourse to lies and calumnies."

Nevertheless, like David Mitchell and Commissioner Lea, De Smet believed that the peace council at Fort Laramie offered the best opportunity for the western tribes to secure a place in the future of the republic before their country was overrun by settlers. He told the Mandan headmen that peace would be made between all the tribes. Territorial boundaries would be established for the first time, boundaries that would be recognized by the Great White Fathers in Washington, and that future generations of Mandan, Hidatsa, and Arikara children would reap the benefits of this difficult but important journey. He himself could not promise them peace, but he knew David Mitchell well, and he could vouch for the commissioner's honesty and honorable intentions.

The headmen retired to counsel among themselves. If this Big Smoke was an opportunity to make lasting peace with the Yankton and Lakota Sioux, Cherry Necklace argued that they must attend. In the end, the headmen came to a consensus. The Hidatsa chose their young war chief, Four Bears, to accompany the Black Robe to Fort Laramie. The Arikara tapped their elder chief, Gray Prairie Eagle, and the revered Red Roan Cow and Raven Chief would speak for the Mandan.

On the last day of July, with a small herd of horses and two wagons, Alexander Culbertson, Father De Smet, and the small band of chiefs and their families woke before dawn and set off from Fort Union on the five-hundred-mile overland trek to Fort Laramie. The weather was beautiful, and the sky itself seemed to bend at the middle to touch the distant horizons. After several days march up the Yellowstone River, a country lush with tall grass, orchards of wild plums, cherries, and gooseberries that grew in profusion amid immense blankets of wild flowers, fields of flowers so vast they seemed to drape the entire world in shimmering colors, the little band crossed into the Big Horn country of the Crow. Here, where the Hidatsa's first cousins had made their homeland for many centuries, De Smet doubted that there was any finer country for the chase. Twenty years before the arrival of the "Iron horse," and thirty before the first homesteaders, De Smet described the Big Horn Valley as an Eden, and it was seen by few white men before it was divided by steel rails and vanquished beneath plows. "I was for seven days among innumerable herds of buffalo. Every moment I perceived bands of majestic elk . . . , white clouds of antelope took flight before us with the swiftness of arrows. . . . The ashata, or bighorn alone seemed not to be disturbed by our presence. These animals rested in flocks or frolicked upon the . . . crags, out of gunshot. Deer are abundant, especially the black-tailed . . . [and] all the rivers and streams that we crossed in our course gave evident signs that the industrious beaver, the otter and the muskrat, were still in possession of their solitary waters, and through all the country there was no lack of ducks, geese, and swans."

After a brief stop at Fort Atkinson, the party turned due south and departed Crow country by skirting the eastern flank of the Big Horn Mountains. Here they were stepping off into a forbidding and lifeless country that was wild and unfamiliar. For the next two weeks they wandered from sunrise to dusk along the desiccated arroyos of a harsh, treeless land given over to rattlesnakes and jackrabbits. By the third week they had lost the wagons, and by the fourth, all were afoot. But whatever difficulties the country presented to their progress, they were spared the news that arrived by telegraph and courier at Mitchell's camp on the first of September. Two days after the *St. Ange* left Fort Clark on its return trip down the Missouri, cholera had broken out among the Arikara. Their agent, Alexander Kipp, reported: "Yesterday twenty-five Indians died, and today I hear of thirty-seven more fatal cases. . . . Two attempts have been made to kill me . . . the Indians now regard me as one among the crowd of evil-doers."

Had the killing fever broken out weeks earlier, no amount of diplomatic finesse could have persuaded the elders to send representatives to Fort Laramie. Mitchell was not only alarmed by the news, but he was also burdened with an unsettling dilemma. If and when the Black Robe and Culbertson finally arrived, should he withhold the news from the Indians or should he tell them, knowing he would likely lose their audience at the council?

As they wandered south across the trackless wasteland claimed by the Sioux, De Smet and Culbertson were oblivious to these concerns. Both men decided they had been given a bad map by tricksters at Fort Atkinson, but the only thing to do was conserve water and press ever southward. On September 2, as Mitchell and Fitzpatrick were meeting with the council of chiefs to determine a new venue for the council, De Smet and his little band stepped out of the wilderness onto the Oregon Trail at a place called Red Buttes and then turned east for the last sixty miles to Fort Laramie. There, sparing Mitchell the sorrowful task, they learned that the cholera had arrived in their villages and killed many. Details were sketchy, but it was known that hundreds had perished in the first days, and others had fled onto the plains in search of buffalo. Their first impulse was to turn about, yet, as De Smet reminded them, never before had so many Indians been gathered in one place. They had come far, too far, across very difficult country, to turn back now. So, the following day, their hearts heavy with an unsettling ambivalence of grief, foreboding, and relief, they pressed on in silence toward the gathering at Horse Creek.

For all considerations both diplomatic and social, the broad grassy plain surrounding the confluence of the North Platte and Horse Creek could not have been better suited for the peace council. In the four directions lay a broad pasture dotted intermittently with swales of cottonwoods and immense fields of virgin grass. To ensure the peace—though by this time even the Snake had been invited to feast with the Cheyenne—Fitzpatrick assigned each of the tribes a spot for their camps on the north side of the river. Mitchell set up his headquarters tent on the south side, on a triangle of land where the rivers joined, and Fitzpatrick moved his about a mile upstream, where he was joined by other traders and interpreters. There they knew there would be some respite from the incessant feasting and dancing that was soon to begin. The Snake camp was placed on the south side of the river, adjacent to the dragoons, where their separation from the main camp was less likely to provoke trouble with their enemies.

Since more Indians were arriving by the hour, the encampment grew each day by hundreds of teepees and thousands of horses. By Saturday, September 6, the day De Smet and the representatives of the three tribes arrived at Horse Creek, the gathering had swollen to a throng of some fifteen thousand Indians. Mitchell, who was becoming increasingly anxious about the absence of the Crow and the missing gifts, thought it best to use the situation as an excuse to buy more time. Accordingly, he declared Sunday to be "the white man's Medicine Day," when no business would be conducted (though no one—apart from De Smet—was particularly religious), in hopes that the Crow would appear. They had agreed months ago in St. Louis that it was perfectly feasible to proceed without the Blackfeet, who occupied a remote country on the fringe of the known world. But it was difficult for either Fitzpatrick or Mitchell to imagine—no, it defied imagination—a treaty of this magnitude without the Crow, a fearsome tribe known to themselves and their many enemies as the Children of the Long Beaked Bird. The Crow, who occupied the keystone piece in the commissioners' million-square-mile puzzle of Indian homelands, occupied the prime buffalo country between the Tongue and Yellowstone rivers. They were surrounded on all sides by the homelands of their blood enemies, the Blackfeet, Cheyenne, and Sioux, who had coveted Crow territory ever since they arrived on the plains. Yet rather than give ground, the Crow—outnumbered five to one—had successfully repulsed thirty years of hostilities by becoming the most fearsome warriors and finest horsemen on the northern plains. Even without the Crow, Mitchell and Fitzpatrick had decided they would have no choice but to establish boundaries for their homelands. Otherwise, there would be no hope of brokering a meaningful peace with their many enemies.

The Indian women spent the Sunday hiatus setting up their camps, building council fires, and roasting dogs for an evening feast. Bands of young hunters rode off onto the plains in search of buffalo, while Cheyenne and Sioux elders observed the formalities of treaty making by erecting the formal council arbor in the shade of the cottonwoods. The arbor was a simple affair—a canopy of cottonwood branches and animal skins arranged in a large circle—one that served the dual purpose of providing shade and, more important, avoiding diplomatic pitfalls. All who gathered here would be equal, and none could claim a superior position in the negotiations. For his part, Mitchell ordered a flagpole raised at the headquarters tent and told the chiefs that each day's council would be called to order by the deep-throated "bark" of the cannon.

The Indians saw the council as an end in itself, but for the Great White Fathers and their bureaucratic representatives, treaty councils were commonly viewed as requisite preambles to a signed document, the obligatory ritual to be endured before securing a final agreement and fixed signatures. By the standards of European law, signed treaties were the prize to be won by staging a successful council ceremony, but for the tribes, the council, the gathering, the speechmaking, and the feasting were in and of themselves the desired end. For all the Plains tribes, politics was the process of achieving consensus. Without consensus there could be no decision, and with it, no vote was necessary, for the council *was* itself the expression of agreement. Conversely, from the white man's point of view, success was proved by words on a page. As the Supreme Court would be obliged to point out, many times, to mystified literalists in the coming century, this was a concept utterly alien to the Indian, and therefore legally groundless. Treaties, like other laws, said the high court, must take account of the world as it is—a meeting of dramatically different systems of symbols, languages, and ideas. Since treaties were assembled from the symbols, language, and legal constructs of the white man, they must be interpreted—to the extent possible—in the manner in which the Indian would have understood them at the time they were signed and ratified. For the Plains tribesmen, whose framework for the enterprise of human society was dramatically different from that of their white counterparts, symbols on a piece of paper were meaningless scratch marks, yet no point of honor was more sacred to them than a man's word. "The heavens and earth are my heart, the rising sun my mouth," declared New Corn, the Pottawatomi chief. "Do not deceive us in the manner of the French, the British, and Spanish. . . . Be you strong and preserve your word inviolate. . . . I am old, but I shall never die. I shall always live in my children, and my children's children."

Despite these differences and distinctions, on the eve of the council's first day, expectations for a successful outcome ran high on both sides of the river. A. B. Chambers, the *Missouri Republican* editor who had accompanied David Mitchell across the plains, spoke for all in a story he sent by courier to the nearest telegraph: "Its [the council's] results, we have reason to believe, will be satisfactory to all, and highly beneficial to the people of the United States, as well as to the Indians. Its importance, as being the first attempt at a new policy towards the tribes of the Plains, a policy which has become essentially necessary from considerations of humanity and economy, render it important that all the attendant circumstances should be detailed."

With everything ready and well prepared, the Indians devoted Sunday to visiting their friends in other camps and to feasting and dancing. The Ogallala held a dog feast for the Snake, Arapaho, and Cheyenne, followed at twilight by dances, which lasted through the night. De Smet, who was welcomed into the Ogallala's camp as a guest of honor, noted in his journal that the flesh of dogs was "very delicate and extremely good; it much resembles that of a young pig. The portion they bestowed on me was large; the two thighs and the paw, with five or six ribs; the law of the feast required me to eat it all."

Feasts and dances were given in most of the other villages as well, and "the sound of the drums and unmeaning chants of the Ogallala made sleep impossible," wrote B. Gratz Brown, who staggered back across the river to his own tent in the wee hours of the morning. It seemed that the drums were still going soon after dawn, when the entire prairie came alive at the roar of the cannon. Brown's sleep-deprived senses were so reenergized by the scenes transpiring around him that his powers of observation were brought sharply into focus.

When the cannon had given forth its thunder, the whole plains seemed to be covered with the moving masses of chiefs, warriors, men, women and children, some on horseback, some on foot. Until the signal was given for the Council to assemble, the masses had remained at a distance from the temporary arbor prepared for the occasion. But when the whole body commenced moving to the common centre, a sight was presented of the most thrilling interest. Each nation approached with its own peculiar song or demonstration, and such a combination of rude, wild, and fantastic manners and dances, never was witnessed. It is not probable that an opportunity will ever again be presented of seeing so many tribes assembled together displaying all the peculiarities, features, dress, equipments, and horses.

They came out this morning, not armed or painted for war, but decked out in all their best regalia, pomp, paint and display for peace. The Chiefs and Braves were dressed with punctilious attention to imposing effect . . . [and] it must be confessed that the Prairie Dandy, after his manner, displays quite as much sense and taste as his city prototype, with his advantage. . . . In their bearings, and efforts to show pride of dress and tinsel, they are on par.

The squaws were out in all the richness and embellishments of their "toggery." . . . The "belles" were out in all they could raise of finery and costume, and the way they flaunted, tittered, talked and made efforts to show off to the best advantage before the Bucks, justly entitled them to the civilized appellation we have given them. . . . Even more than ordinary care had been bestowed on the dress of the children. . . . Some were decked out in all the variety of finery that skins of wild animals, beads, porcupine quills, and various colored cloths could suggest. Others were in more simple costume, a string of beads round the neck, and a string round the loins. . . . A novice in this wild country, surrounded by the excitement of transpiring scenes, has scarcely the time to put all he observes on paper.

When the crowd had assembled, it was announced that only the principal or headmen of the nation were expected within the circle prepared for the Council. The others took positions on the plains, generally in the rear of the part assigned to their chiefs and braves. The council ground was a circle—about a third of it facing east was left open . . . [t]he tribes were arranged around—the Sioux first, north and west of the entrance, then the Cheyenne, followed around by the Assiniboines, Shoshone, Arikara, Gros Ventres, Mandans, Arapahos.

In the center, beneath another canopy of cottonwood thatch, were gathered the commissioners, several officers of the dragoons, and the various interpreters, including Alexander Culbertson, Jim Bridger, and Father De Smet. This was "as fine a field for a painter or daguerreo-typist as could anywhere be found," noted Brown, but in the haste of making final arrangements in St. Louis, none had been invited. Once all the tribes had seated themselves on the surrounding prairie, the only sound to be heard was the chirping of birds. "For quietness, decorum and general good behavior, on such occasions, the Indians might be made models for more civilized society," wrote Brown. "Although they were closely pressed together, many thousands of them, everything was as quiet as in a church."

When each of the chiefs had been greeted and welcomed by the commissioners, the contingent of dignitaries that accompanied Mitchell as official witnesses arrayed itself in a circle around the perimeter of the council. De Smet sat in silence and marveled at the historic moment unfolding before his eyes. In fact, as he surveyed the faces around the arbor, he realized that he knew them all and noted that the only person who looked out of place in this council was the commissioner himself. Mitchell, with his short body, thick shoulders, and ponderous brow, struck De Smet as an undistinguished presence, one that had wandered in off the plains by accident into this dignified assembly of chiefs. He also realized that for the first time in American history nearly all of the chiefs of the great western Indian nations were assembled peacefully in one place.

After the dignitaries were settled and order was restored, David Mitchell asked that the council commence the proceedings by passing the pipe. "The Great Spirit sees it all and knows it. Now, I do not wish any Indian to smoke with me that has any deceit or lies in his heart—or has two hearts—or whose ears are not ready to hear what his Great Father at Washington has to propose, and perform whatever is agreed upon. All such as those will let the pipe pass. I don't want them to touch it.

With that, all watched in silence as the bowl of the red stone pipe was packed with the customary mixture of tobacco and kinnekinnick. Mitchell then drew fire into the bowl, disappearing momentarily in the cloud of smoke that enveloped the three-foot-long stem. With that, the opening ceremony commenced, and once again, the ceremonial pipe, decorated with beaded ornaments, eagle feathers, ermine skin, and various talismans intended to assure all gathered of each chief's honesty, was handed first to Terra Blue, and then along to the Cheyenne, the Assiniboin, and around finally to Four Bears of the Hidatsa and Cut Nose of the Arapaho. No one passed, but just as this ceremony was concluding, another incident of "great excitement and thrill of feeling," wrote Brown, suddenly seized the crowd of thousands. Cries went up from the silent throng, and when all heads turned from the center to find its cause, a Cheyenne woman, leading a horse mounted by a ten-year-old boy, stepped through the entrance and into the arbor. "The interruption was sudden," wrote Brown, "and for a few minutes not understood. . . .

Some years previously, one of the Shoshones, a Snake chief, who was then in the Council, had killed her husband, leaving this boy, then an infant, fatherless. She now came to present the boy and the horse to the Snake chief, by which, according to their customs, the boy becomes the adopted son of the Snake, and entitled to all the rights and privileges of that tribe. The Snake chief had no right, by their customs, to refuse receiving the gift, and upon [acceptance] became bound to treat the boy, in every respect, as his own child."

Once the interruption had subsided, the woman quietly left the circle and returned to her tribe. Mitchell signaled the various translators to take their positions with their assigned chiefs, then rose to address the council with his opening remarks. He noted that none had passed on the pipe, and he was satisfied that all would speak the truth. Mitchell and Fitzpatrick had called them here, he said, to make a new kind of peace, because, as they all knew, their condition was now changed from what it had been not long ago.

> Your Great Father at Washington has sent me and my white-haired brother [Major Fitzpatrick] to make peaceful arrangements with you for your own benefit. . . . We do not come to you as traders; we have nothing to sell you and do not want to buy anything from you. We do not want your lands, horses, robes, nor anything you have; but we come to advise with you, and make a treaty with you for your own good.
>
> The ears of your Great Father are always open to the complaints of his Red Children. He has heard and is aware that your buffalo and game are being driven off, and your grass and timber consumed by the opening of roads, and the passing of emigrants through your countries. For these losses he desires to compensate you. He does not desire that his White Children shall drive off the buffalo and destroy your hunting grounds, without making you just restitution. . . .

In times past you had plenty of buffalo and game to subsist upon, and your Great Father well knows that war has always been your favorite amusement and pursuit. He then left the questions of war and peace to yourselves. Now, since the settling of the districts west of you by the white men, your condition is changed . . . it is now necessary that you should make and maintain peace between nations and bands as well as with the whites. Diseases, famine, and the vices of bad white men are carrying your people off fast enough without the aid of war. Your Great Father does not want your lands, your horses, your robes, nor anything you have. He wants to drive the bad white men out from amongst you, and I therefore expect you will freely give me the names of any bad white men in your country. . . . Your Great Father [also] desires that his white children shall pass along these roads without molestation of any kind, and when depredations are committed he don't want to be told that they were by a war party of one nation in the territory of another.

Mitchell's calculating review of recent events achieved its intended effect. All the chiefs were listening intently now, waiting to hear about the Great Father's willingness to trade demands and expectations. In short, carefully constructed sentences that could be easily translated without confusing nuance and preconditions, Mitchell assured the tribes that their complaints would be heard, that they would be compensated for resources destroyed by white settlers with gifts amounting to fifty thousand dollars per year for fifty years, and that they would punish any white men who came into the Indians' country and did them harm. In exchange for these things, the Great Father expected safe passage for the white children on the Oregon and Santa Fe trails, reserved the right to build military posts in their country to protect those trails, and expected the tribes to establish boundaries for their homelands and agree to peace among themselves and with the whites. There were many bands among them, said Mitchell, and since the Great Father could not recognize all of these divisions, he wanted the bands of several nations to make peace with each other and form one nation. "Your Great Father will only treat with the whole nation or tribe when united, not with any band, however large or powerful. For this purpose I desire that each nation shall select one suitable man to be chief of the whole nation . . . [and] through him your Great Father will transact all Government business. The man you select for Chief of the nation shall be a good man, and fit for the place."

After reassuring them once again that "a large train of ox wagons is on the way, containing a large amount of presents and provisions," Mitchell said that he had spoken his piece. He now wanted them to return to their camps to talk and smoke over what he had proposed. When they returned to council, two days hence, they should be prepared to name their head chief. Until then, he wanted them to hold councils among themselves and to "make peace, and visit each other."

Fitzpatrick followed Mitchell with a brief farewell, inviting the tribes to come to them with any questions. And then it was over. As one, fifteen thousand Indians rose to their feet. Terra Blue stepped forward to shake hands with both commissioners, addressing Mitchell through his interpreter.

"We have heard you were coming, ever since the grass began to grow," the old warrior told him. "Now you are here, and I have not two hearts—my ears have been open to all you have told us. It seems good to me. I believe our Great Father is good; but I will go home and talk to my people about it—we will think of it."

Following the others, Terra Blue then turned to rejoin his people. Chief Washakie of the Shoshone then shook Mitchell's hand.

"We have come a great distance to see you and hear you, and like our friends the Arikara and the Gros Ventre, I throw my family too, away, to come and listen, and I am glad and my people are full of your words. We will talk them over again in council."

Mitchell's presentation, translated one fragment at a time, had taken several hours, but more had been accomplished that morning than either he or Fitzpatrick had dared to hope. As the great throng dispersed and returned to the camps in the surrounding hills, both men were buoyed by the morning's events, by the pageantry and decorum. Their only disappointment was the absence of the Crow.

The prairie night erupted once again in feasts in all the camps. The Indian drums pounded out songs from every quarter of the surrounding prairie. Fitzpatrick and the interpreters retreated to the relative peace of their upstream camp, while B. Gratz Brown, temporarily revived by an afternoon nap—and heartened to learn that the Shoshone refused to eat the flesh of dogs—set off with De Smet and Chambers to witness a "scalp peace" ceremony between the Snake and the Cheyenne.

The ceremony commenced at the Cheyenne camp, where hundreds of warriors, chiefs, women, and children from both tribes were gathered expectantly around a large feasting fire. As the crowd stood by in hushed silence, a thousand watchful eyes followed the brother of the two Indians who had been killed en route to Fort Laramie to the center of the circle. There, he took his place, seated on the ground between two principal Snake chiefs. "The scalps [of his brothers] were then presented to him; they had been dried and prepared after the Indian fashion," Brown wrote. "The brother looked quite sorrowful, and upon receiving the scalps evinced deep emotion, but when the goods were presented, his countenance changed, he embraced the murderer of his relatives—a general whoop went up, followed by numerous interchanges of friendship, speeches, and a general giving of presents. In the midst of their wild revelry, I left them," he wrote, hoping to get some sleep. But it was not to be, as the feast soon moved to the Snake encampment, near his own, "and made the night horrible by their dances and songs."

The following day was one of rest for the camps of the white men. As Mitchell had requested, chiefs of all the nations gathered in their own councils to discuss the Great Father's proposals. Of course, the most important thing they heard in Mitchell's speech was the Great Father's promise to protect the tribes from depredations by white settlers and traders who came into their country. But the business about picking one chief to represent all the bands of Sioux and all the bands of Cheyenne was a problem for the larger tribes like these. For some years, particularly along the Oregon Trail, Terra Blue's loose confederacy of tribes had been the most troublesome on the plains. Rather than organizing themselves around a central council of elders, the Sioux were little more than a tangled web of blood relationships, shared rituals, overlapping territories, and nebulous political alliances that could be formed one day and broken the next. As the day wore on, Mitchell learned from his interpreters that the Sioux were having difficulty with the idea of selecting one chief. Just as he had feared, this was the stubborn knot that would somehow have to be cut in order to achieve a meaningful peace.

As he had promised, Fitzpatrick rose before dawn on Wednesday morning, September 10, 1851, and rode downstream to the headquarters camp and raised the Stars and Stripes. Already, the smoke of a thousand cooking fires made a blanket haze that hung low over the shallow valley. Mitchell, who had tossed and turned and wrestled with his doubt through a long sleepless night, had finally sought oblivion with a strong dose of brandy. Now, he rolled out of bed looking tired and haggard, had a bite of breakfast and a bracing mug of coffee, then struck a match to the cannon's primer. Strangely, after the cannon had roared, the surrounding country lay utterly still. Mitchell's darkest fears, the very fears he had conquered with brandy, raced again to the fore. This must be their answer. "They're going home," he muttered to Fitzpatrick. "We've asked too much."

Shoulder to shoulder, Fitzpatrick and Mitchell gazed in consternation at the silent city of teepees across the North Platte. They seemed to stretch from horizon to horizon, the thousands of skin lodges clustered around as many fires, and countless thousands of grazing ponies. But before either man could panic, a solitary voice yelled out with a message, a piece of news that had already swept over all the country from the camp of the Snake, and accounted for the silence. *"The Crow are coming . . . it's the Crow . . ."*

Mitchell and Fitzpatrick shot each other an astonished glance, then sprung to their horses. With spurs flailing and leather snapping, the two men charged across the river at a gallop and raced, withers to withers, up the flank of the nearest hill for a better vantage of the surrounding country. What they saw in the distance, wrote B. Gratz Brown, who chased behind them, abruptly brought both men to a halt, for marching down the road from Fort Laramie, after a journey of eight hundred miles, was a vision, a hope, that both men had already abandoned. Brown recorded the moment in his journal later that same morning.

> The Crow were all mounted and their horses, though jaded and reduced by the long trip, were beautiful animals, certainly more beautiful than any we had seen. It must be admitted that the Crow Indian rides better than any other, and he sits his horse with ease and elegance. This is much the finest delegation of Indians we have yet seen, as they came down the plain in a solid column, singing their national melody. . . . They were dressed with more taste, especially the headdresses of the chiefs, than any other of the tribes, and though they rode down into the midst of their enemies the whole plain seemed now alive with a moving mass of redskins, and amidst it all, riding through the middle, they were not the least disturbed or alarmed.

As the Crow warriors rode triumphantly over the hill and down through the widely scattered Indian villages of their enemies toward Mitchell's camp, thousands of Indians fell in behind them and followed on foot. The entire procession was accomplished in the most respectful fashion, as probably no more than a few Cheyenne and Sioux had ever seen these warriors, the Children of the Long Beaked Bird, the mountain raven, up close, yet all who were gathered here knew the stories of their prowess in battle and their legendary endurance. Like their own warriors, these were large men with broad muscular shoulders, narrow waists, and lean powerful legs, men who seldom felt any need for shelter from the sun, wind, or intense cold. Only the Crow were bigger still, like their Hidatsa cousins, most six feet tall and larger, men who made the whites—half a foot shorter on average, with much smaller frames—appear scrawny and skeletal in contrast.

The commissioners rode back down the hill and across the river and were in position to receive them when the two Crow headmen swung down from their mounts at the government's camp. Mitchell gave a brief speech of welcome and then invited the Crow to set up their lodges in the open field next to his. Dutifully, without a word of prompting, the women set off with the travois to set up camp, while the warriors hobbled their horses in the stand of cottonwoods beside the arbor. Then, as if by an invisible cue, all the chiefs made their way forward to the familiar council arbor. Once all were assembled and seated, the Crow chose two seats at the east end of the circle, beside their Arapaho friend Cat Nose. Mitchell then reopened the proceedings by acknowledging the Sioux.

Terra Blue was the first to speak, but his message this morning was short and soon echoed by all the others, a unified front that rekindled Mitchell's anxieties. "We want a chief for each of our bands," the Brulé chief demanded. "The white father does not understand. We are many bands, and if you make two chiefs for each band, it will be better for you. It is not possible to make one chief speak for the many."

Another, a chief named Big Yankton, who reminded Chambers of the fulsome, everyday orators in Congress, told Mitchell that this was the third time the Yankton had met with the whites, but they were still confused by the white man's manner and his choice of words. "You tell us to behave ourselves on the roads and make peace, but it is your own people who make the trouble by stealing our grass and making the buffalo scarce. I am willing to shake hands and make peace with the whites and all the Indians, but we ask, 'Why do you not give your people grass of their own?' They have destroyed our timber, and we can't hunt where we used to hunt. We used to own all this country and went where we pleased."

Then the Yankton named Painted Bear rose to his feet and asked to be recognized. He stood proudly erect and began his speech in a bold and derisive tone, first reminding the commissioners that the western tribes were as free as soaring birds. They could go where they wished, and when they wished it—so why should they allow the Great Father to tell them where they should live, when the Great Spirit had already given them this home? Did the Great White Father think he was more powerful than the Great Spirit? How could this be so? "We have moved around in this country with the freedom of the wind, and we intend to keep it this way."

Painted Bear's speech bristled with anger and hostility and threw down a sobering challenge to Mitchell's entire proposal. In few words, the proud Sioux elder let the commissioners know that Indian leaders in the West were not going to play obsequious pawns to self-proclaimed authorities living in the land beyond the rising sun. He also demonstrated the Indians' political astuteness. They had diplomatic tools of their own and would use them to call Mitchell down for daring to compare the cosmology of the white man with that of the Indian. The white fathers had sent other men long before him to smoke and make peace, and the promises they made were never kept. How, then, since it was already known that the white man's word had little power, could he dare to put the Great White Fathers in Washington on an equal footing with the Indian's Great Spirit, the master of life? This was a ploy that would not work to bring them into the circle of peace. If Mitchell hoped to make peace with the Sioux, he should start by realigning the metaphors in his thinking, because up until now, it was difficult for the Indians to see what they would gain by touching the pen to this agreement.

When Painted Bear sat down, a charged silence hung over the arbor for long, uncertain moments. All present seemed to weigh and absorb the aging chief's defiant words. Finally, the Arapaho's Cat Nose rose unsteadily to his feet and lifted his large dark eyes to meet those of the commissioners.

"I thank the Great Spirit for putting us on this earth," he began. "It is a good earth. We Arapaho hope there will be no more fighting on it. We are tired of the fighting, but we are glad to fight when we must. But we hope it will be no more. We hope that the water will fall from the sky and make the grass grow and bring plenty of buffalo. I come to tell you that we have heard your words, and we think there is much good in what you say. We will go home from here satisfied if we do not have to watch our horses at night, or be afraid for the safety of the women and children. We have to live on these streams and in the hills. I would be glad if the whites would pick out a place for themselves and not come into our country anymore. We have chosen our chief as you asked. Whatever he does we will support him in it, and we expect the whites to support him also. That is all I have to say."

With each speech being carefully translated, this round of Indian oratory took up most of the day. Toward late afternoon the Cheyenne and Arapaho presented the chiefs they had selected to represent them, and the Mandan, Hidatsa, and Arikara heads were also named in council, along with Washakie, the revered Snake leader. With that, Mitchell asked the tribes to continue discussing the matter of selecting a chief and then adjourned the talks for the day.

The following morning, while the Sioux were holding private councils, hunters from all the camps rode off in the four directions in search of hairy hump-backed four-legged beasts. De Smet, the first to rise and the last to retire, held mass each day of the council and baptized hundreds of children at a small makeshift chapel. By this time the stench rising from the sprawling encampment was overpowering human senses, so much that dragoons and other officials in Mitchell's camp began packing up their wagons and scurrying off in search of relief, farther up

Horse Creek. As he watched the hunters ride off, merging finally with the thin blue horizon, Mitchell paced the ground in front of his tent and struggled to contain his private fury over the delayed gifts and provisions. Continual glances toward the east refused to bring relief, and more worrisome yet was the fast vanishing supply of comestibles. There was none left to be had from the quartermaster at Fort Laramie. The dried beef had run out, and the Indians were now slaughtering their dogs at an alarming rate to keep up with the evening feasts. "No epoch in Indian annals," wrote De Smet, "probably shows a greater massacre of the canine race."

Mitchell used this interlude to meet in private with the Crow. Through their interpreter, Robert Meldrum, a man "who has been many years among them, and is . . . an intelligent man, and understands their language perfectly," he reviewed the proposal he had made on the opening day of the council. Alexander Culbertson, a man the Crow also knew well and trusted implicitly, joined in the discussion, and after all their questions were heard and answered, they retired to their camp to make a council. "At a late hour the cannon was fired, the flag hoisted, and the Indians once again assembled in General Council."

The Sioux, beginning with Terra Blue, opened with a round of speeches that sought to demur the selection of a principal chief for the whole nation. Each band wanted its own chief—the large bands because they were strongest, and the smaller bands because they were weak—the very conundrum, of course, resolved at the Constitutional Convention in 1787 by the Founders' Great Compromise. But here, there was to be no middle ground. Despite their pleas, Mitchell explained that he lacked the power to change the terms dictated by the Great White Fathers. They had set these conditions on the first day of the council, and was certain that if the Indians smoked together more in earnest they would find a path to agreement. Then, "after all this had been gone through, the Crow returned to the council and took their places."

Mitchell recognized their leader, the man they called Big Robber, who asked permission to address the council. As he rose, Chambers scribbled his impressions of the moment: "Big Robber, the Crow chief, very elegantly dressed, as fine a specimen of a man, large, well developed and symmetrical, with as intelligent a face as I ever saw, was introduced . . . and made the most sensible speech I heard from the Indians."

"Father," he began, "we are a small nation, and these that are with me here have been selected to come and see you, and do whatever is most for the good of the Children of the Long Beaked Bird. We live a great way off, many days travel from here, and we have but little to do with the whites, but we are willing to be at peace with them. We believe it would be for the good of all to be at peace and have no more war. We listened to our elders. They told us to come and see you and to listen to what you had to tell us. Father, what I promise I will perform, and my people will sustain me. For our part, we will keep the peace, and honor the boundaries of the others' homelands. We only ask that they do the same. I have been asked to speak as the voice of my people. The sun, the moon, and the earth are witnesses of the truth, and all that I have promised here will be fulfilled."

With Big Robber's speech, the geopolitical world of the western Indian was changed forever. Henceforth, the western plains would be shaped by the plan envisioned by their friend Broken Hand in St. Louis earlier that spring. The Crow's willingness to accept territorial boundaries permanently altered the terms of the political debate that had reached an impasse around the Sioux's council fires. Because the Children of the Long Beaked Bird owned and controlled the best grasslands and buffalo commons north of the white man's Medicine Road and had warriors sufficient to protect those boundaries, their declaration of unity with the Great Father's proposals put Terra Blue—and all Sioux subchiefs—under enormous pressure to join the peace. The guidance given to Big Robber by his Crow elders would now compel the Sioux to begin dealing with Congress in good faith. Although the Crow leadership could not have anticipated this coercive effect,

Fitzpatrick, who understood the political alignments of these nations better than any man in America, had read the game board well. If Terra Blue could not yet see the map of the world realigning itself in the peace council, he would soon realize that he risked his tribe's survival by having both the whites and the Crow as enemies. After this, the Sioux's only alternative to acceptance of Mitchell's proposal was to go home empty-handed and prepare for war with all of their neighbors.

This was a propitious turnabout in the negotiations that neither Fitzpatrick nor Mitchell would have dared to predict two days before. Mitchell seized the moment to resolve the Sioux's stubborn impasse over leadership by selecting a man named Frightening Bear to be their "big chief." Frightening Bear, a brave of the highest reputation, told the council that he was not afraid to die, but that they were putting him in a very difficult position. "If I am to be chief, I must be a Big Chief, or in a very few moons I will be sleeping [dead] on the prairie. I have a squaw and papoose that I do not wish to leave. If I am not a powerful chief, my opponents will be on my trail all the time. . . . I will try to do right to the whites, and hope they will do so to my people."

The Sioux challenges were now settled. An emboldened Mitchell announced that the council's deliberations would begin taking a different form the following morning. Each chief was asked to bring five or six principal headmen to the arbor. There, the individual tribes would begin meeting with the interpreters and commissioners to lay out the boundaries of their homeland. The task of establishing these boundaries would fall in the main to men they trusted and knew well: Broken Hand, Culbertson, Meldrum, the Black Robe, and Jim Bridger. Between them, these five were matchless in their knowledge of the tribes and the myriad unmapped geographic details that comprised the American West. Without their collective knowledge and diplomatic wisdom, the entire enterprise would have come to ashes before the wind.

The smoking ceremony had no sooner ended the following morning than Terra Blue made one final attempt to salvage some diplomatic dignity from the failed protests of the previous day. The chiefs had all met again, as Mitchell requested, and now they were very concerned that disputes over boundaries between the Arapaho, Cheyenne, and other Sioux tribes were certain to lead to war. Boundaries could not work for the Indians, the venerable chief argued, since they were all accustomed to traveling where they wished, under the whole sky, not just a piece of it.

In this speech Terra Blue was using a political tool that showed the Indians to be far more shrewd as negotiators than they wanted to let on before the prize was in view. The dispute over boundaries became a diplomatic canard, one, in this case, that conveniently concealed the Sioux's determined efforts to reclaim bargaining power lost to the Crow by laying claim to a territory that was far out of proportion to their customary homelands. The Platte was a natural border between the Arapaho and the Sioux, but Terra Blue wanted to claim lands on both sides of the Platte, and the Brulé demanded the right to hunt as far south as the Republican Fork of the Kansas. The Ogallala, represented by Black Hawk, rose to challenge the boundaries with a territorial claim that would reach into the land of the Crow. So, with mounting concern and heightened anxiety, Mitchell and Fitzpatrick left the bait untouched and let the Indians talk.

Terra Blue was hoping to neutralize the Crow's influence on the business of mapmaking by coaxing their enemies into a boycott of tribal boundaries. Before he fully understood what was happening, Mitchell found himself juggling a growing litany of claims and counterclaims. Although each tribe occupied territories generally recognized by the others, hard and fast boundaries were alien constructs for these nomads. Hoping to stem the mounting dissension, Mitchell recessed the council and withdrew to his camp with Fitzpatrick. The two men sat down over lunch, reviewed the Sioux's strategy, and then reconvened the chiefs in the afternoon.

Mitchell preempted any planned protests by restating the government's purpose for demarcating tribal territories. Acting on Fitzpatrick's advice, Mitchell explained that boundaries were simply the formal recognition by the Great White Fathers of the Indian world as it already existed. Boundaries agreed upon at Horse Creek would not limit any tribe's right of passage, or the right to hunt, in the country of another nation. As long as they remained at peace with one another and caused no harm to white settlers, they would be free as the wind to travel and hunt as they had always been accustomed.

This seemingly insignificant caveat devised by Fitzpatrick was enough to allay the leaders' fears. While it neutralized the trap set by the Sioux, Mitchell was keenly aware that he had departed from the protocol set for him by Commissioner Luke Lea and Congress. He was freelancing on the subject of boundaries. But in light of John Marshall's ruling on the sanctity of usufructuary rights—the right to hunt, gather, and fish on ancestral ground—Congress would come to its senses when it got down to balancing those concerns against its desire to avoid war. For without this caveat, there would be no peace on the Oregon Trail. Yet this simple concession, one that was easily and reasonably granted in the peace council, would still be frustrating state governments and confounding state and federal courts in the twenty-first century.

With that crisis passed and the Sioux's challenge effectively turned back, the headmen of the tribes spent the following days huddled with their interpreters as they worked to establish the boundaries of their ancestral homelands. Wisely, Raven Chief, Four Bears, and Gray Prairie Eagle agreed to band together for the purpose of establishing a contiguous homeland for their three nations on the Upper Missouri River. Negotiations at the arbor filled the days, while dancing and feasting went on each night until dawn. No one was more impressed by the Indians' well-mannered decorum than De Smet, who had worked himself into a general state of exhaustion baptizing thousands of Indian children. "During the twenty-three days of the assembly there was no disorder," he wrote. "On the contrary, peaceable and tranquil . . . [the tribes] seemed all to form but a single nation. Polite and kindly to each other, they spent their leisure hours in visits, banquets and dances; spoke of their once interminable wars and divisions as past things to be absolutely forgotten, or 'buried,' to use their expression. There was not a remark in all of their conversations to displease, and never did the calumet pass in peace through so many hands."

By week's end, B. Gratz Brown and the commissioners, dragoons, and interpreters were delirious from lack of sleep. Their collective weariness seemed all the more pronounced in contrast to the Indians, who appeared unaffected by the diplomatic and ceremonial demands of the council. Day by day, Bridger and De Smet, the chiefs and their interpreters, gathered around a large sheet of parchment and began assembling a blueprint for governance, one that translated the abstractions of John Marshall's foundation of federal Indian law into an operational model for federalism that formally recognized the American Indian tribes of the West as possessing guaranteed powers of self-government, and fixed homelands.

As the deliberate and painstaking process unfolded, De Smet and Bridger found themselves embroiled in a world of geographical nuance and arcane oral histories, all of which had to be squared, as neatly as possible, on the sheet of parchment showing dozens of merging boundaries. Day by day, one river, one mountain range or valley at a time, the geographic features of a new American West began to shape a map that was unlike any other previously drawn. As the mapmakers called the roll of the tribes, each group of chiefs and subchiefs gathered around the parchment. Bunched together in the shade of the cottonwood thatch, the unlikely band of adventurers, priests, traders, Indian chiefs, interpreters, and bureaucrats knelt shoulder to shoulder in the dust. When the task was completed, the boundaries laid down by De Smet, Fitzpatrick, and Bridger had legally described a dozen new tribal territories that covered a contiguous swath of the North American continent that was larger

—by a hundred thousand square miles—than the entire Louisiana Purchase. The 1.1 million square miles of land divided among the "wild and savage tribes" of the Far West that attended the Big Smoke at Horse Creek would one day envelop twelve states and corral the future cities of Denver and Fort Collins, Kansas City, Billings and Cheyenne and Casper and Sheridan, Cody and Bismarck, Salt Lake City, Omaha and Lincoln, and Sioux Falls and Des Moines.

While the conclusive map was being drawn for presentation to Congress, fifteen handwritten copies of the formal agreement for the Treaty of Fort Laramie were prepared for the final signing ceremony. On September 17, 1851, the council was convened at midmorning in the accustomed manner. That day, as on the first, the chiefs were accompanied to the arbor by their tribes. When all had gathered, the throng of thousands sat in expectant silence on the surrounding prairie. Mitchell then rose and informed them that the purpose of this gathering was to formally touch the pen to the documents of peace. He then read them the text, line by line, and asked that the interpreters be certain to explain all the meanings to the chiefs whose names would be affixed to the final document. "Every effort was made, and successfully too, to give them the full and just import of each article," wrote Brown.

The preamble stated that this solemn agreement had been made by the republic of the United States of America and the chiefs and braves of Indian nations residing south of the Missouri River, east of the Rocky Mountains, and north of the boundary lines of Texas and New Mexico. Article 1 stated that the object of the council was to make a firm and lasting peace between these parties, and the second stated that the Indians recognized the right of the United States government to make roads and to build military posts within their respective territories. The third, in consideration of the former article, promised the Indians that the Great White Fathers would protect them from encroachment and atrocities by whites in their homelands, and fourth, the Indians similarly agreed to make restitution for any wrongs committed against whites by any band or individual, and promised to remain at peace with one another. In Article 5, the Great Fathers formally recognized the homelands of the tribes that were signatory to this treaty, and promised that white settlers would be prohibited from settling in those territories for "as long as the rivers shall flow." The territory of the Crow, for example, commenced "at the mouth of the Powder River and the Yellowstone— thence up the Powder River to its source—thence along the main range of the Black Hills and the Wind River Mountains, to the headwater of the Yellowstone—down the Yellowstone to the mouth of Twenty-Five Yard Creek—then to the head waters of the Muscle Shell—thence down the Muscle Shell to its mouth—thence across the headwater of the Big Dry Creek, and down to its mouth." In the sixth article, the Indians bound themselves to respect and sustain their named leader, and the seventh stipulated that the government, in consideration for the right of way through their lands and for the damages the tribes had sustained, would annually deliver fifty thousand dollars worth of merchandise, provisions, domestic animals, and agricultural implements, to be distributed among the signatory tribes each year for the next fifty years. The eighth and final article reserved for the president of the United States the right to withhold these payments if the Indians violated the terms of the agreement. Then, "In testimony whereof the said D. D. Mitchell and Thomas Fitzpatrick commissioners as aforesaid, and the chiefs, headmen, and braves, parties hereto, have set their hands and affixed their marks, on the day and at the place first above written," the peace was concluded.

For the Mandan, Hidatsa, and Arikara, the treaty council at Horse Creek was a formal recognition by the Great White Fathers of the world as they had known it for eight centuries. The boundaries of their homelands encompassed twelve million acres, including numerous rivers, religious sites, and traditional hunting grounds. After all the chiefs had touched the pen and made their marks on the many copies of the treaty, each tribe was given its own copy. Then, several of the older chiefs used the occasion to make speeches to the young warriors. Cat Nose, for one, told the Arapaho braves to be "wide awake, attentive to the promises we have made here, for long after we are gone, you will be bound by this peace." Similarly, Terra Blue told the Sioux warriors—of all the bands—that they must make peace not only with the whites but also with each other. The time for war had come and gone.

The ritual celebrations that marked the end of the gathering at Horse Creek went on for two days. On the evening of September 20, the long-awaited supply train appeared on the horizon, and there was a great rejoicing in the hills above the North Platte. The following day, Mitchell rose early and raised the flag, and one final time he discharged the cannon to bring the Indians into council. There, where dragoons had worked late into the night unloading the twenty-seven wagons, awaited the treasure of promised gifts and provisions. Once the Indians had all flocked in to take their accustomed places, dressed now in the gayest of costumes and painted with "glaring hues" of their cherished vermillion, Mitchell presented the principal chiefs with gilt swords and the uniforms of generals. Then, each band was called forward to claim its gifts, and "the arrangement was characterized by benevolence and justice, and the conduct of this vast multitude was calm and respectful. Not the slightest index of impatience or of jealousy was observed during the distribution."

For almost three weeks, fifteen thousand tribal nomads had set aside their ancient animosities and camped together in a spirit of peace and friendship at the confluence of the North Platte and Horse Creek. By now, the vast herd of horses had nibbled the last blade of grass down to roots. The slightest zephyr raised a cloud of choking dust that engulfed the sprawling encampment in airborne refuse and human wastes. Once the presents were distributed, the women struck the teepees, loaded the prairie buggies, and gathered up their newly baptized children for the long journey home. "Glad, or satisfied, but always quiet," Brown wrote in his journal that evening, the tribes gathered their horses and one by one slipped away over the horizon. Alexander Culbertson accompanied the Village Indians—the Mandan, Hidatsa, and Arikara—back home to the Upper Missouri, while Fitzpatrick and a group of chiefs made their way across the continent to Washington for an audience with President Millard Fillmore. Father De Smet agreed to return to St. Louis with Mitchell to prepare a formal map for the ratification process that was soon to commence in the U.S. Senate.

With quiet elation, the Indians' good and faithful friend Broken Hand watched from the solitude of his camp as the last bands of Sioux, Cheyenne, and Arapaho struck their villages. Despite his ambivalence about the Indians' future, Thomas Fitzpatrick had worked with persistent and solitary diligence for many years to persuade the western tribes to meet in a formal peace council with the Great White Fathers. Certainly no one's diplomatic skill or intimate knowledge of the tribes—their many languages, unique customs, and the country they occupied—had been more instrumental in bringing the council to a successful conclusion. Like the Indians themselves, particularly the old men like Cat Nose and Gray Prairie Eagle, Fitzpatrick was well aware that this was the first gathering of its kind in the great American West, and that most likely it would be the last. Events they could not possibly foresee on that September afternoon in 1851 affirmed their clairvoyance in the coming decades. No spectacle equal to its grandeur and pageantry, or its diplomatic promise and goodwill, would ever again be convened on the high plains of North America.

For the moment, however, such reflections were luxuries to be enjoyed by white men, white men in distant towns, villages, and cities whose proxies had at long last claimed their coveted prize—safe passage for settlers through Indian country to the Oregon Territory and the new state of California. The road to Canaan, unburdened of legal encumbrances and threats of hostile attack by "wild and savage tribes of the plains," was now open to the restless multitudes of Christendom. For the Indians, the true test of the Great White Fathers' solemn promises made at Horse Creek lay not in words on a sheet of parchment or in the ashes of the council fire, but in deeds done on an unmarked day in an unknowable future. The old men knew that in one fashion or another, that test would come just as surely as winter snows would soon fly over the short-grass prairie.

As they quietly bundled up their lodges and prepared to leave, Cheyenne hunters rode back into camp with stirring news. A large herd of buffalo had been sighted in the country of the South Platte, two days' travel to the southeast. Waves of excitement raced through the villages. The Cheyenne and the Sioux, with their enormous encampments, were particularly eager to make one last chase before the first snows drove them into their winter villages at Belle Forche and Sand Creek.

From their separate camps, Fitzpatrick, Mitchell, De Smet, and Brown watched the last members of Terra Blue's band ride away in the late afternoon. Before long, after leaving behind swirling motes of dust on a grassless plain, the nomads merged with the southern horizon. The broad and familiar sweep of the North Platte country was suddenly forlorn and strangely hushed. It was as if the grand kaleidoscopic pageant of their gathering—an event unique in the pages of America's rapidly unfolding story—had been nothing more than a colorful prelude to a feast of bones for the coyotes, raptors, and implacable wolves.

SIX

Monsters of God

While Thomas Fitzpatrick was busy escorting the tribal leaders from the Horse Creek council on a tour of the seats of power and industry along the Atlantic seaboard, Father De Smet returned to his bookkeeping duties at the Jesuit residence at St. Louis University. Cloistered in semi-seclusion at the abbey, he spent two and a half weeks drawing a formal map that would be presented to Congress, along with Mitchell's final report on the Fort Laramie treaty. During most of that time, Alexander Culbertson was on the trail with the Village Indians, finally arriving back at Fort Union in a whiteout blizzard on October 31. Each step of that arduous journey seemed to harden Culbertson's opinion that Mitchell had made a serious blunder in choosing Frightening Bear to be the *ex parte* representative for the nine principal bands of Sioux. For the veteran trader and diplomat, this was another lamentable example of how Washington's ethnocentric view of the world seemed utterly incapable of solving one problem without creating half a dozen more. As much as Culbertson wanted to believe that Horse Creek marked the beginning of a new day in Indian country, the veteran bourgeois feared that its undoing was already built into the treaty itself. In his view, Mitchell and Fitzpatrick would have been wise to hold each band of Sioux accountable through chiefs that represented each distinct band.

Mitchell, meanwhile, went into isolation of his own to write an account of the treaty and to compose his annual report to Commissioner Lea and Congress. On October 25, he wrote a preliminary memorandum assuring Lea that he and Congress had not acted a moment too soon in treating the wild tribes of the prairies. Horse Creek had vanquished all doubt that their "sorry state" was the direct result "of the evils they charge, and I suppose justly, upon the whites."

Father De Smet, an irrepressible optimist by nature, had ridden away from Horse Creek in high spirits. To his monastic brethren in St. Louis he returned confidently predicting a "new era for the Indians—an era of peace, [for now] the Indian will have little to dread from bad white men, for justice will be rendered to him." Also, he was certain that the map he was drawing would be an essential component in the blueprint for the Indian's survival, one that would advance the goal of peaceful coexistence between these dramatically dissimilar, antagonistic civilizations. But his optimism was not naive or simplistic. While he was certain in his own mind that the peace accords at Horse Creek promised to be a turning point for both societies, he argued that the treaty's success would largely depend on the will and integrity of the white man. If Congress honored its pledges, all would be well. If the government was faithful to its commitment to protect the tribes from attacks and encroachments by white settlers and delivered the promised annuities on schedule, this would be the Indians' last best opportunity to transition out of a life dependent on the chase, into a more settled existence in their accustomed homelands.

On November 10, De Smet presented to Mitchell the carefully drawn product of his labors. The finished treaty map—fifty-four inches wide and thirty-six high—showed a region of the American plains bordered on the south by the 36th parallel and on the north by the 49th (the newly established Canadian border). In the east, the map began at 91 degrees longitude and extended west to 119 degrees, on the Pacific flank of the Rocky Mountains. As Mitchell had requested, it also displayed territorial boundaries as of 1851, including Oregon and the northern portion of the state of California, and the designated homelands of the Indian tribes as described in the corpus of the treaty. When Mitchell bundled up his report, the map, and the final text of the treaty for shipment to

Commissioner Lea and the United States Senate, he noted for their benefit, "The accompanying map, upon which these national boundaries are clearly marked and defined, was made in the presence of the Indians, and fully approved and sanctioned by all."

Mitchell then proceeded to devote much of his report on the treaty to the conditions and promises made by the Indians but, counterintuitively, chose to downplay the government's new obligations. It seemed that everyone in government, even the commissioner of the Indian Office in Washington, was concerned that justice and humanity be shown to the Indians—so long as this deference did not come at the expense of the financial and material interests of the Great White Fathers or their children. Ever mindful of the political clout of the latter, Mitchell's annual report called for "a new day in Indian policy" by proposing that the Indian Office and Congress begin drawing a realistic distinction between the border tribes—those living on the white frontier in Missouri, such as the Choctaw and Sac and Fox—and the "wild Indians of the prairies and mountains."

When Congress debated the final language and conditions of the Kansas-Nebraska Act in the spring of 1854, lawmakers took up Mitchell's recommendation—though he had since been replaced by a new superintendent appointed by the incoming president, Franklin Pierce —and appropriated fifty thousand dollars for the purpose of extinguishing title to the lands held in whole or in part by the border Indians in the newly created territories. Implementing this policy fell to President Pierce's new commissioner of Indian affairs, George W. Manypenny, a former newspaper man from Ohio. Unlike his predecessor, Luke Lea, Manypenny was a formidable defender of Indian rights throughout his tenure. But when he took the oath of office on March 28, 1853, he had no inkling of the policy upheavals and frontier turmoil that awaited him.

In mid-April, Manypenny received instructions from Congress to begin negotiating with northern border tribes for half of their territory. To fulfill the request, Manypenny was instructed by his new boss,

Secretary of the Interior Robert McClelland, to persuade tribal leaders
to abrogate treaties that were scarcely a decade old—treaties that contained solemn pledges by Congress that expressly forbade the creation
of any new "organized territories" in the Indians' midst. In the view of
Congress, the nation stood on the threshold of a bright new morning,
and those treaties had been ratified before Manifest Destiny revital-
ized expansionism with its providential sanction. Whatever promises
had been made to these removed tribes by President Jackson were the
bleached bones of the past. Now that the government's march across
the continent was following a divine blueprint, the new theocratic ethic
had manifold uses, including the suspension of the government's treaty-
bound commitments.

Manypenny was deeply alarmed by the amnesia epidemic on Capitol Hill. Rather than battle the ghosts of the past, he immediately left
Washington to take a personal fact-finding tour of the Indian reserves
on the Missouri frontier. Upon his return to Washington he threw down
the gauntlet to Secretary McClelland. "By alternative persuasion and
force some of these tribes have been removed, step by step, from mountain to valley, and from river to plain, until they have been pushed
halfway across the continent," he wrote. "They can go no further; on
the ground they now occupy the crisis must be met, and their future
determined."

Just as the Choctaw's Colonel Folsom had predicted when he snubbed
Andrew Jackson's offers of peace twenty years earlier, tribes that had
been removed from their homelands in eastern forests were again being targeted for a second wave of removal. Despite Manypenny's protests, the calculus of treaty making perfected in Georgia and the Ohio
Valley would now be used to rid the new Indian country set-asides in
Missouri, Kansas, and Nebraska of their native inhabitants in order to
promote white settlement. Congress established the Territory of Nebraska knowing full well that it was ignoring its promises to the Indians
and throwing off its fiduciary responsibility to protect their lands. Thus

caught in the jaws of a vise, the Indian Office itself—an agency created to oversee the government's trust responsibilities to the tribes—was shaped into the point of the wedge that Congress would use to fulfill its Manifest Destiny in the Indian country annexed by President Jefferson in 1804. "The Indian is placed between the upper and nether millstones and must be crushed," declared one congressman in response to Manypenny's protests. "Humanity may forbid it, but the interest of the white man demands their extinction."

The U.S. Senate initially ratified the Treaty of Fort Laramie on May 24, 1852, but not before adding a significant amendment to Article 7. At the last minute, lawmakers decided to reduce the amount of the annual payments from fifty thousand to twenty-five thousand dollars, and to cut the annuity's term from fifty years to ten. When De Smet heard of these changes he was instantly alarmed. How would the tribes react? What was going to stop them from accusing the agents of trickery and going to war? Mitchell, on the other hand, after arguing the previous spring that fifty years was a minimum term for the concessions being requested, had revised his thinking. "This modification of the treaty I think very proper, as the condition of these wandering hordes will be entirely changed during the next fifteen years." In contrast to the missionary, it seemed that the superintendent's determination to close a deal that was "entirely for the Indian's benefit and future welfare," as he had written to Luke Lea the year before, had undergone a sobering encounter with this new political dynamo called Manifest Destiny.

Like his famous predecessor William Clark, David Dawson Mitchell bewailed the lot of the Indian. But despite his well-intentioned efforts on behalf of the tribes under his protection, Mitchell seldom challenged the brahmans of Washington with a vigorous defense of the Indians' interest. In this respect, Mitchell, like most of the government's Indian-country diplomats, was a creature of his time. As the Jesuit scholar John J. Killoren has observed, most of the Great White Father's emissaries to the western tribes infected the government's many long-standing treaty relationships with an erosive paternalism that served the needs of Congress rather than its trustees, an approach that dictated federal Indian policy into the late twentieth century. On one hand, Superintendent Mitchell and many of his contemporaries supported the tribes against the onslaught of European civilization, but at the same time they undermined the Indians' ability to adapt to a rapidly changing world.

After returning to St. Louis in March 1852 from his travels with tribal leaders, Fitzpatrick promised Mitchell that he would personally present the amended treaty to the Horse Creek tribes. Mitchell knew that success in this adventure would ride on Fitzpatrick's reputation among the tribes as an honest broker and trader. But the Senate's tardiness in amending the treaty forced Fitzpatrick to delay the reckoning for another year. This loomed as a serious problem, since the terms of the original agreement called for annuities to be delivered during the summer following the peace council. Wisely, Commissioner Lea approved a requisition for eight thousand dollars worth of goods for the Sioux tribes of the Upper Missouri, at Fort Pierre. Similarly, annuities were subsequently delivered to the Brulé Sioux, Cheyenne, and Arapaho, on the Arkansas and the North Platte. For the time being, the delivery of goods to the Upper Missouri gave the appearance that the Great White Fathers were committed to fulfilling their end of the bargain. This was a promising omen to the tribal headmen, and throughout the first year Indian agents and trail bosses reported that peace was holding on the Oregon Trail. In early May 1853, Congress at last returned the amended treaty to Mitchell's successor, Alfred Cumming, who was instructed by Manypenny to circulate the amendment among the tribes as soon as possible, and to dispatch the proper agents to obtain the signatures of the tribal leaders. Lawmakers had sent the new amendments to Manypenny with a stern proviso: Fitzpatrick and Culbertson, the agents who would be responsible for obtaining most of those signatures, were to withhold all further annuities until the amendments had been signed by the appropriate headmen. Accordingly, annuities were purchased and shipped from St. Louis and distributed to various forts around the West, but under no circumstances were they to be distributed until the proper chiefs had "touched the pen" to the amendments.

The delayed delivery of annuities in 1853, combined with congressional foot-dragging, put Fitzpatrick in a difficult spot. As the one man responsible for maintaining peace along a thousand unprotected miles of the Oregon and Santa Fe Trails, he had little choice but to put his shoulder to this humiliating task and hope for the best. But added to this diplomatic challenge of the amendment was the responsibility for enforcing a thinly veiled policy of blackmail. On what would be his last trip across the plains, Broken Hand's plan was to meet with the Comanche and Apache tribes on his way to the mountains, then treat with the Platte River tribes wherever he could find them. His hope was to persuade the chiefs to sign by appealing to their wisdom—that the agreement was still in the best interests of their children's grandchildren.

By August 2, Fitzpatrick had managed to conclude a new treaty of friendship with the Comanche, Kiowa, and Prairie Apache at Fort Atkinson on the Arkansas River—a mirror of the compact made at Horse Creek. That accomplished, he pressed north to Fort St. Vrain, on the South Platte, where he brought the Cheyenne and Arapaho the latest news from Washington. If the tribes wanted the annuities that were being held for them by the fort's quartermaster, they had no choice but to sign the amendment. Both tribes agreed and touched the pen, but when Fitzpatrick tracked down Terra Blue in the Wyoming Territory, the Sioux chief spoke for many when he shrugged and asked the unanswerable question. "Where is our incentive to comply with these conditions, Broken Hand? The White Fathers change every agreement to suit their own needs! What will the next changes be? You tell us the whiskey traders are bad white men because they tell us the White Fathers are making these treaties in order to steal our lands. It seems to us only the bad white men tell the truth."

As Fitzpatrick expected, Sioux leaders were nearly unanimous in their fury over the meddling of Congress. As he was approaching Fort Laramie from the east on September 10, word reached Fitzpatrick that the Brulé and Ogallala were in a foul mood and were waiting at the fort in full attendance. Earlier that summer, it seemed, a band of wild Miniconjou Sioux had arrived from the Cheyenne River for a visit with their cousins on the Platte. A warrior from the Miniconjou camp had asked a soldier in a skiff for permission to cross the Platte. When permission was denied, the Indian fired on the boat. Troops were sent from Fort Laramie to the camp to arrest the Indian, but what resulted was a skirmish that left four Indians dead. As calls for vengeance circulated among the Platte River tribes, Fitzpatrick was arriving with his news from Washington.

Thanks only to his good name and high standing, Fitzpatrick was able to persuade the Brulé and Ogallala chiefs to set aside their threats of hostility, and to make their marks on the amendment. At the same time, Alexander Culbertson was engaged in a similar diplomatic challenge with the chiefs of the Upper Missouri Sioux tribes, at Fort Pierre. Securing the many signatures of tribal leaders—scattered across hundreds of square miles of open country—was an assignment that could be accomplished only on horseback. Because the process was slow and haphazard, misleading interpretations of the amendments often preceded the agents to the next council. Some, such as the Crow, were off on summer hunts that made them difficult to find; the Crow, in fact, did not even see the amendments until the fall of 1854, but in the end, five of their most influential headmen agreed to touch the pen.

In the years that followed some of the descendants of the widely scattered leaders would remember different things about the amendment, while others would forget it altogether. When General William Tecumseh Sherman sued Red Cloud for peace on the Bozeman Trail in 1868, the venerable Ogallala chief, Man Afraid of His Horse, told Sherman that Mitchell and Fitzpatrick had promised annuities for fifty years. Though Man Afraid was present at Fort Laramie when Fitzpatrick explained the new terms in September 1853, his memory failed to capture the revised terms of the treaty. Unfortunately, misunderstandings and faulty interpretations became the rule of treaty making. The congressional penchant for making last-minute additions and deletions to complex conditions, coupled with details that were lost in translations into many Indian languages, were destined to combust into bloody hostilities between the Indians and the whites in coming decades. This alone was reason enough for the U.S. Supreme Court to later rule that Indian treaties, which were written in the language and symbols of the interlopers, must therefore be interpreted in the manner in which the Indians would have understood them at the time they were made.

If the hammer and saw can be said to be the principal tools of home building, the peace council and the Indian treaty were the main tools of empire building on the North American continent. The republic's first era of treaty making was characterized by many dozens of hastily arranged deals that secured land cessions from hundreds of eastern tribes. Since the young republic was not yet in the business of taxing its citizens, acquiring cheap land and selling it to speculators and settlers was the bankrupt nation's primary means for paying off its lingering war debts. After many dozens of land cessions from the eastern tribes and the wilderness between the Appalachians and the Mississippi had been cleansed of native inhabitants, the first era came to a close when the last Indians were removed to the territory known as the Louisiana Purchase. During that seventy-five-year period, which stretched from the War of Independence to the peace council at Horse Creek, the U.S. Senate ratified almost two hundred treaties. During the second era, from ratification of the Fort Laramie treaty to the Nez Perce treaty of 1868—the last Indian treaty to be ratified—Congress nearly doubled that number.

Like the treaty made at Horse Creek, most of the compacts during the later era were originally designed to secure and promote mutual peace and friendship. Instead of acquiring new lands—which it would later accomplish by force and legislative malfeasance—the government offered the tribes annuities in exchange for peaceful coexistence. Also, a feature common to most of the treaties made during the second era was the recognition by the government of native-owned homelands that were protected by the supremacy clause of the U.S. Constitution for "as long as the waters shall flow." But as most western tribes were soon to discover, water seldom flowed for more than ten or fifteen years in the land of the White Fathers. To the Indians, it seemed that one treaty had no sooner been signed than Congress was sending new agents with new agreements. Each successive treaty renewed the call for peace for more annuities and, eventually, for a reduction of the Indians' homelands.

The great Indian leaders of that era, men like Red Cloud and Sitting Bull, Black Kettle and Plenty Coups, were not fooled by the blizzard of contradictory offers, or by the unceasing requests for new treaty councils. The Kansas-Nebraska Act, coming on the heels of the Great Smoke at Horse Creek, had taught their fathers that the concessions and promises the government gave with one hand were soon taken away by the other and turned over to settlers and homesteaders. "We saw that the white man did not take his religion any more seriously than he did his laws," said the Crow chief Plenty Coups, "and that he kept both of them just behind him, like Helpers, to use when they might do him good. . . . These were not our ways. We have never understood the white man, who fools no one but himself."

In the beginning the only thing Congress wanted from the western tribes was a guarantee of peace. "In order to get that, they were pretty much willing to guarantee the Indians anything they wanted, such as perpetual access to their hunting grounds," says University of Montana professor of Indian law Raymond Cross. Little could nineteenth-century lawmakers imagine that those same usufructuary rights would one day morph into enormous federal lawsuits between tribal governments and multinational mineral and energy corporations in the twenty-first century.

By the time the second era of treaty making was over, most western tribes had signed four and five compacts with new and overlapping conditions and promises. When the century-long era of Indian treaty making finally ended in 1869, Congress had assumed responsibility for 371 treaties and recognized more than 500 Indian nations. Virtually all of the white men who brokered and ratified those treaties believed the Indians would be vanquished by the dawn of the twentieth century. By then, however, most of the men who made those treaties were dead themselves, but the treaties—and the millions of descendants of the Indian leaders who made them—were still active and legally binding.

Ultimately, a fiercely ethnocentric society lured west by a national policy of expansionism—a policy its people (and many of their elected leaders) presumed to be biblical and ordained by God—became the dominant energizing force behind the cultural upheavals and Indian wars of the second half of the nineteenth century. Indian removals in the East, and the cataclysmic wars and cross-cultural turmoil that succeeded them, were a natural and inevitable outgrowth of the nation's stubborn and vituperative dissonance over settling on a workable solution to the imbalances embedded in federalism. Following Horse Creek, had the national government set its course according to its legal obligations to the Indians rather than the insatiable appetites of its citizens—as De Smet, Fitzpatrick, and Mitchell had urged—the Indian wars and all of the misery that flowed from them into the twentieth century would undoubtedly have resulted in a different national narrative. Instead, as treaty expert Francis Paul Prucha has observed, agreements and compacts with Indian nations in the second half of the nineteenth century were increasingly viewed by lawmakers as necessary political anomalies. As time went on and the terms of one compact yielded to the terms of another, the Great White Fathers found it increasingly easy to view the treaty "as a convenient and accepted vehicle for accomplishing what United

States officials wanted to do. . . . By treaty, the government could provide Indian segregation on small reservations and throw open the rest of the territory to white settlement and exploitation." What the United States wanted to do was march across the continent. Beneath the red, white, and blue banner of Manifest Destiny, treaties with Indians became the new republic's legal stepping-stones for building the road to empire in its determined quest to reach the Pacific Ocean.

The United States took one large step along that road on May 30, 1854, when President Franklin Pierce signed the Kansas-Nebraska Act into law. This uneasy compact between northern and southern lawmakers sought to resolve the politically explosive issue of slavery in the western territories. Although it postponed the inevitable reckoning over slavery for another six years, the law marked an important turning point in the republic's convulsive expansion. The final set of compromises— four years in the making—would further aggravate those convulsions by creating two new territories that spanned the length and breadth of the high plains. These territories now extended from the thirty-sixth parallel in the south to the Canadian border in the north, and from the western banks of the Missouri River to the Rocky Mountains.

The two huge new parcels of public lands, separated by the fortieth parallel, were to be managed by independent territorial governments. Residents of both territories were already looking ahead to statehood, even though the law specifically declared that the rights of the Indians were "not to be impaired" and that land already assigned by treaty to the tribes "shall be excepted out of the boundaries, and constitute no part of the Territory." However, embedded in the law was a familiar caveat: these provisions would remain in force only "so long as such rights shall remain unextinguished by treaty." In other words, Congress had already named the tool that it would use to effect "the removal of the Indian barrier to the summit of the Rockies." This would be a tall order in Nebraska, as the Indians already owned most of that territory.

In view of the sinister subtext, Commissioner Manypenny took every opportunity to remind Congress that "the rights of person or property now pertaining to the Indians in said Territories" were inviolate, and that no part of Indian lands could be alienated from them, or included in the new public domain, until the Indians chose, voluntarily, to cede them by treaty.

With great reluctance, Congress was awakening fitfully from the somnambulistic torpor induced by its long-standing misconceptions about the Louisiana Purchase. The phrase itself, the Louisiana Purchase, was a sublime misnomer, one whose true meaning would remain concealed indefinitely behind the veil of legislative expedience and populist myth making. Men like Manypenny were beginning to realize that the federal government's $15 million payment to Napoleon had bought them clear title to no more than a few dozen square miles of land in New Orleans and St. Louis. Beyond those trifling parcels of strategically valuable real estate—and despite the hollow claims to the contrary made by the third president and his successors—the government had acquired little more than free access to the region's rivers, and the unrestricted right to negotiate new deals for more settlement lands with the territory's rightful owners—the American Indians. To the astonishment of many lawmakers, it was fast becoming clear that the Indians held a monopoly on the western landscape from Westport Landing, on the Missouri River, to the ramparts of the Pacific Ocean. Furthermore, because these native lands fell within the new territorial boundaries of the United States, the federal government, as the Indians' trustee, had assumed a solemn fiduciary obligation to protect the integrity of the tribes' landholdings above all other competing interests.

But two years on the job would retool Commissioner Manypenny into a political realist. In 1855, he reported back to Congress that his bureau had successfully advanced Manifest Destiny onto the high plains and into the Pacific Northwest by concluding no fewer than fifty-two new treaties. The combined cessions in the removal treaties amounted to

174 million acres of new public lands. "In no former equal period of our history," boasted the commissioner in his annual report, "have so many treaties been made or such vast accessions of land obtained." Nevertheless, congressional insistence on removal for the border tribes had forced Manypenny to work against his own convictions. Henceforth, he would openly argue that removal was inhumane and impractical. The only sensible solution to the inevitable expansion across the continent was to give the Indians permanent homes that would remain inviolate before the mounting tide of white humanity. "The main cause for strife, violence, disorder, and murder that is now so common between the frontier settlers and the Indians," wrote Manypenny, had to be laid at the feet of Congress. White lawmakers in Washington made promises to the Indians they had no intention of keeping, so the daily reports that reached his office telling of butchery and mayhem on the frontier were the inevitable consequence of the federal government's refusal to fulfill its solemn obligations to the tribes. Fitzpatrick's grim predictions about the white blood that would be shed on the Oregon Trail—resulting from the government's failure to observe its treaty commitments—had come to pass.

A year later, the gruesome consequences of Manypenny's wholesale treaty making would temper the initial celebrations in Congress at having acquired so much land. In his subsequent report, Manypenny conceded with alarm and contrition that racial volatility on the frontier had resulted in serious harm to the Indians. "Trespass and depredations of every conceivable kind have been committed on the Indians. They have been personally maltreated, their property stolen, their timber destroyed, their possessions encroached upon, and diverse other wrongs and injuries done to them. Their rights and interests seem thus far to have been entirely lost sight of and disregarded by their neighbors." Despite its many promises, Congress did not dispatch a single company of dragoons to protect the Indians from encroachment by lawless emigrants.

No one was more distraught over the passage of the Kansas-Nebraska Act than Pierre De Smet. "Whites are already pouring in by the thousands," he wrote. "All hasten to take possession of the best sites. The law has just passed; no steps are yet taken to protect the Indians, and already fifty new towns and villages are in progress. . . . I did not think that the moment of invasion was so near."

By late 1853, Fitzpatrick and Culbertson feared there was little hope that the Horse Creek peace would hold. Atrocities were inevitable on both sides. Within a year, Nebraska's eastern bulwark crumbled under the weight of illegal incursions and encroachments by whites. Land speculators lusted after Indian lands, and the government, in a deliberate abdication of its fiduciary obligations, turned a blind eye to the sacking of Cheyenne and Pawnee homelands. Settlers who rushed in to occupy tens of thousands of little squares on government surveyors' plat maps vanquished the vast buffalo commons of northern Kansas and southern Nebraska in weeks. Farther west, the winter camps of the Cheyenne and Arapaho, on the eastern slope of the Rockies, were soon overrun by a new wave of gold diggers headed for the Colorado goldfields. With the Civil War brewing in the East, Congress was reluctant to send federal troops into the Wild West to keep the peace, and those it sent to protect remote trading posts, such as Fort Laramie, were mostly young, inexperienced, and often conscripted into service as they stepped off the boat from Ireland, Switzerland, and Italy. Consequently, each successive year throughout the 1850s saw an increase in violent conflicts, an ominous trend that was further exacerbated by the fact that neither the Indians nor the emigrants showed any willingness to back away from spilling the others' blood.

Over the next thirty years, the wheels of the Conestoga wagons wore ten-inch grooves into the limestone bedrock in eastern Oregon, yet the western tribes were not about to stand idly by as the endless river of settlers destroyed a world that had sustained them for centuries. Like something once dreamed of in a state of youthful exuberance, the West that Fitzpatrick, Bridger, and Culbertson had known as beaver men, just two decades earlier, had already disappeared beyond horizons that only a handful of white men could claim to remember.

In his final annual report to Congress, written in November 1853, less than three months before his ignominious death at the age of fifty-five from a bout with influenza in a Washington hotel room, Broken Hand was wrestling with the harsh terms of the rapidly approaching denouement. More poignantly, he also seemed to recognize that his own enthusiastic promotion of white settlement and the Oregon Trail, and his ambivalence toward the Indians, had inadvertently played a role in setting their tragedy into motion. "The Indians will perish before the land thrives," he wrote, with characteristic insight and bluntness. "Indeed, examples of all their race who have preceded them on the continent, would point to a condition of poverty, of humiliation, of extinction, as the natural result of the foster policy of the government. The emaciated remains of the great tribes, who hover in parties upon the borders of Missouri and Arkansas, are evidences that cannot be ignored. But must it always be thus? Must the same system, which has resulted so unfortunately heretofore, be pursued remorselessly to the end? Must the course of removals from place to place, and successive contractions of territory, and perpetual isolation, which has thus far been fraught with such enormous expense, be likewise applied to the nations of the interior?" This new wave of removals, he told Congress, must be called by its name: "the legalized murder of a whole nation. It is expensive, vicious, inhumane, and producing these consequences, and these alone." Leaders of the republic must realize, he warned, that humanity would judge its policies by its fruits, not by the gloss of its high-toned words.

Then, as if restless fates had set out to underscore Fitzpatrick's salient points, on August 17, 1854, a cow owned by a Mormon emigrant strayed off the Oregon Trail and wandered into a camp of four thousand Brulé and Ogallala Sioux. The Indians were camped near Fort Laramie, where they were awaiting the arrival of their annuities from St. Louis. The wayward cow proceeded to wreak havoc in the camp, so a young Brulé warrior shot the animal and wasted no time dividing the spoils. When the cow's owner discovered its fate, he raced ahead to Fort Laramie and reported the incident as a theft to the fort's commandant.

Unfortunately, the commandant ignored the provision in the Horse Creek treaty that called for restitution of Indian thefts from their annuities. Instead, he reacted hastily and ordered a high-spirited second lieutenant named John Lawrence Grattan, a patrol of twenty-nine mounted soldiers from the U.S. Sixth Infantry Regiment, and one interpreter to apprehend the thief at a nearby Brulé encampment. Grattan, a hot-tempered West Point graduate who was openly contemptuous of the Sioux's reputation for bravery, had only recently arrived on the frontier. He rode off into the hot afternoon at the head of his column of soldiers, itching for the opportunity to immortalize his own name in battle.

When the soldiers arrived at the village, Lieutenant Grattan's first mistake was in failing to account for the stature of the head chief. In fact, this was Frightening Bear (also known as Conquering Bear), the same man Mitchell had selected three years earlier to represent all of the Sioux nations. Grattan's interpreter, a Frenchman drunk on whiskey, aggravated the tense situation by taunting the chief's warriors with foul-mouthed insults. Hoping to diffuse the situation as quickly as possible, Frightening Bear offered to give up the offender, but when Grattan decided to make a show of the white man's justice and rode into the Indian camp to arrest the man himself, Frightening Bear rose to his feet in protest. A rifle shot rang out, and the battle that ensued became memorialized in the U.S. military annals by an incendiary malapropism—the Grattan Massacre. Of the thirty soldiers and one civilian who rode into the Brulé camp, none rode out. The bloody melee was over in minutes, but the ground was littered with blue coats and writhing, half-dead horses. Warriors rushed in to take scalps and guns, while others carried away the dead body of Frightening Bear—a U.S.

Army bullet through his back—the same man who had predicted his own death in his speech at Horse Creek.

"We knew him [Frightening Bear] well," a memorial essay written by A. B. Chambers in the *Missouri Republican* of St. Louis began, "and a better friend the white man never had. He was brave, and gentle, and kind—a wise ruler, a skillful warrior, and . . . one of the most high-toned and chivalric of all the Indians we have known."

Father De Smet was so incensed by the news of this incident that he wrote a scathing satire titled "Will You, in Europe, Believe This Tale of a Cow?" Unfortunately, rumors preceded facts, and the incident was soon a rallying cry for vengeance on the frontier. In Washington, the secretary of war, Jefferson Davis, told Congress that it must "punish the offenders quickly." General William S. Harney, on leave in Paris, was called back to Washington and immediately sent west with orders to subdue the savages. Harney rode off with his troops from St. Louis declaring: "By God, I'm for battle—no peace!"

General Harney's campaign finally ended at a small defile on Blue Water Creek, called Ash Hollow, near the North Platte. Harney's troops surrounded the Brulé camp, led by Chief Little Thunder, and provoked the Indians to put up resistance. Little Thunder obliged, and after dozens of women and children had been slaughtered by indiscriminate fire from the dragoons, Harney's men took seventy of the surviving women and children as hostages before moving on to challenge other Sioux bands on the Platte. De Smet bewailed the carnage as the senseless aftermath of a stolen cow. In a letter to Secretary McClelland, he lamented simply: "And yet, such is the origin of a fresh war of extermination upon the Indians."

Thus began the initial spate of bloody skirmishes, provocations, and retributions that would lead to two decades of full-scale war between the principal signatories to the treaty of peace and friendship made at the Great Smoke at Horse Creek. Although the encounters were relatively small and intermittent for the first ten years, General Harney's ruthless behavior at Ash Hollow taught the tribes that the peaceful coexistence promised in the 1851 treaty was a chimera. Henceforth, the white man would regard the Medicine Road as the exclusive property of the United States government. With no direction from Congress or the Indian Office, Harney took it upon himself to tell a gathering of Sioux chiefs that the Horse Creek treaty was nothing more than "molasses and crackers," a meaningless piece of paper. Henceforth, he warned them, the Indians "must not obstruct or lurk in the vicinity of roads traveled by the whites," or he would again teach them the lessons of Ash Hollow and "sweep them from the face of the earth."

The chiefs who had been at Horse Creek soon realized that the Great White Fathers had little control over their own citizens. Time and again, as whites demonstrated brazen contempt for the laws and treaty obligations of their government, Washington either turned a deaf ear to the pleas of the tribes or sent troops to punish them for retaliation. Attack and counterattack became the dominant pattern of cultural interaction on the Great Plains. To the Arapaho, Sioux, and Cheyenne, it seemed as if the Great White Fathers now looked upon the Fort Laramie treaty as another worthless document signed by people who were nothing more than obstacles to the march of empire. Like the treaties that preceded Horse Creek and all that followed in the next twenty years, the ground-breaking agreement forged between the Great White Fathers and the tribes of the American plains could fulfill its promise through rigid enforcement, but there is scant evidence to suggest that serious consideration was ever given to this aspect of treaty making by officials in Washington. And no single event of that period attested to the solemn consequences of Washington's neglect more than the Sand Creek massacre of November 29, 1864.

When he heard that Chief Black Kettle's band of Cheyenne were settled into their winter camp a few miles northeast of the frontier town of Denver, a firebrand Methodist minister, Colonel John Chivington, led his mounted command on a nightlong march in search of the Indians.

Having recently signed a new treaty of peace, Black Kettle had been promised protection by the U.S. Army from other bands of Indians that were trying to wrest away the Cheyenne hunting ground in eastern Colorado. Black Kettle, whose camp of a hundred lodges was made up of mostly women, children, and old people, had proclaimed his neutrality in all the skirmishes being fought on the countryside around his winter camp. With nothing to fear, the members of his band lay peacefully asleep as dawn broke on a cold winter morning.

When Black Kettle stepped from his lodge and saw the frieze of blue coats arrayed on the cut bank above the village, he quickly raised the American flag on a standard to display his neutrality, but the gesture was ignored. When Colonel Chivington was asked what they should do about the women and children, he ordered his men to kill them all. Then, he waved his saber in the air and ordered his troops to open fire.

"And then the scene of murder and barbarity began—men, women, and children were indiscriminately slaughtered," reads the report of the official congressional investigation. "In a few minutes all the Indians were flying over the plain in terror and confusion. A few who endeavored to hide themselves under the bank of the creek were surrounded and shot down in cold blood. . . . From the sucking babe to the old warrior, all who were overtaken were deliberately murdered. Not content with killing women and children who were incapable of offering any resistance, the soldiers indulged in acts of barbarity of the most revolting character; such, it is to be hoped, as never before disgraced the acts of men claiming to be civilized. No attempt was made by the officers to restrain the savage cruelty of the men under their command, but they stood by and witnessed these acts without one word of reproof."

When the sound of gunfire finally yielded to the unnerving silence, after the screams and wails of the dying had fallen quiet and the last crying babies had been run through with bayonets, the sordid mayhem of the troops commenced in earnest. As their commander looked on from the bluff above the village, Chivington's troops worked their way through the village from lodge to lodge, lopping off ears and fingers as they went, and gathering ornaments and scalps from the victims' bodies. Then came the signature atrocity of these massacres, the dissection of the women's genitalia with bayonets and Bowie knives. Commonly, the eviscerated body parts were stretched over the soldier's caps and worn as hatbands—the prized souvenirs of battle. When Chivington and his men rode into Denver, they were welcomed by the governor and a throng of citizens as conquering heroes, all hats bristling. The God-fearing women of Denver then collected the scalps and mutilated genitals of the Cheyenne women and children and hung them like Christmas ornaments over the stage at the Denver opera house.

Later, the official investigators called Chivington's interpreter, John S. Smith, to submit to cross-examination before members of Congress.

INVESTIGATOR: Were the women and children slaughtered indiscriminately, or only so far as they were with the warriors?

SMITH: Indiscriminately.

INVESTIGATOR: Were there any acts of barbarity perpetrated there that came under your own observation?

SMITH: Yes, sir, I saw the bodies of those lying there cut all to pieces, worse mutilated than any I ever saw before, the women all cut to pieces.

INVESTIGATOR: How cut?

SMITH: With knives; scalped; their brains knocked out; children two or three months old; all ages lying there, from suckling infants up to warriors.

INVESTIGATOR: Did you see it done?

SMITH: Yes sir, I saw them fall.

The government's investigation concluded: "As to Colonel Chivington, your committee can hardly find fitting terms to describe his conduct. Wearing the uniform of the United States, which should be the emblem of justice and humanity, . . . he deliberately planned and executed a foul and dastardly massacre which would have disgraced the veriest savage among those who were the victims of his cruelty . . . [and] took advantage of their inapprehension and defenseless condition to gratify the worst passions that ever cursed the heart of man. . . . Whatever may have been his motive, it is to be hoped that the authority of this government will never again be disgraced by acts such as he and those acting with him have been guilty of committing."

Despite the blistering verdict of congressional investigators, neither the minister-colonel nor any of his subordinates were ever fined, court-martialed, or punished for their deeds at Sand Creek. Churchgoing citizens in western frontier settlements were joined in their belief that the extermination of the Indian should be helped along. As men like Chivington reminded them from the pulpit, "Joshua upon entering the promised land had been ordered by God to exterminate the Canaanites, an Indian-like people, and [Joshua] was punished for hesitating." The United States government promised to compensate the Cheyenne and Arapaho for the massacre committed at Sand Creek, but when the treaty reached the Senate for ratification, the Select Committee on Indian Affairs quietly deleted that provision. "Indians [today] remember that the United States Army, led by a Methodist minister, ruthlessly slaughtered nearly five hundred defenseless Indians," wrote the late Sioux legal scholar Vine Deloria Jr., in *Of Utmost Good Faith*. "Before there can be any warm feelings that we are all 'one people,' the United States must make compensation to the Cheyenne and Arapahos for Sand Creek."

News of Sand Creek spread across the prairie faster than an electrical storm. Rather than convince the Indians that they should retreat before the ever growing wave of settlers, the massacre spawned outrage among all who heard of it. The few remnants of goodwill that remained among the western tribes from the council at Horse Creek were destroyed in less than an hour by a righteous, hot-headed Methodist minister and his troops. The Sioux and Cheyenne renewed their blood oaths of friendship and vowed to fight to the last man to exact revenge. In the ensuing years the many successful Sioux attacks on military outposts on the "bloody Bozeman" trail in Montana, all in response to Sand Creek, led to the second peace council of Fort Laramie, in 1868, when General Sherman sued the Lakota Sioux's war chief, Red Cloud, for peace. But the Great White Father broke that treaty, too, just six years later, when President Ulysses Grant sent Colonel George Armstrong Custer, with a thousand cavalry soldiers, from Fort Abraham Lincoln in North Dakota into Red Cloud's beloved Black Hills in search of gold. Grant ordered this calculated transgression on the thin hope that a gold strike might relieve the banking crisis that had suspended construction of the transcontinental railroad. Gold was found, and the Lakota Sioux's prized homeland was soon swarming with a stampede of prospectors.

By the spring of 1876, terms and promises made to Red Cloud and the Lakota in the Fort Laramie treaty of 1868 had been thoroughly abrogated. Under the protection of federal troops, gold miners in the Black Hills were throwing up the frontier towns of Deadwood and Rapid City. Sitting Bull, Big Foot, Crazy Horse, and Gall concluded from this that the Great White Fathers had no intention of living by their agreements. The treaty made at Horse Creek now seemed no more tangible than a winter night's dream. White men they had once known and trusted, Mitchell, Fitzpatrick, and De Smet, had all died and been replaced by General Harney, Colonel Chivington, and Colonel Custer. Bridger, having survived a thousand deaths, was now a reclusive old man living in a cabin in Kansas, where he eventually passed into oblivion, in 1881, as unobtrusively as he came.

Although the Indians still roamed the West at will, their leaders realized they now stood alone against an overwhelming force, and their time was fast running out. There would be no returning to the life on the plains that they had known for the previous century. As Fitzpatrick and Manypenny had stated years ago in their reports to Congress, the Indian Trade and Intercourse Acts, first passed by Congress in 1790, through abuse and neglect had become the ineffective mainstay of a disgraced Indian policy. Just months before the battle of the Greasy Grass—also known as the Battle of the Little Big Horn—Sitting Bull said to General Alfred H. Terry: "Tell them at Washington if they have one man among them who speaks the truth to send him to me, and I will listen to what he has to say."

The battle of the Greasy Grass took place on a hazy sweltering afternoon in June 1876, one week before the United States Centennial Exposition opened in Philadelphia. Custer hoped that news of a great victory against the implacable Sioux would steal President Grant's thunder in the upcoming elections. Personal ambitions aside, the Battle of the Little Big Horn was a collision of civilizations made inevitable by a history of broken promises, hubris, and the Eurocentric society's difficulties in abiding by its own laws. At the time, the nation's spirits were soaring on the wings of irrepressible optimism. Throughout the month of June, foreign leaders arrived from all over the world to take part in the republic's centennial celebration, a once-in-a-lifetime gala affair. After an evening of drinks and small talk with foreign dignitaries, Grant and the organizers were about to sit down to a seven-course meal when a courier arrived with an urgent message for the president.

The message had traveled twenty-five hundred miles from the Montana Territory, by foot and horseback, then steamboat, and finally through a copper wire over a succession of telegraph relays. The piece of paper itself seemed to knock Grant off balance. The man being courted to replace him as president, who had stood beside him at the surrender of the Confederacy at Appomattox, George Armstrong Custer, along with his entire command in the Seventh Cavalry, had been massacred at the Little Big Horn by an overwhelming force of hostile Indians led by the Sioux's war chief, Sitting Bull, and the Cheyenne chief Gall. The man who had cast a philosophical eye across nine thousand dead bodies on the battlefield at Cold Harbor, Virginia, was stunned to silence by the unnerving image of Custer's locks hanging from the coup stick of a Cheyenne warrior.

This singular event, a battle that took less time, said Sitting Bull, "than it takes a man to eat a meal," would soon prove to be a dramatic turning point in the nation's history. Perhaps no other hillside or valley in America conjures deeper or more ineffable meanings, more bewildering and disorienting paradoxes, than that eerily silent piece of windswept sweetgrass overlooking the Little Big Horn River, at the heart of Crow country.

In spite of the Indians' stunning victory, this climactic clash marked the beginning of the end of a way of life for the once great nomadic tribes of the American plains. "Had there been no Indian," writes historian Stanley Vestal, "there could have been no frontier, no wars, no pillage, no adventure, only a mob of lusterless clodhoppers moving into the empty wilds a little farther each season." But there were Indians, and within two years, most of the wandering savages would be rounded up and corralled behind stockades on remote reservations. Conversely, this marked the end of the beginning for white migrants, who—with the passage of the Dawes Act of 1887, which threw open vast tracts of Indian country to white settlement—were free to populate and inhabit two million square miles of the unfenced West that had been promised less than a generation earlier to the tribes "for as long as the waters shall flow." From Lodgegrass to Peoria, from Shiprock to Boston, this clash of civilizations was a reckoning with ideological, social, and geographic paradoxes that would remain embedded in mainstream American society well into the next century and beyond.

According to Wallace Stegner: "Behind the pragmatic, manifest-destinarian purpose of pushing western settlement was another motive: the hard determination to dominate nature that historian Lynn White, in the essay 'Historical Roots of Our Ecologic Crisis,' identified as part of our Judeo-Christian heritage. . . . God and Manifest Destiny spoke with one voice urging us to 'conquer' or 'win' the West; and there was no voice of comparable authority to remind us of Mary Austin's quiet but profound truth, that the manner of the country makes the usage of life there, and that the land will not be lived in except in its own fashion."

And so it was, in such an unlikely but unrelenting manner, that a long-forgotten legal relic passed down from Pope Innocent III, via Spanish philosophers and English lawyers of the Age of Discovery, became the officially sanctioned engine for westward expansion on the North American continent. Once the signatory tribes to the Horse Creek treaty were captive on widely scattered reservations, the government in 1883 created the Indian Religious Crimes Code, a new law written by Methodist ministers that outlawed all Indian religious ceremonies, including the Plains Indians' sacred Sun Dance—a suspension of First Amendment rights for natives that would not be repealed by Congress until 1978.

Four years after the Religious Crimes Code, Congress in 1887 declared that it would henceforth be the final arbiter of its red children's civil rights—an edict that would have been unthinkable to James Madison, Benjamin Franklin, or George Washington. But having exhausted its own ideas and resources in a series of failed policies over eight decades, Congress turned over the management of the Indian Office to the care of Methodist and Congregational missionaries. With the lawmakers' blessings, the missionaries scattered out over Indian country and commenced the practice of abducting Indian children from their homes and sending them off to boarding schools, sometimes thousands of miles away. This was done, said the missionaries, in hopes of "killing the Indian to save the man."

A few years later, after the Seventh Cavalry had exacted tribute for the Little Big Horn by slaughtering Big Foot's band of Ghost Dancers beside a creek called Wounded Knee, the United States census of 1900 quietly gave evidence of the toll that had been levied against native peoples. Where millions of "savages and infidels" had prospered and flourished three centuries before, fewer than 240,000 had survived their encounters with the Europeans. America's century was just beginning, and Manifest Destiny, the tireless engine of providence driving the expansion of America's democratic faith from sea to shining sea, could now look to more distant horizons. In a speech titled "Expansion and Peace," Theodore Roosevelt closed out the nineteenth century and stepped boldly into the twentieth by declaring America's destiny to be a visible, but incomplete, reality. "It is only the warlike power of a civilized people that can give peace to the world," declared Roosevelt, arguing that this meant a victory for law, order, and righteousness, forcing "the barbarians" to recede or be conquered. The peace that follows such a conquest, he claimed, "is due solely to the power of the mighty civilized races which have not lost the fighting instinct, and which by their expansion are gradually bringing peace to the red wastes where the barbarian peoples of this world have held sway."

A few weeks later, on January 9, 1900, Senator Albert Beveridge amplified Roosevelt's themes for the benefit of his Senate colleagues, in a speech that might have been written by a pope in the Middle Ages, or by a crusading American president in the twenty-first century. "God has not been preparing the English-speaking and Teutonic peoples for a thousand years for nothing but vain and idle self-contemplation and self-admiration," Beveridge declared. "No! He has made us the master organizers of the world to establish system where chaos reigns. He has given us the spirit of progress to overwhelm the forces of reaction throughout the earth. Were it not for such a force as this the world would relapse into barbarism and night. And of all our race, He has marked the American people as His chosen nation to finally lead in the regeneration of the world. This is the divine mission of America, and it holds for us all the profit, all the glory, all the happiness possible to man."

Midway through the twentieth century, yet another Indian removal era commenced on the northern Great Plains. By 1950, the Great White

Fathers' political strategies were more polished and sophisticated than they had been a century earlier. Also, thanks in large part to the nation's outrage over the notorious findings of the Meriam Report in 1928, the legal methods Congress used for exerting its will in Indian country were less crude and bloody than they had been in the time of missionaries and cavalry soldiers. On balance, however, the consequences of the federal government's strong-arm tactics were just as devastating for the tribes in the Eisenhower era as they had been during the presidency of Andrew Jackson. With the passage of the Pick-Sloan Plan and the Flood Control Act of 1944, Congress signaled a return to the broader legislative tactics of the Jackson era—to the familiar business of forcibly removing Indian tribes from their treaty-protected ancestral homelands.

Since a succession of homestead acts and executive orders had succeeded in opening Indian lands to white settlement in the late nineteenth and early twentieth centuries, the government's chief objective for the latest phase of removal was to make way for massive public works projects in the Upper Missouri River basin—a million square miles of America's high plains desert. Congress was determined to wrestle the Big Muddy into unconditional surrender, but to claim that prize, lawmakers were obliged to abandon their long-standing constitutional and fiduciary obligations as trustees to the collective welfare of their native beneficiaries. The first Indians to be removed from the Upper Missouri were the Mandan, Hidatsa, and Arikara tribes, a socially complex intermingling of semi-sedentary cultures whose members had been intermarrying, sharing languages, and blending social customs for nearly five centuries. Of the dozens of tribes and Indian bands that called the Upper Missouri River basin home, most had signed the treaty negotiated by Thomas Fitzpatrick and David Dawson Mitchell at the Great Smoke at Horse Creek in 1851.

In the decades that followed the nineteenth-century Indian wars, the Three Affiliated Tribes looked on in a kind of helpless limbo as successive homesteading acts and executive orders (many of which were later ruled illegal) reduced their treaty-protected homelands from twelve million acres to less than one million. Nevertheless, by the end of World War II, a cataclysm that introduced many of the three tribes' young men and women into mainstream American society through the armed services, the Mandan, Hidatsa, and Arikara people were the only self-sustaining Indian nations in the United States. Their economic independence and vitality was due largely to their ancestral ownership of the richest farmland in America. But the building of Garrison Dam—the keystone flood control impoundment in the Pick-Sloan constellation—meant they would lose another 156,000 acres of that farmland to what members of the three tribes still refer to as "the flood." As the Missouri's waters inundated the world they had known for nine centuries, thousands of Mandan, Hidatsa, and Arikara people were forcibly removed to the desolate windswept wasteland of the surrounding high plains—that forbidding no-man's-land of desiccated hardscrabble that was home to rattlesnakes, jackrabbits, and silver sage—known simply as "on top."

As the formal taking of their lands under the Fifth Amendment was being legally engineered in backrooms in Congress, Martin Cross was returning from service in the Army Air Corps to resume his life as a family man and cattle rancher in Elbowoods, North Dakota. Once home, Cross reluctantly donned the mantle of leadership pressed on him by the elders of his tribes, a solemn duty that compelled him to turn about and squarely face the daunting challenges and uncertainties of the future. For twelve years Cross threw himself into a battle against the U.S. Congress and the Army Corps of Engineers in a heroic effort to save his people's homelands. With the U.S. Constitution and long-settled federal Indian law on his side, it was a battle he and the tribes were nevertheless destined to lose to the formidable bulwark of historical precedent, malfeasance, and legislative sleight-of-hand.

In the winter of 1964, twenty years after he was first elected tribal chairman, Martin Cross made his last trip to Washington, D.C., on official business for the tribal council. On a frigid February day, he climbed into his pickup truck and drove north from his ranch near Raub, North Dakota, to the small wind-blown railroad town of Minot, some seventy miles away. After parking his truck in the gravel lot beside the train station, he once again boarded the Northern Pacific's Empire Builder, a muscular transcontinental passenger train whose clitter-and-clack had become more familiar to Martin Cross than the sound of his own mother's voice.

After a four-year hiatus from tribal politics, Martin had decided to come out of retirement in 1960, at the age of fifty-four. Lonely and destitute out on the ranch, he threw his hat over the wall for one last run at the tribal council. He won easily. By this time the Garrison Dam's broad shoulders were bowed against a lake that ran two hundred miles upstream, all the way to the Montana border and the river's confluence with the Yellowstone. In the decade that had passed since the taking, via eminent domain, of his tribes' homelands, the Sioux, the Assiniboin, the Crow, and the Cheyenne had subsequently lost their battles and homelands to the Pick-Sloan scheme. To the high plains Indians it seemed that all of the tribal signatories to the Treaty of Fort Laramie in 1851 were destined to drown, either alone or together, behind the government's flood control and hydroelectric dams on the Upper Missouri River and its tributaries.

By luck, pluck, and perseverance, the Mandan, Hidatsa, and Arikara people had survived the immediate trauma of dislocation and relocation, but like most tribal governments in the West, theirs struggled from week to week to remain solvent and intact. The three tribes had just barely survived the termination era of the 1950s, a little-known campaign sponsored by Representative Reva Beck and Senator Arthur Watkins, both Utah Mormons, that called for the cessation of all U.S. trust responsibilities to the hundreds of federally recognized tribes. In a cruel twist of syntax and legalese, Beck, Watkins, and their allies in Congress planted a flag on ersatz moral high ground by citing altruism as their driving motivation. Their helpful goal, they declared, was simply to free the Indians from the wretched imprisonment of perpetual wardship.

What got less attention during this noisy campaign was the strategy devised by mineral and resources consortiums, and their many friends in Congress, to divest western tribes of a treasure chest of resources—gold, uranium, coal, oil and gas, timber, copper, zinc, and silver—all of which were now known to lie beneath the unwanted wastelands where most of the Horse Creek tribes had been removed in the nineteenth century. Until senators Barry Goldwater of Arizona and Lee Metcalf of Montana finally put an end to the termination movement by calling on Congress to repeal these laws, including P.L. 280 and House Resolution 108, in late 1958, the Three Affiliated Tribes were on the government's short list for dissolution as a formally incorporated legal entity. Throughout those dark years, Martin Cross was a semi-permanent resident of backstreet hotels in Washington, fighting to preserve the vestiges of nationhood. Even though he had lost the war with the Corps of Engineers in 1949, he succeeded in guiding the three tribes safely through the stormy nights of termination. By 1960, the Garrison Dam had forced the removal and relocation of his people "on top," but despite the cataclysmic social trauma endured by the Village Indians, their tribal government, the formal legal apparatus that secured their nationhood, was still intact.

At the same time Martin Cross was battling termination, dozens of tribes around the country were beset by yet another "relocation" program, a scheme that was instigated as an adjunct to termination by President Truman's commissioner of Indian affairs, Dillon Myer. Commissioner Myer, a well-known face around Washington, was a career bureaucrat whose previous incarnation had been as Roosevelt's chief administrator for the internment of Japanese Americans during World War II. With hopes of emptying the reservations and assimilating native people into mainstream American society, Myer's solution to the government's perennial "Indian problem" was to load them on buses and trains and drop them off en masse in large western cities. The brazen new commissioner assured his receptive congressional audience that once they were relocated, the Indians would follow the example of the Japanese Americans and begin blending into the surrounding society. Tens of thousands of Sioux, Cheyenne, Crow, Arapaho, Blackfeet, and Hidatsa, including Martin's own children, were given one-way bus and train tickets to Chicago, Los Angeles, Seattle, and San Francisco— where they were handed vouchers to skid-row hotels and flophouses and told to go start new lives. Before long, the path from the Upper Missouri River, from the Crow and the Rosebud and the Northern Cheyenne reservations, among many others, became a well-worn groove to urban centers in the Midwest and on the West Coast.

"There were a lot of tragedies in those years that will never get into the history books," says Alfred Cross, who himself went on relocation in the late 1950s and has lived in California and New Mexico since then. "Who knows how many thousands of Indians were dumped off in the cities? Years later you'd hear about the suicides of friends from back home, in a bar on the North Beach, or from somebody who knew somebody, or from headlines in the newspapers. NAMELESS INDIAN JUMPS OFF THE GOLDEN GATE BRIDGE, or, NO NAME JOE LEAPS FROM WINDOW. No known origin. No known survivors. No name, or, for that matter, no country."

As members of the three tribes were being scattered across the American landscape by federal agents implementing Dillon Myer's relocation program, Martin's leadership responsibilities began to take a heavy toll on his health and his personal life. After trying unsuccessfully to work things out on top during the chaotic years of removal and relocation, he and his wife, Dorothy, were divorced in 1954. With two young children in tow Dorothy moved into a small house in Parshall, North Dakota, where she took odd jobs and the kids attended school. Martin, a rancher from the crown of his hat to the heels of his boots, escaped from the hurly-burly of town and moved onto a barren piece of high plains that he inherited from his father. The small white ranch house was miles from nowhere, and once he was out of politics and living alone, Martin tended to drink more than he should, and his life fell apart. Like everything else around him, his body was breaking down, and there weren't enough days in the week to turn his small-time cattle business into a profitable venture. On top, ranching was a one-way street to financial ruin. With ranchers selling off their livestock to buy propane and groceries just to get through the winters, it seemed that no amount of effort could keep the tribes' cattle operations—which had thrived on the bottomlands—in the black. In March 1964, Martin returned home from Washington to get ready for spring calving. Three weeks later, on April 4, on a fine spring morning with clear skies and the sound of songbirds drifting through the open windows, he laid down on his bed, took a deep sigh, and died. "His heart opened up like a zipper," the coroner told his eldest son, Crusoe. At fifty-eight, Martin Cross had worn it out.

It wasn't until he was a high school sophomore in California that Martin's youngest son, Raymond, born in Elbowoods in 1948, was old enough to appreciate his father's years of sacrifice. Martin Cross, he realized, had been the last of the old and the first of the new, a bridge between the nineteenth and twentieth centuries, the last connection between himself and the men who had signed the treaty at Horse Creek. By sheer force of will, his father had overcome the twin entropies of a limited education and a parochial upbringing. Over the course of his career in tribal politics, and as a founding member and first vice-president of the National Congress of American Indians, Martin Cross had personally known four United States presidents, along with countless senators, congressmen, and state governors. As the last of the old, he had accepted the loneliness and isolation that came with leadership, and he did so without complaint. As the first of the new, he was in the vanguard of those who could see over the horizon into the future, and he struck out for that horizon with deliberate and bold resolve, determined to bring his people into the modern age.

"If you look at Plato's response to the Sophists, Plato says, 'I can show

you that the only way to have a just man is to create a just society,'"
says Raymond Cross, now a professor at the University of Montana's
school of law. "I think this points to where American society has so often
broken down. We build capable individuals like Frederick Douglass,
Cesar Chavez, and Martin Cross, but then we deny them the resources
to build a just society."

By 1964, the Indians were not the only ones struggling to cobble
together a life out of the limited resources left to them by Pick-Sloan.
White farmers on the high plains were growing increasingly restless,
impatient, and angry. The million acres of irrigation that had been promised to them by politicians who needed their support to pass the Flood
Control Act in 1944 had still not materialized. Irrigation, it seemed, had
been nothing more than a carrot used to lure them into a high-stakes
game that was a rigged lottery favoring farmers and barge operators
in downstream states. Just as the Hoover Report had warned in 1949,
dry-land farmers across the high plains had unwittingly volunteered
to become hostages to two federal agencies fighting for control of the
Missouri River. Once the big dams were built—all with enormous cost
overruns—no one in Washington was clamoring to spend billions more
on irrigation projects. The Pick-Sloan Plan, wrote the editorial board of
the *St. Louis Post-Dispatch*, was on a fast track to becoming "the most
gigantic boondoggle in American history." The public works project
that was originally projected to cost $3 billion had topped $20 billion,
with no end in sight.

Once Sioux and Crow lands were being inundated in the 1960s, federal investigators decided this would be a good time to update their files
on the Mandan, Hidatsa, and Arikara. Specifically, the Bureau of Indian
Affairs wanted to know how they were adjusting to the challenges of life
on top. President John F. Kennedy had recently characterized the living
conditions of Native Americans as a disgraceful blight on the conscience
of the nation. The BIA's investigation found nothing at the Fort Berthold
Reservation, where they were living, to brighten that assessment. Their

poverty, coupled with the isolation of many in the remoter parts of the reservation, had created a situation in which starvation was a real possibility for many of the tribal members, the report said. There was no avoiding the conclusion that the forced relocation of these Indians—once the most prosperous tribes in the nation—from their homelands had undone a century of progress in less than ten years. The government, the report warned, should expect a similar plague of conditions and afflictions to visit the Sioux, the Cheyenne, and the Crow.

"See, what you have now is this Indian," says Alfred Cross, "this creature who is a product of all those policies of the federal government, all the removals, the broken treaties and the wars, the allotment era and the missionaries, and then termination and relocation. The Indian is now a product of all that—he's a creature of the federal government."

The once-vibrant governments of high plains tribes during the New Deal era had drifted into a collective state of governmental paralysis. Of all the Horse Creek tribes, the Crow's homeland was most intact, a condition that is commonly ascribed to their fierce neutrality during the Indian wars of the previous century. But their wealth was in the land, not in cash. All the tribes were destitute. Infant mortality on reservations was five times the national average, and 95 percent of their members fell below the national poverty level. In 1969 the nation's native population was approaching one and a half million, but fewer than five hundred Indian children were enrolled in schools of higher learning.

Then, when the future looked as bleak as it had at any time since the 1890s, words American Indian tribes had been waiting to hear for two centuries came from a most unlikely source. On July 8, 1970, Richard M. Nixon became the first president in history to deliver a speech to Congress on the subjects of federal Indian policy and Native American rights. After characterizing the termination era of the Eisenhower administration as "a national disgrace," Nixon challenged lawmakers to join him in writing a new story for Indian country. "The American Indians have been oppressed and brutalized, deprived of their ancestral lands, and denied the opportunity to control their own destiny, yet their story is one of endurance and survival, of adaptation and creativity in the face of overwhelming obstacles. The time," he declared, "has come to break decisively with the past." In President Nixon's view, the policy evils of paternalism and chronic governmental malfeasance had deprived millions of Indians of life, liberty, and the pursuit of happiness for nearly two hundred years. Henceforth, he declared, "Indians can become independent of federal control without being cut off from federal concern and federal support."

Nixon's speech reverberated like summer thunder across the high plains. Apart from fulfilling a campaign promise to native leaders, the president's proposal was a powerful reaffirmation of John Marshall's federal trust doctrine for these "domestic dependent nations," and an equally powerful challenge to state governments that were perennially jealous of tribal resources and governmental sovereignty. The conditions Nixon laid down for correcting the ill effects of federal paternalism also mirrored the very demands for self-determination that had been echoed by native leaders ever since the Great Smoke at Horse Creek. It was as though someone in Washington, this unlikely Republican Quaker from California, had finally heard their pleas.

Nixon asked James Abourezk, a progressive U.S. senator from South Dakota and the son of Lebanese immigrants who had settled on the Sioux's Pine Ridge Reservation fifty years earlier, to assist him in writing an Indian Self-Determination Act. This landmark legislation was a comprehensive reimagining of federal Indian policy, one that was connected in Congress with the Indian Education Act of 1972. Henceforth, federal and state funds would be made available to tens of thousands of young college-bound Indian students. Shortly after Nixon was driven from the White House by the Watergate scandal, Congress fulfilled its promise—over a loud chorus of protests from western governors and state legislators—by passing the Indian Self-Determination Act. By the late 1970s, Nixon's far-reaching initiatives had sparked the first social revolution in Indian country since the Founders gathered in Philadelphia in 1787. But the optimism it spawned across Indian country was to be short-lived. The election of Ronald Reagan in 1980 prompted an abrupt and dramatic return to the nihilistic paternalism of the past. The cause for that turnabout was neatly summarized in an article published in *Forbes* magazine that observed, with searing, atonal irony, "Now, at a time when the United States seems to be running out of practically everything, Indian reservations constitute one of the least-known repositories of natural resources on the continent."

The Reagan administration quietly convened a secret committee made up of industry experts and their counterparts in conservative think tanks, such as the Rand and Heritage foundations, called the Strategic Minerals Consortium. The SMC was charged with the task of studying the problem of mineral scarcity and finding a way to gain easy access to mineral treasures in Indian country, a mission that clearly echoed William Tecumseh Sherman's century-old assessment of the federal government's attitude toward the sanctity of Indian land titles: "An Indian reservation is a tract of land set aside for the exclusive use of the Indian, surrounded by thieves." While the SMC was busy devising grand schemes, Secretary of the Interior James Watt came up with a plan of his own, one that was eerily reminiscent of the strategy devised by Congresswoman Beck, Senator Watkins, and Commissioner Myer thirty years earlier. Watt proposed that Congress use its plenary power over the tribes to declare all treaties null and void. Then, the Indians should be moved off their reservations and into closer proximity to white citizens, in urban centers, where they could be more easily assimilated into mainstream society.

Fifty years earlier, before the tribes had the financial resources to mount an effective defense against such a plan, the Reagan administration's schemes might have succeeded. By 1983, however, most tribes had stepped into the modern era. By then, thanks to the Indian Education Act passed by Congress a decade earlier, thousands of young Indians had been trained as chemists, biologists, and lawyers in the white man's colleges and universities. Rather than disappearing into urban America after graduation, many returned to their reservations with the intent of protecting their natural resources, their treaties, and their tribal sovereignty. Among those many thousands was Raymond Cross.

After earning a bachelor's degree from Stanford University and a law degree from Yale University in 1973, Raymond Cross went to work for the Native American Rights Fund, based in Boulder, Colorado, and served his apprenticeship in federal courts on the West Coast. Then, after winning the landmark Indian water law case known as *Adair v. Oregon* for the Klamath tribe, he returned to Fort Berthold in 1982. Privately, he hoped an opportunity would arise to resume his father's fight for just compensation for the taking of the tribal trust lands. That opportunity came in 1984 when Congress convened a commission to investigate the negative effects of Pick-Sloan on the state of North Dakota. As that commission's work was being completed and presented to Congress, simultaneously, in 1986, Raymond appeared twice before the U.S. Supreme Court to argue *Three Affiliated Tribes v. Wold Engineering*, an appeal of a lower court ruling that resulted in a 6–3 victory for the tribes, and a forceful reaffirmation of Chief Justice Marshall's federal trust doctrine. Then, culminating an eight-year campaign to win just compensation for the 1949 taking of their homelands, in 1992 Raymond's quiet but relentless efforts in Congress resulted in a $149.6 million award to the Three Affiliated Tribes for the violation of their treaty rights and the unconstitutional taking of their homelands. Martin Cross's devastating defeat in 1949 had been overturned, and his dream redeemed, forty-three years later by his son Raymond. In addressing Cross and the members of the Senate Select Committee on Indian Affairs, Chairman Daniel Inouye scornfully declared that the story of the Three Affiliated Tribes was unfortunately only one of many in a sad and tragic chapter of the federal government's long history of deceit and deception. "Of the three hundred seventy treaties that this Senate, our predecessors, ratified, the United States government violated provisions in every one of them," Inouye said. "It is a very sad chapter, and as one senator, as chairman of this committee, I can assure you that we will do our best to see that no further violations are carried out in this country."

"These old laws [treaties and statutes] emanate a kind of morality profoundly rare in our jurisprudence," writes the preeminent Indian law scholar and writer Charles Wilkinson. "It is far more complicated than a sense of guilt or obligation, emotions frequently associated with Indian policy. . . . Somehow, those old [treaty] negotiations . . . are tremendously evocative. Real promises were made on those plains, and the Senate of the United States approved them, making them real laws. My sense is that most judges cannot shake that. Their training, experience, and, finally, their humanity—all of the things that blend into the rule of law—brought them up short when it came to signing opinions that would have obliterated those promises."

By the year 2007, farmers on the high plains were still waiting to see the first trickle of Pick-Sloan water. The guarantees Congress had made to their grandfathers fifty years before were still so many flyblown words on long-forgotten reams of paper. Ever since the Flood Control Act was passed in 1944, the O'Mahoney-Milliken Amendment—that backroom deal that promised farmers they would be first in line for Pick-Sloan water—had been held hostage to an uncertain (and dry) future by downstream politicians who controlled important transportation committees in the U.S. Senate and the House of Representatives. No amount of howling from high plains politicians seemed to make any difference. As drought-stricken farmers looked on from the parched stubble of their devastated grain fields, millions of acre-feet of water were drawn down from Garrison Dam each year to keep barges floating between St. Louis and Sioux City, Iowa. And in ways—and for reasons—not visible or very well understood until the mid-1970s, General Lytle Brown's ominous predictions about the long-term consequences of building dams on the Upper Missouri—predictions presented to Congress in 1934—were proved tragically prescient seven decades later.

Just as Brown and his engineers had warned, the Big Muddy's well-known penchant for siltation could not be abated or avoided by any conventional or financially feasible means. In fact, the same sediments that gave the river its famous nickname had been the primary building block for the barrier islands at the mouth of the Mississippi, in the Gulf of Mexico, ever since the last Ice Age. For more than ten thousand years the same mineral-rich silts that once made the Mandan corn and squash plantations a source of wonder and wealth had steadily built up and replenished the forty-mile-wide belt of islands that absorbed energy and storm surges from hurricanes and tropical storms on the Louisiana coastline. When the floodgates closed on the five Missouri River dams, tens of millions of cubic yards of silt, once transported by the river's currents to the mouth of the Mississippi, began settling behind the Army Corps of Engineers' stair-step impoundments across the high plains.

By the mid-1970s, marine biologists on the Gulf of Mexico were sounding a quiet but persistent alarm. For inexplicable reasons, the barrier islands were disappearing at an alarming and increasing rate. Their warnings were well founded. Within twenty years the barrier islands off the coast of Louisiana were all but gone, vanished in a blink of geologic time. When Hurricane Katrina stormed ashore in August of 2005, the cities of Mobile and New Orleans, and the entire Gulf coastline, had been rendered defenseless. The taking by eminent domain that had violated the Indians' constitutional guarantees to their homelands in 1949 had also resettled the Gulf Coast's barrier islands behind the Pick-Sloan dams and laid them out in blankets of thick, river-choking silt along nine hundred miles of river bottom on the northern plains.

Just a few years earlier, as mineral and gas corporations continued to circle Indian reservations across the West, a feisty middle-aged Blackfeet woman named Elouise Cobell decided that the time had come to begin a long-overdue accounting of mineral royalties on Indian lands. What started as a mere suspicion—a hunch that the federal government and mining corporations had been stealing from the poor and giving to the rich—soon germinated in actualities and took root in the law to become a formal complaint. Once her suit was filed in federal court in 1996, the case, currently known as *Cobell v. Kempthorne*, evolved into a class-action suit involving three hundred thousand plaintiffs across western Indian country. The list of plaintiffs included tens of thousands of the descendants of the Indians who had attended the Great Smoke at Horse Creek.

Cobell's suit argued that the U.S. Department of the Interior, in collusion with energy and mineral extraction companies, had neglected its solemn fiduciary responsibilities to the Indians by absconding with mineral royalties since the late 1800s. "The significance of Indian trust funds as a source of capital for American industrialization cannot be overemphasized," the economic historian Craig Miner has written. Indian trust funds managed by the federal government became one of the principal sources of capitalization for emerging extractive industries during the twentieth century. Many casual observers noted that the strength and influence of those mineral corporations grew in inverse proportion to that of the Indians whose resources they were exploiting. The chronic long-term abuse of the trust funds severely undermined the popular "argument that this change was inevitable because God intended a new culture to rise, and it raises the question whether money held in trust for the protection of the Indians ought to have been used to support the instrument of the ultimate doom of their sovereignty."

Accountants for the firm of Price-Waterhouse conducted the initial review of the government's books. Their report minced no words: it appeared that as much as $50 billion had gone missing, and maybe more. In 2003, a conservative judge from Texas by the name of Royce Lamberth, who from the beginning had presided over the case in federal district court in Washington, D.C., ruled in favor of the plaintiffs. Along the way, he three times cited sitting secretaries of the interior for contempt of court because of their chronic foot-dragging, malfeasance, and bureaucratic double-talk. Once the basic question of culpability was settled, the protracted and contentious accounting nightmare could begin in earnest.

"Alas," declared Judge Lamberth in words seldom heard from a federal bench, "our modern Interior Department has time and again demonstrated that it is a dinosaur—the morally and culturally oblivious hand-me-down of a disgracefully racist and imperialist government that should have been buried a century ago, the last pathetic outpost of the indifference and Anglocentrism we thought we had left behind. . . . For those harboring hope that the stories of murder, dispossession, forced marches, assimilationist policy programs, and other incidents of cultural genocide against the Indians are merely the echoes of a horrible, bigoted government-past that has been sanitized by the good deeds of more recent history, this case serves as an appalling reminder of the evils that result when large numbers of the politically powerless are placed at the mercy of institutions engendered and controlled by a politically powerful few." In 2005, at the insistent urging of the White House and the Interior Department's lawyers, who accused Judge Lamberth of being "too harsh on the government" in a twenty-three-page motion seeking his dismissal, Judge Lamberth was removed from the case.

Louise Holding Eagle, the high-spirited young mother who drove to town for groceries and returned to find that her house and family had vanished on that long ago spring evening in 1951, lived to be a funny, and wise, and beautiful spitfire of a little old lady in her longtime hometown of Parshall, North Dakota, population: 862. A few days before Christmas in 2003, while remembering the Christmases of her childhood in Elbowoods in a speech to members of her community, a tiny bubble let go in a blood vessel in her brain. Her shoulders slumped and she tumbled to the floor behind the podium. Over the next several days, the last of the life she had lived with cheerful dignity and indomitable optimism slowly seeped out of her. She never recovered from the aneurysm, which was a shame, because three months later, on a brilliant morning in March, the pyramidal granite tip of that permanent fixture on the American landscape, the eighteen-foot-tall obelisk raised to the memory of the chiefs who attended the Great Smoke at Horse Creek, augured its way through the vast landscape of ice covering Lake Sakakawea. In the spectral brilliance of a high plains sunrise, the tribes' monument to peace and friendship with their white neighbors and the Great White Fathers became visible once again for the first time in fifty years. And Louise would have liked that.

APPENDIX

Treaty of Fort Laramie (Horse Creek), 1851

Articles of a treaty made and concluded in the Indian Territory, between D. D. Mitchell, superintendent of Indian affairs, and Thomas Fitzpatrick, Indian agent, commissioners specially appointed and authorized by the President of the United States, of the first part, and the chiefs, headmen, and braves of the following Indian nations, residing south of the Missouri River, east of the Rocky Mountains, and north of the lines of Texas and New Mexico, viz, the Sioux or Dahcotahs, Cheyennes, Arrapahoes, Crows, Assinaboines, Blackfoot, Piegans, Gros-Ventre [Hidatsa], Mandan, and Arrickaras, parties of the second part, on the seventeenth day of September, A.D., one thousand eight hundred and fifty-one.[1]

ARTICLE 1: The aforesaid nations, parties to this treaty, having assembled for the purpose of establishing and confirming peaceful relations amongst themselves, do hereby covenant and agree to abstain in future from all hostilities whatever against each other, to maintain good faith and friendship in all their mutual intercourse, and to make an effective and lasting peace.

ARTICLE 2: The aforesaid nations do hereby recognize the right of the United States Government to establish roads, military and other posts, within their respective territories.

ARTICLE 3: In consideration of the rights and privileges acknowledged in the preceding article, the United States bind themselves to protect the aforesaid Indian nations against the commission of all depredations by the people of the said United States, after the ratification of this treaty.

ARTICLE 4: The aforesaid Indian nations do hereby agree and bind themselves to make restitution or satisfaction for any wrongs committed, after the ratification of this treaty, by any band or individual of their people, on the people of the United States, whilst lawfully residing in or passing through their respective territories.

ARTICLE 5: The aforesaid Indian nations do hereby recognize and acknowledge the following tracts of country, included within the metes and boundaries hereinafter designated, as their respective territories, viz;

The territory of the Sioux or Dahcotah Nation, commencing the mouth of the White Earth River, on the Missouri River, thence in a southwesterly direction to the forks of the Platte River; thence up the north fork of the Platte river to a point known as the Red Butte, or where the road leaves the river; thence along the range of mountains known as the Black Hills, to the head waters of the Heart River; thence down the Heart River to its mouth, and thence down the Missouri River to the place of beginning.

The territory of the Gros Ventre [Hidatsa], Mandans, and Arrickaras Nations, commencing at the mouth of the Heart River; thence up the Missouri River to the mouth of the Yellowstone River; thence up the Yellowstone River to the mouth of the Powder River in a southeasterly direction, to the head-waters of the Little Missouri river; thence along the Black Hills to the head of the Heart River, and thence down Heart River to the place of beginning.

The territory of the Assinaboin Nation, commencing at the mouth of Yellowstone River; thence up the Missouri River to the mouth of the Muscle-shell River; thence from the mouth of the Muscle-shell River in a southeasterly direction until it strikes the head-waters of Big Dry Creek; thence down that creek to where it empties into the Yellowstone River, nearly opposite the mouth of Powder River, and thence down the Yellowstone River to the place of beginning.

The territory of the Blackfoot Nation, commencing at the mouth of the Muscle-shell River; thence up the Missouri River to its source; thence along the main range of the Rocky Mountains, in a southerly direction, to the head-waters of the northern source of the Yellowstone river; thence down the Yellowstone River to the mouth of Twenty-five Yard Creek; thence across to the head waters of the Muscle-shell River, and thence down the Muscle-shell River to the place of beginning.

The territory of the Crow Nation, commencing at the mouth of the Powder River on the Yellowstone; thence up Powder River to its source; thence along the main range of the Black Hills and Wind River Mountains to the head-waters of the Yellowstone River; thence down the Yellowstone River to the mouth of Twenty-five Yard Creek, thence to the headwaters of the Muscle shell River; thence down the Muscle-shell River to its mouth; thence to the head-waters of Big Dry Creek, and thence to its mouth.

The territory of the Cheyenne and Arapaho, commencing at the Red Butte, or the place where the road leaves the north fork of the Platte River; thence up the north fork of the Platte river to its source; thence along the main range of the Rocky Mountains to the head-waters of the Arkansas River; thence down the Arkansas River to the crossing of the Santa Fe road; thence in a northwesterly direction to the forks of the Platte River, and thence up the Platte River to the place of beginning.

It is, however, understood that, in making this recognition and acknowledgement, the aforesaid Indian nations do not hereby abandon or prejudice any rights or claims they may have to other lands; and further, that they do not surrender the privilege of hunting, fishing, or passing over any of the tracts of country heretofore described.

ARTICLE 6: The parties to the second part of this treaty having selected principals or head-chiefs for their respective nations, through whom all national business will hereafter be conducted, do hereby bind themselves to sustain said chiefs and their successors during good behavior.

ARTICLE 7: In consideration of the treaty stipulations, and for the damages which have or may occur by reason thereof to the Indian nations, parties hereto, and for their maintenance and the improvement of their moral and social customs, the United States bind themselves to deliver to the said Indian nations the sum of fifty thousand dollars per annum for the term of ten years, with the right to continue the same at the discretion of the President of the United States for a period not exceeding five years thereafter, in provisions, merchandise, domestic animals, and agricultural implements, in such proportions as may be deemed best adapted to their condition by the President of the United States, to be distributed in proportion to the population of the aforesaid Indian nations.

ARTICLE 8: It is understood and agreed that should any of the Indian nations parties to this treaty, violate any of the provisions thereof, the United States may withhold the whole or a portion of the annuities mentioned in the preceding article from the nation so offending, until, in the opinion of the President of the United States, proper satisfaction shall have been made.

In testimony whereof the said D. D. Mitchell and Thomas Fitzpatrick commissioners as aforesaid, and the chiefs, headmen, and braves, parties hereto, have set their hands and affixed their marks.

NOTE
1. This treaty as signed was ratified by the Senate with an amendment changing the annuity in Article 7 from fifty to ten years, subject to acceptance by the tribes. Assent of all tribes except the Crows was procured (see Upper Platte C., 570, 1853, Indian Office) and in subsequent agreements this treaty has been recognized as in force.

NOTES

Text is identified by page number and the first few words of the passage referred to in the note.

CHAPTER 1. REDEEMING EDEN

1 *"I don't know what we would have eaten":* Louise Holding Eagle, interview by the author, June 2002.

2 *This was, by all accounts, the richest:* Holder, *The Hoe and the Horse,* 29–42, gives an excellent analysis of the migration patterns of the Village Indians (the Mandan, Hidatsa, and Arikara tribes) and a thorough description of their horticultural expertise.

2 *Surveyed by government engineers:* VanDevelder, *Coyote Warrior,* 76–77.

3 *Even in a region accustomed to extremes:* Fitzharris, *The Wild Prairie,* 7–10. Vestal, *Short Grass Country,* 190, tells of a four-month period in Dodge City when the average velocity of the wind was 11 miles per hour; maximum velocity, 45; duration of the south wind, 1,420 hours; calm, 27 hours.

3 *The Elbowoods Warriors:* Phyllis and Al Cross, interviews by the author, June 2002.

4 *It weighed more than five tons:* Meyer, *Village Indians of the Upper Missouri,* 200, 238.

5 *"I don't know how long I sat there":* Louise Holding Eagle interview. Also, see Macgregor, "Attitudes of the Fort Berthold Indians Regarding Removal," and Macgregor, "Social and Economic Impacts of Garrison Dam."

6 *In 1951, Louise's people were organized:* See Meyer, *Village Indians of the Upper Missouri,* for further details on the Three Affiliated Tribes Corporate Charter, ratified April 24, 1937, and the Indian Reorganization Act Constitution and bylaws, approved June 29, 1936.

6 *the only self-sustaining Indian tribes:* Meyer, "Fort Berthold and the Garrison Dam," 229–233. Also, see *Report on House Resolution 108 Authorizing the Committee on Interior and Insular Affairs to Conduct an Investigation of the Bureau of Indian Affairs,* H.R. Report 2680, September 20, 1954. This report was published during the middle of relocation, termination, and dislocation. The Department of the Interior found that "less than fifty percent of the approximately six hundred and fifty Fort Berthold Indian families have

demonstrated the ability to support themselves by their own efforts." Just ten years earlier, the BIA's report of 1943 found that *all* of the Fort Berthold families were self-sufficient. With the tribe fully enveloped in the effects of dislocation resulting from the construction of Garrison Dam, the 1954 report states: "It is the conclusion of the bureau of Indian Affairs field staff, and this conclusion is supported by anthropologists independently of Federal personnel, that to a considerable extent a substantial percentage of Fort Berthold Indians suffer from the mental conflicts which develop in the process of transition from the earlier Indian cultural environment to the environment now being imposed on these people by a dominant non-Indian culture with its differing social and economic system of values. As a result of this situation it is probable that any program under which the great majority of Fort Berthold Indians were permitted to assume full responsibility for independent management of their own affairs, would result in rapid depletion of existing assets followed by widespread dependence upon welfare assistance."

6 *Unlike tribes that had been pushed out:* For a thorough description of tribal migration patterns out of the eastern woodlands in the eighteenth century, see Gibson, "Great Plains as Colonization Zone," 19–37.

6 *the Mandan people had migrated out:* Professor Raymond Wood, interview by the author, February 2002. Also, see Wood and Thiessen, *Early Fur Trade on the Northern Plains,* and Holder, *The Hoe and the Horse,* 2–10.

6 *highly complex clan-based matrilineal society:* Bowers, *Hidatsa Social and Ceremonial Organization,* and Peters, *Women of the Earth Lodges.*

6 *these socially sophisticated peace-loving farmers:* Holder, *The Hoe and the Horse,* 29–42.

7 *So prominent was their reputation as masters:* Wood and Thiessen, *Early Fur Trade on the Northern Plains.*

7 *On maps drawn in 1718 by the leading French:* Wheat, *Mapping the Trans-Mississippi West,* 1:48–63.

7 *The purpose of this claim was to open:* Ibid.

7 *With the eastern forests under the control of the British:* Ibid.

8 *As battles raged in the forests of a distant continent:* Ibid.

8 *In pre-Columbian times, the Mandan people:* Wood and Thiessen, *Early Fur Trade on the Northern Plains.* Also, see Bodkin, *Our Natural History,* and Ronda, *Lewis and Clark Among the Indians,* 67–80.

8 *most seventeenth-century trade routes:* Wood and Thiessen, *Early Fur Trade on the Northern Plains.*

8 *Pierre Gaultier de Varennes, the Sieur de La Vérendrye:* Smith, *Explorations of the La Vérendryes.*

9 *In 1781, after traveling north from the central valley:* Each new inquiry into the role of epidemics contributes important information to the overall picture of the decline of the native populations in the Americas. According to Dobyns, *Their Number Become Thinned,* the native population in the Western hemisphere reached 100 million by 1492. An investigation conducted by the Smithsonian Institution documented ninety-three widespread epidemics among native peoples in the post-Columbus Americas. Smallpox is believed to have first come ashore in 1519 with a sailor from the expedition of either Hernán Cortez or Pánfilo de Narváez; Verano and Ubelaker, eds., *Disease and Demography in the Americas.*

9 *Bewildered and terrified, the surviving leaders:* Ken Rogers, ethnographer, interview by the author, October 2000. Also, see VanDevelder, *Coyote Warrior,* 79–84.

9 *When Lewis and Clark made their way:* Ronda, *Lewis and Clark Among the Indians,* 67–80.

9 *Unwittingly, says noted historian James Ronda:* Ibid.

10 *Before the sun went down, her land:* Louise Holding Eagle, interview by the author, June 2002.

10 *"We certainly didn't need anybody to tell us":* Ibid.

10 *It put horns on frogs, forced deadly snakes to slither:* Webb, "The American West," 26.

10 *From the hundredth meridian west:* Webb, *The Great Plains,* 3–9, and VanDevelder, *Coyote Warrior,* 27. Also, Wilkinson, *Crossing the Next Meridian.*

11 *fifteen inches of "god-water":* Reisner, *Cadillac Desert,* 46–48, 148–159.

11 *one look at that sky, one moment surrendered:* Vestal, *Short Grass Country,* 3–5.

11 *"Above its vague and receding horizons":* Ibid.

12 *filled the surveyors' "little squares with people":* Reisner, *Cadillac Desert,* 43–46, and Webb, *The Great Plains,* 418–431.

12 *The homestead acts of 1870 and 1887:* Webb, *The Great Plains,* 418–431.

12 *They came by train and on foot:* VanDevelder, *Coyote Warrior,* 86. Also, see Raban, *Bad Land,* 1–55.

12 *The Northern Pacific's hard sell:* Raban, *Bad Land,* 20–34, and Reisner, *Cadillac Desert,* 40, 41.

13 *In Powell's ground-breaking* Report: Powell, *Report on the Lands of the Arid Region.* Also discussed in Webb, *The Great Plains,* 418, and Powell, *Seeing Things Whole.*

13 *He urged Congress to scrap:* Webb, *The Great Plains*, 418. Because he was in complete agreement with Powell, Webb's seminal work on the Great Plains was viewed by many westerners as heresy. Nevertheless, Webb was as secure in his thinking "as a Christian holding four aces."

13 *Land units in irrigation districts:* Webb, *The Great Plains*, 418–431.

13 *Powell's report came with a bold-faced warning:* Ibid. By the time he made his prediction it was already too late. Large landowners and corporations swept into the West and bought up the water rights to the major rivers and tributaries in the late nineteenth century.

14 *when it passed the Desert Lands Act:* Reisner, *Cadillac Desert*, 43–46.

14 *Wedged without appeal between a rock:* Webb, *The Great Plains*, 420–425.

15 *"the largest contingent to the asylums":* E. V. Smalley, "The Isolation of Life on Prairie Farms," *Atlantic Monthly*, December 1893. Also, see C. W. Thornthwaite, "Climate and Settlement in the Great Plains," *Climate and Man: Yearbook of Agriculture* (Washington, D.C.: GPO, 1941).

15 *Since turn-of-the-century lawmakers were hesitant:* Reisner, *Cadillac Desert*, 114–115.

16 *Throughout the 1920s, congressmen:* Ibid., 120–124.

16 *But civilian engineers were every bit as reluctant:* VanDevelder, *Coyote Warrior*, 86–87.

16 *"Of all the variable things in creation":* Hart, *The Dark Missouri*, 120.

17 *The Army Corps' chief engineer:* A letter from the Secretary of War, referred to the Committee on Rivers and Harbors, February 5, 1934, as ordered by the Flood Control Act of January 21, 1927.

18 *In May 1935, a storm struck:* Hart, *The Dark Missouri*, 118–136.

18 *Coincident with this request:* Reisner, *Cadillac Desert*, 189–199, and Hart, *The Dark Missouri*, 122–128.

19 *Soon, word filtered up through channels:* Meyer, "Fort Berthold and the Garrison Dam," 240–243.

20 *At first, nothing about the March deluge:* Hart, *The Dark Missouri*, 122–128.

20 *Then came the downpour:* "Residential and Industrial Areas in Omaha Inundated," *New York Times*, April 13, 1943.

20 *President Roosevelt put out an urgent call:* Reisner, *Cadillac Desert*, 189–199, and Hart, *The Dark Missouri*, 122–136.

20 *Glenn Sloan's unfinished master plan:* Reisner, *Cadillac Desert*, 189–199, and Hart, *The Dark Missouri*, 122–136.

21 *President Roosevelt was an instant convert:* Ibid., and VanDevelder, *Coyote Warrior*, 98.

21 *As the floodwaters rose in the streets outside:* VanDevelder, *Coyote Warrior,* 99.

21 *Pick's proposal, a scant ten pages long:* Meyer, "Fort Berthold and the Garrison Dam," 239.

22 *As soon as he got wind of Wheeler's legerdemain:* VanDevelder, *Coyote Warrior,* 98–100.

22 *"an obduracy that is beyond belief":* U.S. Senate Committee on Indian Affairs, *The Missouri River Basin.* Over the next few years, Ickes unleashed a relentless verbal assault on the corps, describing the agency as a "willful . . . self-serving clique in contempt of the public welfare. . . . No more lawless or irresponsible group than the Army Corps of Engineers has ever attempted to operate in the United States either outside of, or within, the law. . . . It is truly beyond imagination." Reisner, *Cadillac Desert,* 181.

23 *States' rights groups immediately mounted:* Meyer, *Village Indians of the Upper Missouri,* 212.

23 *Attempts to break the government's monopoly:* For a full discussion of this fascinating subplot, see Morgan, *Dams and Other Disasters.* Early in his engineering career Morgan was a leading hydrologist for the corps. In time, he was appointed by President Franklin Roosevelt as the government's chief administrator for the TVA.

23 *Upstream politicians favored the Sloan Plan:* Meyer, *Village Indians of the Upper Missouri,* 242–245.

24 *If members of Congress would look closer:* VanDevelder, *Coyote Warrior,* 98–102, and Hart, *The Dark Missouri,* 226–234.

25 *Of the eight hundred square miles:* Hart, *The Dark Missouri,* 226–234.

26 *each side recognized its own obstinacy:* Reisner, *Cadillac Desert,* 192–194, and VanDevelder, *Coyote Warrior,* 104.

26 *No attempt was made in Omaha to consolidate:* Reisner, *Cadillac Desert,* 192–194, and VanDevelder, *Coyote Warrior,* 104.

27 *The president of the National Farmers' Union:* Meyer, "Fort Berthold and the Garrison Dam," 240.

CHAPTER 2. SAVAGES AND SCOUNDRELS

28 *"A lot of guys in Dad's generation":* Meyer, *Village Indians of the Upper Missouri,* 202–205; Al Cross, interview by the author, December 2001.

28 *For many, leaving home to fight in World War II:* Ibid.

29 *The census of 1940 found:* Meyer, *Village Indians of the Upper Missouri,* 234. Also, see *Fort Berthold Agency Report of 1943,* Bureau of Indian Affairs, Regional Office, Aberdeen, South Dakota, 1944.

29 *"That was the toughest year of our childhoods":* Martin Cross Jr., interviews by the author, November and December 2001.

30 *Despite the wartime hardships, the enlistment widows:* Meyer, *Village Indians of the Upper Missouri,* 186–207.

30 *Martin received her letter just days:* Martin Cross Jr., and Al and Phyllis Cross, interview by the author, June 2002.

30 *He was no sooner home than elders started:* Ibid.

30 *The* Sanish Sentinel *newspaper:* Meyer, "Fort Berthold and Garrison Dam," 240.

31 *"they came walking in over the hills":* Martin Cross Jr., interview by the author, November 2001. Also, see VanDevelder, *Coyote Warrior,* 110–114 for individual stories.

31 *Those tragedies had been well documented:* For a detailed discussion of the Meriam Report, see Tyler, *A History of Indian Policy,* 162–163, and Meyer, *Village Indians of the Upper Missouri,* 150–155.

31 *the Dawes Act of 1887:* Also known as the General Allotment Act, ch. 119, 24 Stat. 388 (1887).

31 *"What shall be done about the Indian":* Commissioner of Indian Affairs, Annual Report to Congress, 1872, Serial Set v. 1560, 389.

32 *sovereign "domestic dependent nations":* This legal distinction crafted by Chief Justice John Marshall in *Cherokee Nation v. Georgia,* 31 U.S. 1 (1831) became a keystone concept for federal Indian law.

32 *Early in 1936, the Three Affiliated Tribes:* Three Affiliated Tribes Corporate Charter, ratified April 24, 1937, and the Constitution and bylaws, approved June 29, 1936.

33 *leaders distinguished both sides of Martin's family:* Bowers, *Hidatsa Social and Ceremonial Organization.* Family tree on file with author.

33 *The resulting Treaty of Fort Laramie:* 11 Stat. 749.

34 *the new governor of North Dakota, Fred Aandahl:* Governor Fred Aandahl, letter to Martin Cross, April 2, 1946.

34 *he sent a telegram to William Brophy:* Martin T. Cross to William A. Brophy, January 1945, on file with the Bureau of Indian Affairs.

35 *He quickly dictated a letter to Senator O'Mahoney:* William A. Brophy to Joseph O'Mahoney, April 20, 1945, on file with the Bureau of Indian Affairs.

35 *Brophy suspected that the ultimate aim:* Meyer, "Fort Berthold and Garrison Dam," 245.

36   *"Not one of those guys had a stitch of clothes":* Martin Cross Jr., interview by the author, November 2001.

36   *The Empire Builder passenger train:* This train from Portland, Oregon, and Seattle, Washington, to Chicago was pulled over the Rocky Mountains by the largest steam locomotives in the world at the time. The Empire Builder has been running continuously for almost eighty years.

36   *Cohen, a thirty-seven-year-old Jewish lawyer:* VanDevelder, *Coyote Warrior*, 113–122.

37   *Off the record, Congress viewed the hearing:* Meyer, *Village Indians of the Upper Missouri*, 244.

37   *"Mr. Chairman, Senators," began Martin Cross:* U.S. Senate Select Committee on Indian Affairs. *Protesting the Construction of Garrison Dam: Hearing on S.J. Res. 79 to Establish a Joint Committee to Study Claims of Indian Tribes and to Investigate the Administration of Indian Affairs*, October 9, 1945. This scene has been reconstructed from this and subsequent hearings before the Senate Select Committee on Indian Affairs that had a direct bearing on the federal government's responsibility for protecting Indian trust lands.

41   *"Like the miner's canary," he reminded Congress:* Cohen, "The Erosion of Indian Rights." I have distilled the major points in the depiction of this hearing from the official record and from a variety of other sources, including hearings and reports, and law review articles, in which Cohen squarely challenged the will of Congress by citing its overriding "fiduciary responsibilities" to the tribes as trustee of native resources, including their land.

43   *A century before, John Locke had attempted:* Locke, *An Essay Concerning Human Understanding*, and Locke, *Second Treatise of Government*. Of Jefferson's well-known plagiarism of Locke in the Declaration of Independence, Gore Vidal writes: "Later that most famous summer of 1776, Jefferson wrote the Declaration of Independence, making literature of [George] Mason's somewhat desultory laundry list, consisting of John Locke's garments." Vidal, *Inventing a Nation*, 28.

44   *The end of oppression would not come until:* Ellis, *His Excellency*, 272.

44   *Benjamin Franklin, would forcefully defend:* Weatherford, *Native Roots*.

45   *"I believe all things will come out right":* George Washington to Armand Duplantier, October 7, 1785, *The Papers of George Washington, Confederation Series*, quoted in Ellis, *His Excellency*, 150.

45   *"the people shall have become so corrupted":* Vidal, *Inventing a Nation*, 30.

45   *"venality, corruption, and prostitution of office":* Ibid., 48.

45 *"few legislative bodies in American history"*: Williams, *American Indian in Western Legal Thought*, 288.

46 *"Knavery seems to be so much the striking feature"*: Ibid., 50.

47 *"I must own to you that the daring traits"*: Cappon, *Adams–Jefferson Letters*, 250–252.

48 *"All appeared to be determined to govern"*: Hastings, *The Emigrants' Guide*, 6.

48 *When Madison arrived in the City of Brotherly Love:* Ketcham, *James Madison*, 196–207, 228–229. Ketcham recreates the backroom alliance between Madison, Franklin, and James Wilson. Also, see Vidal, *Inventing a Nation*, 8–12.

48 *The opportunity to preempt the southerners:* See Ketcham, *James Madison*, for a complete discussion of the intrigues at the Constitutional Convention, in which the passage of the supremacy clause was a crucial turning point in bifurcating sovereignty between the states and the federal government. Madison, who was deeply suspicious of the states (but would later forsake his earlier wisdom in support of Jefferson, and live to regret it), had already written a clause that would empower Congress to negate state laws, a power, in Madison's view, that was vital to the survival of a federal government. James Wilson persuaded Madison to drop it in favor of the less contentious wording of the supremacy clause.

50 *Between 1778 and 1871, the federal government:* Walsh, *The American Frontier Revisited;* Kappler, ed., *Indian Treaties;* and Prucha, *American Indian Treaties.*

50 *This was the natural outcome of Revolutionary-era debates:* Williams, *American Indian in Western Legal Thought*, 280.

51 *As early as 1705, the Monhegan Indians:* Costo and Henry, *Indian Treaties*, 6–10.

51 *"If it be meant to say that, although capable"*: Cohen, *Handbook of Federal Indian Law*, 34.

52 *"The [republic's] treaty with the Cherokees"*: Treaty of Hopewell with the Cherokee, 7 Stat. 18, November 28, 1785.

52 *Major Caleb Swan reported:* Hitchcock, *A Traveler in Indian Territory*, 7.

53 *To prevent that from happening:* Cohen, *Felix S. Cohen's Handbook of Federal Indian Law*, 62.

53 *Congress, invoking long-established guidelines:* Wallace, *Jefferson and the Indians*, 162–165. These legal conflicts between tribes and the states grew out of what Madison described as "obscure" and "contradictory" language in the

Articles of Confederation, which gave the states the right to engage in war of self-defense against Indians without the consent of Congress.

Hoping to finesse these problems to a more civic-minded future, Franklin proposed language at the Constitutional Convention that would give Congress the exclusive authority to form alliances, make war, and buy land from the tribes. The compromise language that was offered to console southern states was described by Madison as being "absolutely incomprehensible." Madison in turn suggested even firmer language, arguing that the ambiguities in the Articles had led several southern states to enter into unlawful treaties and wars. Despite these appeals, the final language in the Constitution was even more solicitous of southern prejudices, mentioning Indians only as an afterthought in the section giving Congress the power to regulate commerce. Jefferson's friend Benjamin Hawkins wrote him in Paris predicting that nothing but trouble could come of this constitutional stalemate over federal versus states' rights in the management of relations with Indians. History, as it so often did, bore him out.

53   *Marshall, that "principal inventor of the nation":* Vidal, *Inventing a Nation,* 141. While we might have fared better in our first century without the efforts of many of our original founders, it is safe to say that we would not have survived into our third century without the guiding hand of John Marshall in the first.

54   *"in its language, and in its provisions":* Cherokee Nation v. Georgia, 31 U.S. 1 (1831).

55   *Daniel Webster once described:* Flanders, *Lives and Times of the Chief Justices,* 2:410.

56   *Indian Non-Intercourse Act passed by Congress:* 25 USC 177, adopted July 22, 1790, followed by the Indian Trade and Intercourse Act of 1834, 4 Stats. 729, 730, 734, adopted June 30, 1834. Prucha, *American Indian Treaties,* points out that the 1796 version of the Indian Trade and Intercourse Act created a kind of discrete boundary between whites and Indians. Despite frontiersmen's dissatisfaction with the law that intended to frustrate their direct dealings with, or depredations upon, the Indians, Congress reenacted the statute in 1799 without amendment and with little debate, showing that it valued peace with its Indian allies more than it feared the outrage of its wayward and clamoring citizens. Enforcing the act in the nineteenth century would prove virtually impossible.

56   *"The angry passions of the frontier Indians and whites":* Secretary of War Henry Knox, letter to George Washington; Wallace, *Jefferson and the Indians,* 166.

56   *Congress approved the Northwest Ordinance:* Northwest Ordinance of 1787, 1 Stat. 50, adopted on August 7, 1789.

57   *Southern legislatures cavalierly ignored:* Abel, *The History of Events,* 260–276.

57   *"We the people, in order to form a more perfect union":* John Adams, letter to William Tudor, May 9, 1789, cited in McCullough, *John Adams,* 397.

57   *"The fate of this government":* Ibid.

57   *"philosophical gloss on the violently partisan":* Wallace, *Jefferson and the Indians,* 14.

58   *Later it was discovered that speculators:* Abel, *The History of Events,* 250–252.

58   *pompous pretentions to profound knowledge:* Malone, *Jefferson and the Rights of Man,* 459; also cited in McCullough, *John Adams,* 436.

59   *James Madison felt the president had made:* Abel, *The History of Events,* 255. Madison's first direct opinion on the subject of general removal was directed to William Wirt in connection with the 1824 Cherokee case, wherein he blamed the Georgians (and Jefferson) for what he called their "egregious miscalculation" of the compact of 1802. "The most difficult problem is that of reconciling their interests with their rights. It is so evident that they can never be tranquil or happy within the bounds of a state . . . that a removal to another home, if a good one can be found, may well be the wish of their best friends. But the removal ought to be made voluntary by adequate inducements, presents and prospective; and no means ought to be grudged which such a measure may require."

59   *"The Governor, legislators, and judges of Georgia":* Burke, "The Cherokee Cases."

60   *John Quincy Adams declared:* Cohen, *Felix S. Cohen's Handbook of Federal Indian Law,* 82 n.164.

61   *The Indians "have neither the intelligence":* Andrew Jackson, *Message from the President of the United States to the Two Houses of Congress,* 23rd Congress, 1st. sess., 1833, H. Doc. 1, vol. 1, Serial Set 254, 14–15.

61   *"There is not a friendly Chief of distinction":* Abel, *The History of Events,* 264, note e.

62   *"appeal to fear and avarice":* Ibid., 284.

62   *Behind the Treaty of Doak's Stand:* 7 Stat. 210, January 8, 1821; also, see Abel, *The History of Events,* 287.

62   *"The red people are of the opinion":* Abel, *The History of Events,* 372.

63   *In his first message to Congress:* Cohen, *Felix S. Cohen's Handbook of Federal Indian Law,* 81; Abel, *The History of Events,* 378.

63 *"What good man," he asked:* Andrew Jackson, Second Annual Message to Congress, December 6, 1830, *The American Presidency Project* (http://www .presidency.ucsb.edu/ws/index.php?pid=29472).

64 *were summarily ignored by Congress:* Abel, *The History of Events,* 395–405.

64 *"The union has been preserved thus far":* Quoted from *Chief Justice John Marshall: A Portrait,* Public Broadcasting Service documentary, 2007.

65 *report from the Hoover Commission:* Miller, "The Battle That Squanders Billions."

65 *Writing for the panel, Leslie A. Miller:* Ibid. Also, see Morgan, *Dams and Other Disasters.*

65 *"seems to have gone hog wild":* Ibid.

65 *"to make certain that boondoggles":* Ibid.

66 *The search for replacement lands:* U.S. Public Law 374, 79th Cong., 2nd sess., Statutes at Large 60, May 2, 1946, *Lieu Lands Act for Fort Berthold.* Also, see Meyer, "Fort Berthold and the Garrison Dam," 245.

66 *reduced the compensation package:* VanDevelder, *Coyote Warrior,* 132–138. Also, see U.S. House of Representatives, speech by Representative Lempke on the injustice of the Fort Berthold Takings Act, 81st Cong., 1st sess., *Congressional Record,* October 20, 1950 (Washington, D.C.: GPO, 1950).

66 *the official "taking act":* The Fort Berthold Taking Act, U.S. Public Law 437, Statutes at Large 63, pt. 1, October 29, 1949.

66 *What tribes learned that day:* Cross, "Sovereign Bargains, Indian Takings."

67 *"The future doesn't look good to us": Washington Post,* May 21, 1949.

68 *Father Reinhart and Reverend Case:* VanDevelder, *Coyote Warrior,* 159.

CHAPTER 3. WHITE MEN IN PARADISE

70 *the humanism of Thomas Aquinas:* Newland, *St. Thomas Aquinas,* 29–35. Also, Williams, *American Indian in Western Legal Thought,* 30, notes that St. Augustine argued (like Benjamin Franklin, centuries later) that the need for civil authority grew out of man's essentially sinful nature.

70 *On the final day of meetings at the Council:* Mayer, *The Crusades,* 8–10, and Jones and Ereira, *Crusades,* 214.

70 *the pope's immediate audience:* Ibid.

70 *caused by chronic drought-related crop failures:* Erbstosser, *The Crusades,* 43–44.

70 *In January 1099, an army:* Holt, *The Age of the Crusades,* 16–19.

71 *On the day he was elected pope:* Jones and Ereira, *Crusades*, 196; McCabe, *Crises in the History of the Papacy*, 174.

71 *had a talent for managing details:* Ibid.

71 *"His ideal was power; of love he knew nothing":* McCabe, *Crises in the History of the Papacy*, 201.

72 *"There is only one right way of life":* Ibid., 176–182.

72 *Innocent IV, also known as the Lawyer Pope:* Williams, *American Indian in Western Legal Thought*, 46–60.

73 *papal theorists reasserted the pope's duty:* Ibid., 80–81.

73 *"full, free, and integral power":* Ibid.

74 *In the Spanish universities of Salamanca:* Ibid., 97–102.

74 *Francisco de Vitoria, a reclusive theoretician:* Ibid.

74 *"On the Indians Lately Discovered":* Ibid., 97, and Cohen, *Felix S. Cohen's Handbook on Federal Indian Law*, 50–58.

75 *established the equality of rights of all people:* Williams, *American Indian in Western Legal Thought*, 96–107.

76 *the queen and her lawyers could do whatever:* Ibid., 193–194, 202–204, and Washburn, *The Indian in America*, 82–83.

76 *In 1609, Johnson's widely distributed speech:* Williams, *American Indian in Western Legal Thought*, 210–212.

76 *Popular clerics such as Robert Gray:* Ibid.

76 *Lord Coke bundled all of these arguments:* Ibid.

76 *its "will to empire by normatively divergent":* Williams, *American Indian in Western Legal Thought*, 212.

77 *the doctrine of discovery:* Williams, *American Indian in Western Legal Thought*, 231, 312.

77 *aristocratic members of colonial land syndicates:* Williams, *American Indian in Western Legal Thought*, 55 n.45. "The colonial precedent of purchasing land from the Indians became a cornerstone of federal Indian policy."

78 *In the Proclamation of 1763:* Williams, *American Indian in Western Legal Thought*, 228–231, 235.

78 *Washington viewed the king's claims:* Ellis, *His Excellency*, 55.

78 *"I can never look upon that Proclamation":* George Washington to William Crawford, September 17, 1767, *The Papers of George Washington, Colonial Series*, 8:26–30, cited in Ellis, *His Excellency*, 55.

79 *John Adams wrote five decades later:* Vidal, *Inventing a Nation*, 34.

80 *"elementary: how to survive":* De Voto, *The Course of Empire*, 335.

81 *"Alas for the inconsistency of human nature":* Abel, *The History of Events*, 266.

81   *By making the welfare of the western Indians:* Ellis, *His Excellency,* 212.

81   *"familiar and formidable adversaries fighting":* Ibid.

82   *"Indians being the prior occupants":* Henry Knox to George Washington, July 6, 1789, in Washington, *Papers of George Washington,* 3:123–129; Knox to Washington, July 17, 1789, in ibid., 134–141, and quoted in Ellis, *His Excellency,* 212.

82   *"All the parts of our country will find":* Vidal, *Inventing a Nation,* 123. For a thorough analysis and discussion of Washington's Farewell Address, see Ellis, *His Excellency,* 234–240.

83   *Washington "was going out as he came in":* Ellis, *His Excellency,* 237.

84   *no tribe could make a deal without the imprimatur:* Williams, *American Indian in Western Legal Thought,* 231.

85   *"available to legitimate, energize, and constrain":* Ibid., 316–317.

85   *Napoleon remembered the campaign in Santo Domingo:* De Voto, *The Course of Empire,* 388–389.

86   *San Ildefonso would "change the face of the world":* Ibid., 391.

86   *"There is on the globe one single spot":* Ibid., 392.

87   *"To emancipate nations from the commercial tyranny":* Ibid., 390.

87   *William Coleman, chastised him for playing:* Merk, *Manifest Destiny and Mission,* 11–12.

87   *"Ours is the right to the rivers":* Ibid.

88   *"I renounce Louisiana!":* Ibid., 390–391. Merk sets De Voto (and many other historians) right on the subject of the Louisiana Purchase. Generations of American historians have been content to crown Jefferson with laurels when, in fact, the internal workings of this exchange had much more to do with Napoleon's enmity for the English.

89   *"The historic fact is that practically all of the real estate":* Cohen, *Felix S. Cohen's Handbook of Federal Indian Law,* 55 n.54.

89   *the 909,130 square miles of Louisiana:* De Voto, *The Course of Empire,* 397.

90   *"the implicit significance of the American":* Ibid., 400.

92   *he composed an "Indian Amendment" that he hoped:* Abel, *The History of Events,* 241–246.

92   *"The right of occupancy in the soil":* Ibid.

92   *"In at least one respect Jefferson was":* Ibid., 242.

92   *Removal, as the term is technically used:* Ibid., 244.

92   *Jefferson peers down at us:* Wallace, *Jefferson and the Indians,* vii.

93   *"placed him on the side of Indian-hating, riotous":* Ibid., 16.

93   *"planner of cultural genocide":* Ibid., 18.

94   *The monarchical empire model was:* Ibid., 17–19.

94   *a homogeneous mass of equals in which:* Ibid., 18.

94   *Smith warned Jefferson that guaranteeing:* Abel, *The History of Events,* 247–249.

95   *"the independent nations and tribes":* Wallace, *Jefferson and the Indians,* 165–171.

95   *If the federal government wasn't up to the task:* American State Papers, ed. Bergh, 53–54.

95   *Louisiana Territorial Act simply empowered:* Abel, *The History of Events,* 249.

97   *St. Louis was home to fifteen physicians:* Missouri Historical Society, Population of St. Louis, 1820, 166.

99   *It was on those grasslands, while British:* Gibson, "Great Plains as Colonization Zone," 19–21.

99   *From the northwest, Blackfeet agrarians:* Ibid.

100   *This beast, first acquired by the Comanche:* Wood and Thiessen, *Early Fur Trade on the Northern Plains,* and Raymond Wood, interview by the author, March 2002.

100   *William Crawford, did his best to restrain:* Abel, *The History of Events,* 255–262.

101   *The Indians, who had become well familiar:* Ibid., 288–290.

101   *The subsequent relocation of the tribes:* Gibson, "Great Plains as Colonization Zone," 35.

102   *Jackson was secretly encouraging:* Abel, *The History of Events,* 276–285, 370.

103   *"hogs missed and no bones found":* Ibid., 377.

103   *"equally to be the inheritance":* Ibid., 325.

105   *"We have a perfect and original right to remain":* Getches, Wilkinson, and Williams, *Cases and Materials,* 96.

106   *southern courts and legislators refused:* Deloria, ed., *Of Utmost Good Faith.* Deloria writes an extensive commentary, drawn from the opinions of southern courts, on the legal weight of "Indian sovereignty"—opinions that were diametrically opposed to those of the U.S. Supreme Court and northern courts.

106   *"Missionaries are sent among them to enlighten":* Abel, *The History of Events,* 366.

107   *Just as Jefferson had before him:* Ibid., 370.

107   *"Treaties were expedients which ignorant":* Getches, Wilkinson, and Williams, *Cases and Materials,* 97.

108   *"In appropriating to ourselves their hunting grounds":* Ibid.
108   *Representative Henry R. Storrs of New York:* Abel, *The History of Events,*
      380.
108   *The Indians could either move west:* Ibid., 377–379.
108   *attached an amendment requesting protection:* Ibid.
109   *tribes "now residing within the limits of the states":* Ibid., 379–381.
111   *Marshall invented a solution that reflected:* Ibid., 103.
111   *"ferocious passions, . . . independent spirit":* Ibid., 102.
111   *"It was not until the adoption of our present government":* White, *The*
      Marshall Court, 712–713; Getches, Wilkinson, and Williams, *Cases and Ma-*
      terials, 103.
112   *"We are thus convinced that Mr. Wirt":* Knoxville Register, July 21, 1830;
      Abel, *The History of Events,* 386 n.3.

CHAPTER 4. PIONEERS OF THE WORLD

113   *Since Article IV prohibited the tribe:* Abel, *The History of Events,* 381–382,
      and from the South Carolina decision, see Getches, Wilkinson, and Williams,
      Cases and Materials, 105.
113   *"Humanity must bewail the course":* Getches, Wilkinson, and Williams,
      Cases and Materials, 103.
115   *"[President] Washington said in one of his messages":* Tocqueville, *De-*
      mocracy in America, 351–355.
116   *"If courts were permitted to indulge their sympathies":* Cherokee Nation v.
      Georgia, 31 U.S. 1 (1831). For full discussion, see Getches, Wilkinson, and
      Williams, *Cases and Materials,* 104–112. Also, for a remarkable discussion
      of the theological implications of this case in the context of expansionism, see
      Weinberg, *Manifest Destiny,* 72–99.
116   *justices Story and Thompson claimed it did:* Getches, Wilkinson, and Wil-
      liams, *Cases and Materials,* 109–110.
117   *"without a warrant from any magistrate":* Abel, *The History of Events,*
      397 n.4.
118   *"Your excellency is pleased to intimate":* Ibid., 399 note 3a. Rarely are we
      given such a personal and focused glimpse into the thinking of a defendant in
      a case with such enormous stakes. Since Worcester and Butler's letters fell
      outside the beam of her inquiry, Abel chose to fold this material into very
      extensive and inclusive notes.
119   *Ruefully, Lumpkin reported back:* Ibid., 401 note 3c.
119   *Worcester and Butler's response:* Ibid., 402 note 3c.

120   *Accordingly, Worcester and Butler asked:* Ibid., 400–401.

122   *"The acts of Georgia are repugnant to the Constitution":* Worcester v. *Georgia,* 31 U.S. 515 (1832), and Getches, Wilkinson, and Williams, *Cases and Materials,* 120.

123   *Meanwhile, through the magic of legal logrolling:* Abel, *The History of Events,* 401, n. c, and Cohen, *Felix S. Cohen's Handbook of Federal Indian Law,* 260.

124   *"Doubtless, they [the tribes] would have gone":* Abel, *The History of Events,* 412.

125   *As one eyewitness later reported:* Hitchcock, *A Traveler in Indian Territory,* 7–12.

126   *Hitchcock soon uncovered widespread profiteering:* Gibson, "Great Plains as Colonization Zone," 33–34.

126   *"every other conceivable subterfuge":* Hitchcock, *A Traveler in Indian Territory,* 7–12.

126   *the House should not have the report:* Ibid., 13.

128   *secular "doctrine" known as "national completeness":* Weinberg, *Manifest Destiny,* 72–99.

128   *Like the beaver before it, the buffalo was:* William Clark, letter to Secretary of War James Barbour, March 1, 1825, *American State Papers: Indian Affairs,* 2:653–654. In this famous letter, Clark also told Barbour, "The relative condition of the United States on one side and the Indian tribes on the other" had changed drastically in recent years. Before the War of 1812, the "tribes nearest our settlements were a formidable and terrible enemy; since then, their power has been broken, their war-like spirit subdued, and themselves sunk into objects of pity and commiseration."

129   *General William Henry Ashley and his partner:* For a discussion of the Ashley expedition and Clark's role in the development of the fur trade, see Killoren, *"Come, Blackrobe,"* 36–45.

132   *"But the horse-racing, fine riding":* From the journals of Joseph Meek, published in Victor, *River of the West,* 110–111; also cited in Gowans, *Rocky Mountain Rendezvous,* 67.

132   *It was at Pierre's Hole, in July 1832:* Gowans, *Rocky Mountain Rendezvous,* 64–79. The story of this rendezvous is extraordinary. As the camp was breaking up, word reached the mountain men that a band of Blackfeet was waiting to ambush them as they left for their fall trapping. The battle that ensued lasted two days, and many on both sides were killed. Gowans recreates this battle from the journals of the men who were there, written many years

later in some cases, but nevertheless unique windows into a world that was known by very few white men.

134 *One of them, William H. Gray:* Gray, "Unpublished Journal of William H. Gray," 55–63.

134 *"Dr. Whitman was called upon to perform":* Parker, *Journal of an Exploring Tour,* 80–81.

135 *"We are really a moving village":* Drury, ed., *First White Women,* 152, and Gowans, *Rocky Mountain Rendezvous,* 131.

136 *"Meek, We are done with this life":* Gowans, *Rocky Mountain Rendezvous,* 198.

136 *"Long residence and familiar acquaintance":* Frémont, *Report of an Exploring Expedition,* 41.

137 *"The best years of his life have exposed him":* J. W. Abert, *Journal of Lieutenant J. W. Abert, From Bent's Fort to St. Louis, 1845,* 8.

138 *On September 11, 1846, an editorial:* Hafen, *Broken Hand,* 231 n.4. This appointment was largely due to the enormous influence of John C. Frémont's politically powerful father-in-law, Senator Thomas Hart Benton; ibid., 230.

139 *John Quincy Adams knew Polk:* Sides, *Blood and Thunder,* 55. This portrait of Polk, though brief, is one of the best I've read, rich with detail, irony, and historical context.

139 *But Polk, unimpressed by his own:* Ibid.

140 *When Polk was sworn into office:* Merk, *Manifest Destiny and Mission,* 61.

140 *Whereas politicians in the Monroe and Jackson:* Ibid., 14–17.

140 *Thanks to a technical oversight in the Adams-Onís Treaty:* Ibid., 15–19.

141 *The price of cotton sank to an all-time low:* Ibid., 52–53.

141 *"Young America, awakened to a sense": United States Journal,* May 3, 1845, and Merk, *Manifest Destiny and Mission,* 54. The journal was a champion of many causes, as its editor, the flamboyant Theophilus Fisk, was a left-wing Jacksonian Democrat, anti-clerical, a Calhounist, and a defender of slavery, who also happened to be an ultra-expansionist. He wasn't the only person or publication extolling the vigor of youth. At about the same time the *Boston Times* wrote: "The spirit of Young America . . . will not be satisfied with what has been attained, but plumes its young wings for a higher and more glorious flight. The hopes of America, the hopes of Humanity, must rest on this spirit. . . . The steam is up." *Boston Times,* December 11, 1844.

141 *His secretary of state, James Buchanan:* Weinberg, *Manifest Destiny,* 142.

142 *"one of the most charming companions":* Merk, *Manifest Destiny and Mission,* 27.

142 *"To state the truth at once":* John L. O'Sullivan, "The True Title," *New York Daily News,* December 27, 1845. Also, see Merk, *Manifest Destiny and Mission,* 31–32.

142 *"A free, confederated, self-governed republic":* Congressional Globe, 30th Cong., 1st sess., App. 86–7 (January 12, 1848), and Merk, *Manifest Destiny and Mission,* 29.

143 *"Our national birth was the beginning":* O'Sullivan, "Great Nation of Futurity," and Weinberg, *Manifest Destiny,* 107.

143 *The principal boosters of O'Sullivan's vision:* Merk, *Manifest Destiny and Mission,* 40.

144 *"The patriotic impulses of the United States":* James Bennett, "More, More, More!" editorial, *New York Herald,* September 25, 1845.

144 *"Away, away with all these cobweb tissues":* O'Sullivan, "The True Title."

144 *O'Sullivan's manifesto on westward expansion:* Weinberg, *Manifest Destiny,* 145.

145 *"a higher and better title under the law":* Ibid., 143.

145 *"has invaded our territory and shed American blood":* Merk, *Manifest Destiny and Mission,* 88.

145 *"Does history furnish an example":* Ibid., 93, and *Congressional Globe,* 30th Cong., 1st sess., 211.

146 *"Was any government through its Chief":* Ibid.

146 *The president's former Tennessee neighbor: Congressional Globe,* 29th Cong., 2nd sess., December 16, 1846, 56.

146 *Senator John Dix of New York reported:* John Dix to Martin Van Buren, May 16, 1846, Martin Van Buren Papers, Library of Congress; Merk, *Manifest Destiny and Mission,* 92.

146 *"The most remarkable circumstance of these transactions":* John Quincy Adams to Albert Gallatin, December 26, 1847; Merk, *Manifest Destiny and Mission,* 96.

146 *"easier to plunge a dagger into his own heart":* Merk, *Manifest Destiny and Mission,* 92; *Congressional Globe,* 29th Cong., 1st sess., 796.

146 *"a flagrant . . . desolating . . . usurpation":* Merk, *Manifest Destiny and Mission,* 93.

147 *two-thirds of the country's newspapers: National Intelligencer,* October 20, 1846; see Merk, *Manifest Destiny and Mission,* 89–106, for a full discussion of opposition in Congress to the war with Mexico.

147 *method for towing California into an American port:* Hartford Times, July 24, 1845.

147 *"The great and fertile valley of the Mississippi":* Annual Report of the Commissioner of the General Land Office, November 26, 1851, Serial Set 613.

147 *In 1906, the Texas historian George P. Garrison:* Garrison, "Westward Extension," 207.

148 *Wrapped in a veil of righteous nationalism:* Weinberg, *Manifest Destiny,* 73, and Powers, "Ethics of Expansion," 292.

149 *"The Doctrine of Discovery, the primordial mythic icon":* Williams, *American Indian in Western Legal Thought,* 317.

149 *"my eye was caught by something shining":* There are numerous authoritative accounts of James Marshall's discovery of gold at the sawmill he and his compatriots had built for Sutter on the American River; Limerick, *Legacy of Conquest,* 105.

150 *Newspaper editors in San Francisco could set:* Merk, *Manifest Destiny and Mission,* 50–51.

151 *"Imagine thousands of all countries":* Terrell, *Black Robe,* 241.

152 *"is a free and unmolested passage through":* Thomas Fitzpatrick to Superintendent Thomas H. Harvey, October 6, 1848.

152 *"It is only by some measure of this kind":* David D. Mitchell to Commissioner Orlando Brown, October 13, 1849, Commissioner of Indian Affairs, Annual Report to Congress, 1849.

153 *"nature and extent of [the tribes'] title":* William Medill to Thomas Ewing, June 15, 1849, Commissioner of Indian Affairs, Letters Sent, 1850.

153 *"Through these districts all the great leading":* David D. Mitchell to Luke Lea, September 14, 1850, and Thomas Fitzpatrick to David D. Mitchell, September 24, 1850, Commissioner of Indian Affairs, Letters Sent, 1850.

154 *Their circular, an invitation unique:* Killoren, *"Come, Blackrobe,"* 131–134.

155 *"Understanding that you will shortly start":* Terrell, *Black Robe,* 249.

155 *De Smet wrote that cholera was "raging all around":* De Smet Letter Book, Jesuit Missouri Province Archives, 1849.

156 *Thaddeus McCollum, a westward traveler:* Ibid.; Mattes, *Great Platte River,* 84; and Killoren, *"Come, Blackrobe,"* 123.

157 *Mitchell had witnessed firsthand the scourge:* Meyer, *Village Indians of the Upper Missouri,* 94–97. Fearing that a new outbreak of the pox would devastate the western tribes, William Clark coerced some funds out of Congress and sent a doctor up the Missouri to inoculate as many as he could talk into taking a cure. Unfortunately, this humanitarian act was quickly undone by

the unwillingness of Congress to appropriate funds necessary to accomplish the task. Consequently, Clark's agent ran out of inoculations well before he reached the tribes of the middle and upper Missouri. Also, for a horrific depiction of this plague as it moved through the villages, see Francis A. Chardon, *Chardon's Journals at Fort Clark, 1834–1837*, ed. Annie Heloise Abel (Pierre, S.D.: Department of History, State of South Dakota, 1932), xiv–xlvi.

CHAPTER 5. THE GREAT SMOKE

158   *the Comanche and the Apache would not be attending:* On April 22, 1851, Fitzpatrick left St. Louis and headed for the Platte River via the southern route, the Santa Fe Trail, hoping to find the Comanche and Apache tribes, but he arrived at Bent's Fort without seeing either. By June 1, in the vicinity of Fort Mann (in ruins), the future site of Fort Atkinson, he found scattered about the country small bands of Indians and sent out runners with the circular inviting them to Fort Laramie. The Cheyenne and Arapaho were keen to attend, but the Comanche, Kiowa, and Apache claimed the risks of such a journey were too great. They would be happy to meet with Fitzpatrick in their own camps at a later date, which they did, in the summer of 1852.

159   *His years as a bourgeois at Fort Union:* Culbertson arrived on the Upper Missouri in 1833 with D. D. Mitchell, who was sent by the American Fur Company to build Fort Union at the confluence of the Yellowstone and the Missouri. For an excellent narrative of Culbertson years at Fort Laramie, see Wischmann, *Frontier Diplomats*, 188–196.

159   *Fitzpatrick's own views of what might be gained:* Thomas Fitzpatrick to Thomas H. Harvey, December 18, 1847, Commissioner Indian Affairs, Letters Received.

160   *"I am not one of those who expect and look":* Thomas Fitzpatrick to Thomas H. Harvey, October 1847, Commissioner of Indian Affairs, Letters Received, 1847, cited in Hafen, *Broken Hand*, 265.

161   *Several days before departing:* Luke Lea to David D. Mitchell, May 26, 1851, Office of Indian Affairs, Letters Sent, vol. 42. Killoren, *"Come, Blackrobe,"* 134, quotes this letter at length in making a case for the idea that Congress had already seized upon Indian treaties as the stepping-stones to the Pacific. Writes Killoren: "Embodied in the treaty" should be the understanding that annual distribution of the cooperating tribes would be contingent "upon their good conduct," an evaluation to be made by the government. Thus, the government could use the treaty to take control of the Great Plains.

162 *It was a vision, wrote Pierre De Smet:* Smet, *Life, Letters, and Travels,* 1473–1474; Killoren, *"Come, Blackrobe,"* 138–141.

162 *"He [Fitzpatrick] is a real mountain man":* Dispatch from B. Gratz Brown, secretary to A. B. Chambers (editor of the *Missouri Republican*), who was enlisted by D. D. Mitchell to act as the peace council's official secretary. As there was such interest in this "great smoke" in St. Louis, Brown, in turn, was entrusted with writing dispatches on the proceedings to the newspaper. These are henceforth referred to as Brown dispatches. This dispatch was written on September 1, 1851, and appeared in the *Missouri Republican* on September 26, 1851. Judging from the three dozen plus dispatches sent back to St. Louis from Horse Creek, it appears that Brown and Chambers shared the tasks of writing these reports for the newspaper and performing official duties for Mitchell. In transcribing the letters and dispatches and publishing them as a collection in 1956, the Missouri Historical Society chose to credit the entire collection to Brown and Chambers jointly.

163 *"The Cheyenne, who were formerly looked upon as the best":* Ibid.

165 *"Soon, a long line of Indians came moving":* Lowe, *Five Years a Dragoon,* 79–80.

167 *"The only object today is to ask you":* Brown dispatch, September 1, 1851. On matters of intertribal politics, Mitchell was almost completely dependent on the more knowledgeable Fitzpatrick for guidance. Fortunately the two men, though quite different in both appearance and temperament, had great regard for each other. Each brought indispensable skills and contacts to this challenge; Fitzpatrick was highly regarded among the leaders of the western tribes as a man of great integrity, while Mitchell had the skills to coerce necessary concessions out of Washington.

167 *"I do not want your lands, your robes":* Ibid.

168 *"In every direction over the plain":* Ibid.

168 *To circumvent the long-standing Jesuit prohibition:* Killoren, *"Come, Blackrobe,"* 144.

170 *De Smet held a place of esteem among the Dakota tribes:* Robinson, *History of the Dakota,* 206–207.

170 *De Smet and Hoecken embarked on their new adventure:* There are many accounts of this tragic voyage. Two of the best are Killoren, *"Come, Blackrobe,"* 136–138, and Wischmann, *Frontier Diplomats,* 190–195.

171 *"When our men go off hunting":* VanDevelder, *Coyote Warrior,* 60. This, in fact, was the chronic complaint of the Mandan-Hidatsa, and while the white men had promised to step in and stop these atrocities, little ever came of it. Consequently, the leaders of the Village Indian tribes were naturally suspicious

of new promises of peace with their traditional adversaries. Also, see Meyer, *Village Indians of the Upper Missouri*, 105–106.

171 *"The wicked and the strong always find plenty":* Terrell, *Black Robe*, 281.

173 *"I was for seven days among innumerable herds":* Ibid., 119.

173 *"Yesterday twenty-five Indians died":* Brown dispatch, October 14, 1851; Schlesier, ed., *Plains Indians.* None of the deadly European diseases, such as bubonic plague, smallpox, measles, influenza, diphtheria, scarlet fever, typhus, malaria, and cholera, existed on the North American continent prior to the Age of Discovery. Smallpox, by far the greatest slayer of Indian people, made its debut on American shores in 1519, having crossed the Atlantic on a Spanish galleon. It is believed to have first been transmitted by a foot soldier traveling with Narváez's expedition to Veracruz or with Cortez's attack on the Aztec empire. Between 1519 and 1523, smallpox spread north and south through the most populated regions of the Americas. According to Dobyns, *Their Number Become Thinned*, the first epidemic swept out of Mexico and into the Great Plains of the American West, and south into Mesoamerica and South America.

European explorers who first ventured onto what is now called the Great Plains reported a vast, uninhabited, and bountiful hunting ground. That is undoubtedly what they saw. These explorers likely came along just a few years after the smallpox first swept like a killing fire through the tribes of the southern plains. By the time LaSalle and his surveyors laid claim to the territory of Louisiana midway through the seventeenth century, much of the Great Plains had been cleared of inhabitants by the scourges that ran before them.

In addition to smallpox, it appears that the southern tribes had already met the measles virus by that time. For the next three hundred years, measles and smallpox would be a death sentence for any native people who encountered them. Epidemiologists have listed no fewer than ninety-three epidemics for the period 1520 through 1918. "Whether ten million or one hundred million died, the pall of sorrow that engulfed the hemisphere was immeasurable," says historian Elizabeth Fenn (Charles C. Mann, *1491: New Revelations of the Americas Before Columbus*, 6). "Language, prayers, hopes, habits and dreams—entire ways of life—hissed away like steam. The Americas were filled with a stunningly diverse assortment of people who had knocked about the continents [of the hemisphere] for millennia."

No single force or event played a greater role in the depopulation of native peoples from the North American continent than disease. As Dobyns suggests, by the time European migrants arrived on the eastern seaboard, as much as

90 percent of the native population in the Americas had already perished. William Bradford, the first governor of Plymouth Colony, arrived with his small contingent on the *Mayflower* on November 9, 1620. The widespread death they found in Indian villages they took to be by the hand of God, making the new lands ready for occupation by the God-fearing outcasts from Europe. They found villages in the coastal forests where the Indians had "died on heapes, as they lay in their houses, and the bones and skulls upon the several places of their habitations made such a spectacle that the environs seem to be a new found Golgotha. . . . The good hand of god favored our beginnings, sweeping away great multitudes of the natives . . . that he might make room for us."

A century of data-gathering and on-site research has led anthropologists to conclude that the native population of North America above the Rio Grande River may have reached eighteen million at the time Cortez made landfall in Veracruz, Mexico. This translates roughly into eight persons per ten square miles on the continent. Four centuries later, these conclusions are poignantly ironic to Native Americans, who regard the Euro-American version of westward migration and conquest as mythic nonsense. For more than a century, American historians have taken as *de rigueur* Frederick Jackson Turner's declaration in 1894 that the frontier was closed. Turner, a creative and bold academic, delivered his landmark work at the Chicago Exposition. His thesis borrowed heavily from the census figures of 1890, which showed that population density in the West was two persons per square mile. That, said Turner, was the evidence proving that the frontier had been closed. Based on Turner's own data, Native Americans can argue that the frontier in North America "closed" sometime around the birth of Christ. What erupted on the North American continent with the arrival of Euro-Americans was not a conquest of frontier but a protracted and bloody battle over who would live on reservations and who would live in the suburbs.

176 *The arbor was a simple affair:* DeMallie, "Touching the Pen," 41.

176 *Since treaties were assembled from the symbols:* Ibid., 38–41.

177 *"The heavens and earth are my heart":* American State Papers: Indian Affairs, 7:565, and Miller, *From the Heart*, 186.

177 *"Its [the council's] results, we have reason to believe":* Brown dispatch, October 23, 1851.

177 *"very delicate and extremely good":* Terrell, *Black Robe*, 90–91, and Brown dispatch, October 5, 1851.

177 *"the sound of the drums and unmeaning chants":* Chambers, dispatch from Horse Creek printed in the *Missouri Republican* on October 24, 1851.

178   *"When the cannon had given forth its thunder"*: Ibid., and Hill, "The Great Indian Treaty Council," 90–95. Hill provides a richly detailed description of the scene at Fort Laramie when Mitchell arrived, noting, "Nothing like the great council had ever been attempted, and it is questionable whether a gathering of its kind has ever since been held." The actual number of horses present was an estimate, though likely a very accurate one. When traveling, western tribes made a great show of their horses—their most prized form of personal wealth. A nomadic band of a thousand Cheyenne often had six to seven thousand horses. A great herd of fifty thousand would have made quick work of the grassland surrounding the fort.

179   *"as fine a field for a painter or daguerreotypist"*: Chambers, dispatch from September 8, 1851, printed in the *Missouri Republican* on October 24, 1851.

179   *"For quietness, decorum and general good behavior"*: Ibid.

180   *"The Great Spirit sees it all and knows"*: Brown dispatch, September 8, 1851.

180   *"The interruption was sudden"*: Ibid.

181   *"Your Great Father at Washington has sent me"*: Ibid.

182   *There were many bands among them:* Ibid.

183   *"make peace, and visit each other"*: Ibid.

183   *"We have heard you were coming"*: Ibid.

184   *"The scalps [of his brothers] were then presented"*: Brown dispatch, October 29, 1851.

186   *"The Crow were all mounted and their horses"*: Brown dispatch, September 10, 1851.

187   *"We want a chief for each of our bands"*: Ibid. Each of these speeches was recorded by hand by either Brown or Chambers as it was being translated by the dozen translators attending the council.

187   *"You tell us to behave ourselves"*: Ibid.

188   *Then the Yankton named Painted Bear:* Ibid.

189   *"I thank the Great Spirit for putting us"*: Ibid.

190   *"No epoch in Indian annals"*: Smet, *Western Missions and Missionaries*, 109.

190   *"who has been many years among them"*: Brown dispatch, September 11, 1851.

190   *"At a late hour the cannon was fired"*: Ibid.

190   *"after all this had been gone through, the Crow"*: Ibid.

191   *"Big Robber, the Crow chief"*: Ibid. The Crow's spokesman, Big Robber, told the commissioners that he was a stand-in for the tribe's next chief, who was then only a boy. He was referring to Plenty Coups, who was eight at the

time of the Horse Creek treaty. As a boy, Plenty Coups had already had a vision that was profoundly disturbing to the tribal elders. He dreamed that the country would soon be filled with white men who brought "spotted buffalo" (cattle) with them, and built cities. Plenty Coups, indeed, grew up to become a great chief and was a contemporary of both Crazy Horse and Black Elk. In 1931, Plenty Coups was an old man when he decided to relate his life story to Frank Linderman—about the same time Black Elk was telling his life story to John G. Neihardt. One morning when sitting in the shade of a tree near the old chief's home, Linderman noted that an airplane flew by in the distance. The old chief did not even bother to look up. It was as though he had already seen too much change in his life, and the "flying machine" was simply over the top.

191   *"Father," he began, "we are a small nation":* Ibid.

192   *"If I am to be chief, I must be":* Brown dispatch, September 15, 1851.

194   *Boundaries agreed upon at Horse Creek would not:* Prucha, *American Indian Treaties,* 238–239.

194   *"During the twenty-three days of the assembly":* Smet, *Western Missions and Missionaries,* 109.

196   *"Every effort was made, and successfully":* Brown dispatch, September 17, 1851.

198   *Cat Nose, for one, told the Arapaho:* Brown dispatch, September 15, 1851.

198   *"Glad, or satisfied, but always quiet":* Wischmann, *Frontier Diplomats,* 208. B. Gratz Brown later wrote that when the tribes disappeared over the horizon, a strange stillness and silence descended on the prairie. When darkness fell that evening he could hear the sound of the drums beating from their distant camps.

CHAPTER 6. MONSTERS OF GOD

201   *Cloistered in semi-seclusion at the abbey:* Killoren, *"Come, Blackrobe,"* 177–178. This historic map is in the Americana Collection at the Library of Congress, and it depicts an age that seems scarcely imaginable in our own. Very few white men, no more than a couple hundred, lived through that remarkable twenty-five-year period when the vanguard of European civilization and commerce first penetrated the Rocky Mountain West with the fur men—and chief among them was the maker of these maps.

201   *Each step of that arduous journey seemed to harden:* Wischmann, *Frontier Diplomats,* 210–212.

202   *"of the evils they charge, and I suppose justly":* David D. Mitchell to Luke Lea, October 25, 1851, Commissioner of Indian Affairs, Letters Received, 1851.

202   *"new era for the Indians":* Smet, *Life, Letters, and Travels,* 2:682–684, and Killoren, *"Come, Blackrobe,"* 197. De Smet fervently hoped that this treaty would lead to an era of peace and reconciliation in which the Indians could transition out of their "passion for the chase" and into livelihoods and economies more suited to limited territories.

203   *"The accompanying map, upon which these national boundaries":* David D. Mitchell to Luke Lea, November 11, 1851, Commissioner of Indian Affairs, Annual Report to Congress, 1851, 290.

203   *Mitchell then proceeded to devote much:* Ibid., 290–292.

203   *In mid-April, Manypenny received instructions:* Killoren, *"Come, Black-robe,"* 190–196. For a scholarly overview of the second removal era in the West, see Prucha, *American Indian Treaties,* 235.

204   *"By alternative persuasion and force":* Gibson, "Great Plains as Colonization Zone," 35. Gibson adds a historical footnote to Manypenny's challenge by explaining that passage of the Kansas-Nebraska Act turned "the northern portion of the Indian colonization zone, much of it situated on the Great Plains," into the settlement prize for the Anglo-American pioneer, who was now well on his way to reaching the Rocky Mountains.

205   *"The Indian is placed between the upper and nether millstones":* Miner, *The Corporation and the Indian,* 20. Though it sounds astonishing to us today, statements such as these were not out of the ordinary at the time.

205   *"This modification of the treaty I think very proper":* David D. Mitchell to Luke Lea, October 17, 1852, Office of Indian Affairs, Letters Received. Also, see Prucha, *American Indian Treaties,* 241.

205   *most of the Great White Father's emissaries:* David D. Mitchell, letter to Luke Lea, March 22, 1851, and also to Luke Lea, September 14, 1850; Killoren, *"Come, Blackrobe,"* 188. This simply cannot be stated in terms that properly contextualize the extent to which the government agencies set up to safeguard Indian rights and resources were the very agencies that were looked to by Congress to dismantle the same. "Like the Indian policy he helped to fashion and implement," writes Killoren, "Mitchell stated a regard for the rights of the Indians; in practice, however, that concern was always subordinated to that greater and supposedly divinely determined good—the Manifest Destiny of the United States." Ibid.

206   *Lawmakers had sent the new amendments to Manypenny:* George W. Manypenny to Alfred Cumming, May 5, 1853, Office of Indian Affairs, Letters Sent.

208 *Thanks only to his good name and high standing:* Anderson, "The Controversial Sioux Amendment," 217.

208 *the Crow, in fact, did not even see the amendments:* Ibid., 206 n.9. Anderson notes that the Crow amendment arrived at the Bureau of Indian Affairs on July 6, 1855. Contrary to what most historians have claimed—that the Crow did not sign the amended treaty provisions—they signed on September 18, 1854, almost three years to the date of the original treaty.

210 *"We saw that the white man did not take his religion":* Linderman, *American,* 227–228.

210 *"In order to get that, they were pretty much":* Raymond Cross, interview by the author, March 2002.

211 *"as a convenient and accepted vehicle":* Prucha, *The Great Father,* 318.

212 *These two huge new parcels:* Killoren, *"Come, Blackrobe,"* 194–196.

212 *"shall be excepted out of the boundaries":* Commissioner of Indian Affairs, Annual Report to Congress, 1853, 251.

212 *"so long as such rights shall remain unextinguished":* Ibid., and Kansas-Nebraska Act, U.S. Statutes, 10:277–285.

213 *"the rights of person or property now pertaining":* Kansas-Nebraska Act, and Killoren, *"Come, Blackrobe,"* 198.

214 *"In no former equal period of our history":* Commissioner of Indian Affairs, Annual Report to Congress, 1856, 571. Within weeks of the signing of the Kansas-Nebraska Act, most of the treaties negotiated under Manypenny's watch contained provisions for the division of Indian lands in the new territories.

214 *"The main cause for strife, violence, disorder, and murder":* George W. Manypenny to Congress, Commissioner of Indian Affairs, Annual Report to Congress, 1856, 483–484.

214 *"Trespass and depredations of every conceivable kind":* Ibid.

215 *"Whites are already pouring in by the thousands":* Smet, *Life, Letters, and Travels,* 3:1110–1111.

216 *"The Indians will perish before the land thrives":* Thomas Fitzpatrick to Alfred Cumming, November 21, 1853, Commissioner of Indian Affairs, Annual Report to Congress, 367–371.

216 *Then, as if restless fates had set out to underscore:* There are many accounts of this sordid and tragic affair, but most are extracted from relatively few primary sources, including the annual report of Fitzpatrick's replacement on the Platte, John Whitfield. For a summary of the government's investigation, see Killoren, *"Come, Blackrobe,"* 200–204. For the primary source report, see Commissioner of Indian Affairs, Annual Report to Congress, 1854, 297–306.

When word reached De Smet of the bloodshed that resulted from a stray cow, he wrote: "It matters not how great the provocations and wrongs of the whites against the Indians; the latter are always the dupes and victims." Smet, *Life, Letters, and Travels*, 4:1218–1220. Also, see Utley, *Frontiersmen in Blue*, 110–114.

218 *"We knew him [Frightening Bear] well":* Killoren, *"Come, Blackrobe,"* 204, quoting A. B. Chambers, editorial in the *Missouri Republican*.

218 *"punish the offenders quickly":* Ibid.

218 *"By God, I'm for battle—no peace!":* Bandel, *Frontier Life*, 29–31. By the time he retired, Harney's view of the Indians had changed. In a farewell address, he told Congress that he had spent fifty years on the frontier dealing with the Indians, and never once knew an Indian leader to go back on his word.

218 *General Harney's campaign finally ended:* There are many accounts of the Ash Hollow encounter, but virtually all historians agree with Merrill J. Mattes that the Harney massacre was "one of the most savage of all encounters between red and white men." Mattes, *Great Platte River*, 311–338. Also, see Utley, *Frontiersmen in Blue*, 116–117, and Hafen and Young, *Fort Laramie*, 240–244.

218 *"And yet, such is the origin of a fresh war":* Smet, *Life, Letters, and Travels*, 4:1218–1220.

219 *"must not obstruct or lurk in the vicinity":* Senate Executive Documents, 94, 34th Cong., 1st sess., 2, and Commissioner of Indian Affairs, Annual Report to Congress, 300.

220 *"And then the scene of murder and barbarity began":* House Report on the Massacre of Cheyenne Indians, January 10, 1865, and McMurtry, *Oh What a Slaughter*, 35.

221 *Later, the official investigators called Chivington's:* Ibid. Also, see Sides, *Blood and Thunder*, for a wonderfully told and researched account of Colonel Chivington's murderous adventures in Indian country.

221 *"As to Colonel Chivington, your committee":* Ibid.

222 *"Joshua upon entering the promised land":* Miner, *The Corporation and the Indian*, 2.

222 *"Indians [today] remember that the United States Army":* Deloria, ed., *Of Utmost Good Faith*, 161.

224 *"Tell them at Washington if they have one man":* Jackson, *A Century of Dishonor*, 179.

225 *"Had there been no Indian":* Vestal, *Short Grass Country*, 173.

225 *"Behind the pragmatic, manifest-destinarian purpose":* Stegner, *The American West.*

227 *"It is only the warlike power":* Theodore Roosevelt, "Expansion and Peace," *The Independent,* December 21, 1899.

227 *Senator Albert Beveridge amplified Roosevelt's themes:* Senator Albert Beveridge, Congressional Record, January 9, 1900.

230 *To the high plains Indians:* Lawson, *Dammed Indians,* and Meyer, "Fort Berthold and Garrison Dam."

230 *a little-known campaign sponsored by:* An excellent overview of the termination era is included in Josephy, *Now That the Buffalo's Gone,* and Tyler, *A History of Indian Policy,* 172–181.

231 *Barry Goldwater of Arizona and Lee Metcalf of Montana:* VanDevelder, *Coyote Warrior,* 171. Also, see *Congressional Record,* 85th Cong., 2nd sess., April 17, 1958, 104, pt. 5, 6728. Congressman James Murray called for a complete revision of federal Indian policy and P.L. 280. For Goldwater's speech decrying termination-era objectives, see *Congressional Record,* 86th Congress, 2nd sess., 1958, March 9, 1959. For an analysis of Goldwater and Metcalf's challenges to termination-era legislators, see Tyler, *A History of Indian Policy,* 176–178.

231 *Throughout those dark years, Martin Cross:* Meyer, "Fort Berthold and Garrison Dam," 344.

232 *"There were a lot of tragedies in those years":* Al Cross, interview by the author, June 2002.

233 *"His heart opened up like a zipper":* Martin Cross Jr., interview by the author, November 2001.

234 *"If you look at Plato's response to the Sophists":* Raymond Cross, interview by the author, September 2001.

234 *White farmers on the high plains were growing:* Karl Limvere and Rich Madsen, "Rumblings from the Ditch: A Special Report," *North Dakota Union Farmer,* Summer 1972. (This essay is a must-read for anyone interested in the history of Pick-Sloan.) In the first decade of the new millennium, a severe drought across the Great Plains and Rocky Mountain West destroyed thousands of square miles of crops. Drought-stricken farmers in North Dakota watched helplessly as water levels in Lake Sakakawea were drawn down to keep downstream barge traffic moving without interruption between St. Louis and Sioux City, Iowa. This was the very situation Senators O'Mahoney and Milliken thought they had headed off with their amendment to the Flood Control Act of 1944, stating that upstream farmers would always have priority over downstream barge operators. But it never happened.

234   *The Pick-Sloan Plan, wrote the editorial board:* Ibid.

234   *Kennedy had recently characterized:* VanDevelder, *Coyote Warrior,* 172.

234   *The BIA's investigation found nothing:* Ibid., 173.

235   *"See, what you have now is this Indian":* Interview from *Waterbuster,* a documentary film by Carlos Pienado.

235   *"The American Indians have been oppressed":* Nixon, *Public Papers, 1970,* 223–224.

236   *Nixon asked James Abourezk:* James Abourezk, interview by the author, February 2000. Abourezk revealed that Nixon then asked a member of his senior legislative staff, Judy Tell, to work with Abourezk in writing the American Indian Self-Determination Act. During the Sioux's siege of Wounded Knee, Abourezk was the only politician the AIM leaders trusted to meet with them face to face. Abourezk's parents had emigrated to the Pine Ridge Reservation from Beirut, Lebanon, shortly after World War I and opened a general store on the reservation. For more on this fascinating story, see Abourezk, *Advice and Dissent.*

237   *The Reagan administration quietly convened:* For a comprehensive investigation into the Reagan administration's activities in Indian country, see Al Gedicks, *The New Resource Wars: Native and Environmental Struggles Against Multinational Corporations* (Boston: South End, 1993), 39–45.

238   *and served his apprenticeship in federal courts:* VanDevelder, *Coyote Warrior,* 35–57.

238   *Raymond appeared twice before the U.S. Supreme Court:* Ibid., and *Three Affiliated Tribes v. Wold Engineering,* 476 U.S. 877 (1986). Also, see VanDevelder, "In the Name of the Fathers."

238   *Then, culminating an eight-year campaign:* Ibid. Also, see *Final Report and Recommendations of the Garrison Unit Joint Tribal Advisory Committee,* 100th Cong., 1st sess., March 30, 1987.

238   *Chairman Daniel Inouye scornfully declared:* U.S. Senate Select Committee on Indian Affairs, Hearing on the Three Affiliated Tribes and Standing Rock Sioux Tribal Equitable Compensation Act of 1991, 102d Cong., 1st sess., April 12, 1991. Senator Inouye opened the hearings with the summary of the taking of the Mandan, Hidatsa, and Arikara lands, then concluded with his statement on the "deceit and deception" Congress had used to abrogate hundreds of treaties. This was a very important turning point for the legislation (S.B. 168) that eventually became the compensation act. Also, see U.S. Senate Select Committee on Indian Affairs, Implementing Recommendations of the Garrison Unit Joint Tribal Advisory Committee (S. Rept. 250), 102d Cong., 1st sess., November 26, 1991.

239 *"These old laws [treaties and statutes]":* Getches, Wilkinson, and Williams, *Cases and Materials*, 33.

239 *By the year 2007, farmers on the high plains:* Lawson, *Dammed Indians*, 187. Lawson brings humor to a bitter situation, by explaining: "Navigation, Pick's pet project on the lower Missouri, has become a bad joke. Taxpayers have spent untold millions to float no more than 2.6 million tons of commercial freight up the river each year. The Corps admitted that commercial navigation would no longer be viable after 2000, and in 1973 they admitted that there would not be sufficient water by then to maintain a navigation channel, so they proposed a new plan, with a cost of $60 billion, to constantly dredge the river and extend navigation to Yankton, South Dakota. Congress is still laughing." I happened to be invited to speak to the Dakota Water Users Association annual convention in Bismarck in December 2006, and was surprised to discover that the O'Mahoney-Milliken Amendment is not only very familiar to water users at every strata, from small towns to state government, but universally is associated with much anger and bitterness over unkept promises.

240 *When Hurricane Katrina stormed ashore:* In addition to the problem of vanishing barrier islands, aquatic life has virtually disappeared from a thousand-square-mile region of the Gulf of Mexico as a result of the pollutants that have been flushed down the Mississippi River by industry. Scientists have now declared dozens of spots around the globe as "dead zones" due to hypoxia induced by a variety of factors, including the dumping of industrial wastes. Also, see VanDevelder, "Cauldron of Life," 22.

240 *Just a few years earlier, as mineral and gas corporations:* For a full report on the activities of oil and gas corporations in Indian country, see Gedicks, *New Resource Wars*.

241 *Cobell's suit argued that:* There have been numerous stories published in magazines and newspapers that give a snapshot of the case at a given time as it has moved through the court system. Yet like many high-profile Indian cases, this one has been largely ignored by the public.

241 *"The significance of Indian trust funds":* Miner, *The Corporation and the Indian*, 11.

242 *"Alas," declared Judge Lamberth:* Judge Lamberth's "memorandum and order" was widely reported by the nation's leading news wire services the day after it was issued, on July 12, 2005.

BIBLIOGRAPHY

The personal stories in this book were drawn from dozens of interviews. Where necessary, those interviews were corroborated with original documents, such as letters and transcripts from congressional reports, debates, and hearings. Then there is the living and breathing "stuff"—the ineffable impressions and observations that come from walking miles of ground where the story took place. Those impressions are formed by a borderless collage of images, from paddling the Upper Missouri River to digging wild turnips and picking chokecherries with the elders of the Crow, Assiniboin, Sioux, Cheyenne, Mandan, Hidatsa, and Arikara tribes, to the less specific osmosis that takes place, willy-nilly, through new smells and tastes, and in the sound of laughter at weddings, the beat of drums at feasts, and the bereavement songs at funerals. I was fortunate enough to walk through the ancient villages with descendants of the clans who once lived there, and with the renowned anthropologist from the University of Missouri Raymond Wood, whose lifelong effort to recreate the pre-Columbian world on the Upper Missouri River has bested his own hopes and expectations.

My research arrived at a turning point when I discovered the groundbreaking work of Annie Heloise Abel. Sometime in the late 1890s, she set out to earn a Ph.D. in history from Yale University. Her topic was the Indian removal era of the early nineteenth century, and the extraordinary dissertation that resulted from her dedicated labors, *The History of Events Resulting in Indian Consolidation West of the Mississippi*, was awarded the prestigious Justin Winsor Prize of the American Historical Association in 1906. Two years later it was published. Then, for more than fifty years, while Abel was busy writing other books and teaching, her original work gathered dust in dimly lit stacks, waiting to be rediscovered. Seventy years after the AHA first published it, the second generation of editors of Felix Cohen's own landmark tome, *Handbook of Federal Indian Law*, did just that. In fact, the hundreds of pages devoted to federal Indian policy and removal in the fifth edition of the *Handbook* carry innumerable references to Abel's scholarship.

Frederick Merk's *Manifest Destiny and Mission in American History*, Alfred K. Weinberg's *Manifest Destiny: A Study of Nationalist Expansionism in American History*, and Anthony F. C. Wallace's *Jefferson and the Indians: The Tragic Fate of the First Americans*, were worthy companions and adjuncts to Abel's work. In fact, the first two scholars arrived at conclusions that she had deduced decades earlier, but there is no evidence to suggest that either Merk or Weinberg were familiar with their precursor. Nevertheless, the spirited debate that took place between them on the social forces that gave rise to Manifest Destiny was an invaluable dialogue in which there was much ore to be mined from both sides. Weinberg's facile touch with language and his willingness to wield it with exuberance gave him an early advantage in arguing that Manifest Destiny was a by-product of nationalism, but the weight and common sense of Merk's argument—that it resulted from Thomas Jefferson's failure to reconcile the conflicts embedded in his own political ideology about states' rights, brought him up even with Weinberg at the finish. Merk, a history professor at Harvard for four decades and a lifelong protégé of Frederick Jackson Turner, makes a compelling case around the idea that Jefferson's personal shortcomings, combined with his philosophical inconsistencies and political failures, surveyed the road to the Civil War. Both of these men knew they were on to something big, but then, strangely, mythology swamped their work for nearly four decades and virtually nothing of consequence was written about Manifest Destiny until 2000. Anthony Wallace then accomplished an equally admirable task of connecting dots that were invisible to Abel, Weinberg, and Merk by focusing intently on Jefferson through the telling lens of his relationship to the Indians. Some may argue that whatever was done back then is water under the bridge, but the water that flowed under that bridge in the nineteenth century has now flowed into the twenty-first.

On the history of water policy in the West, Marc Reisner's *Cadillac Desert* is the gold standard. It's both authoritative and a joy to read. Lesser known but still remarkable achievements, *The Dark Missouri* by Henry C. Hart, and *Dammed Indians* by Michael Lawson, filled in many blanks and did so with grace, wit, and admirable scholarship. For case law and Indian legal theory, there are none better than the works of Charles Wilkinson, David Getches, Raymond Cross, David Wilkins, Robert Williams, and Rennard Strickland. The extensive scaffolding erected by these scholars is complemented by Francis Paul Prucha's singularly authoritative works on treaties, *The Great Father: The United States Government and the American Indians* and *American Indian Treaties: The History of a Political Anomaly*. These titles are joined on the top shelf by Raymond J. De-Mallie and Vine Deloria Jr.'s *Documents of American Indian Diplomacy: Treaties, Agreements, and Conventions, 1775–1975*, and *Indian Treaties, 1778–1883*, by Charles Kappler, who spent much of his life compiling these two volumes. The work these authors have performed is both inspiring and humbling.

In addition to tens of thousands of pages of primary source material contained in government reports and transcripts, treasures were culled from the nineteenth-century government publication known to scholars as the Serial Set.

This collection, numbering many hundreds of volumes, is a library unto itself, and was recently indexed by tireless research librarians at the Library of Congress. In its millions of pages are all of the bitter debates over removal, John Wesley Powell's reports on water and the settlement of western lands, the hearings and speeches on the Missouri Compromise, the Kansas-Nebraska Act, westward expansion, Manifest Destiny, the annual reports of Indian commissioners, and reports from agents in the field. While most was fascinating but of little help, the good stuff was invaluable.

BOOKS AND ARTICLES

Abel, Annie Heloise. *The History of Events Resulting in Indian Consolidation West of the Mississippi.* New York: AMS, 1972.

Abernathy, Thomas P. *Western Lands and the American Revolution.* New York: Russell and Russell, 1959.

Abourezk, James. *Advice and Dissent.* Chicago: Lawrence Hill, 1989.

Adams, John Quincy. *The Memoirs of John Quincy Adams.* Edited by Charles F. Adams. New York: AMS, 1970.

Allen, A. J. *Ten Years in Oregon: Travels and Adventures of Doctor E. White and Lady West of the Rocky Mountains.* Ithaca: Mack, Andrus, 1848.

Alter, J. Cecil. *James Bridger, Frontiersman, Scout, and Guide.* Norman: University of Oklahoma Press, 1962.

American State Papers: Indian Affairs. 2 vols. Edited by Albert E. Bergh. Washington, D.C.: Gales and Seaton, 1832.

Anderson, Fred. *Crucible of War: The Seven Years' War and the Fate of Empire in British North America, 1754–1766.* New York: Knopf, 2000.

Anderson, Harry. "The Controversial Sioux Amendment to the Fort Laramie Treaty of 1851." *Nebraska History* 37 (September 1956).

Ashley, William H. "The Diary of William H. Ashley." Edited by Dale L. Morgan. *Bulletin of the Missouri Historical Society* 11:26.

Audubon, John James. *Audubon's America.* Edited by Donald Culross Peattie. Boston: Houghton Mifflin, 1940.

Bandel, Eugene. *Frontier Life in the Army, 1854–1861.* Edited by R. P. Giber. Glendale, Calif.: Arthur H. Clark, 1932.

Berry, Don. *A Majority of Scoundrels: An Informal History of the Rocky Mountain Fur Company.* New York: Harper, 1961.

Berry, Wendell. *The Unsettling of America: Culture and Agriculture.* New York: Penguin, 1995.

Berthrong, Donald J. *The Southern Cheyenne.* Norman: University of Oklahoma Press, 1963.

Bickham, Troy O. *Savages Within the Empire: Representations of American Indians in Eighteenth-Century Britain.* New York: Oxford University Press, 2005.

Bigelow, John. *Memoir of the Life and Public Services of John Charles Frémont.* New York: Derby and Jackson, 1856.

Bodkin, Daniel B. *Our Natural History: The Lessons of Lewis and Clark.* New York: Penguin, 1995.

Bonner, T. D. *The Life and Adventures of James P. Beckwourth.* Lincoln: University of Nebraska Press, 1981.

Bordewich, Fergus M. *Killing the White Man's Indian.* New York: Doubleday, 1996.

Bowers, Alfred W. *Hidatsa Social and Ceremonial Organization.* Lincoln: University of Nebraska Press, 1992.

———. *Mandan Social and Ceremonial Organization.* Chicago: University of Chicago Press, 1950.

Burke, Joseph C. "The Cherokee Cases: A Study in Law, Politics, and Morality." *Stanford Law Review* 21 (February 1969): 500–531.

Cappon, Lester J., ed. *The Adams-Jefferson Letters.* Chapel Hill: University of North Carolina Press, 1959.

Chittenden, Hiram Martin. *The American Fur Trade in the Far West.* 3 vols. New York: F. P. Harper, 1902.

Cohen, Felix. "The Erosion of Indian Rights, 1950–1953." *Yale Law Journal* 62 (1953): 348, 390.

———. *Handbook of Federal Indian Law.* 1st ed. Washington, D.C.: United States Department of the Interior, GPO, 1941.

———. *Felix S. Cohen's Handbook of Federal Indian Law.* 1982 ed. Edited by Rennard Strickland et al. Charlottesville: Bobbs-Merrill, 1982.

Conway, Jill Ker. *True North: A Memoir.* New York: Knopf, 1994.

Costello, David. *The Prairie World.* New York: Thomas Crowell, 1969.

Costo, Rupert, and Jeannette Henry. *Indian Treaties: Two Centuries of Dishonor.* San Francisco: Indian Historian, 1977.

Cox, George. *The Crusades.* New York: Charles Scribner's Sons, 1886.

Cross, Raymond. "Sovereign Bargains, Indian Takings, and the Preservation of Indian Country in the Twenty-first Century," *Arizona Law Review* 40, no. 2 (Summer 1998).

———. "Tribes as Rich Nations." *Oregon Law Review* 79, no. 4 (Summer 2001).

Dale, H. C. *The Ashley-Smith Explorations and the Discovery of a Central Route to the Pacific.* Glendale, Calif.: Arthur H. Clark, 1941.

Damon, Charles Ripley. *The American Dictionary of Dates.* 2 vols. Boston: Gorham, 1921.

Deloria, Vine, Jr. *A Brief History of the Federal Responsibility to the American Indian, Based on the Report "Legislative Analysis of the Federal Role in Indian Education."* Washington: Department of Health, Education and Welfare [Education Division], Office of Education, GPO, 1979.

———, ed. *American Indian Policy in the Twentieth Century.* Norman: University of Oklahoma Press, 1985.

———, ed. *Of Utmost Good Faith.* San Francisco: Straight Arrow, 1971.

Deloria, Vine, Jr., and Raymond J. DeMallie, eds. *Documents of American Indian Diplomacy: Treaties, Agreements, and Conventions, 1775–1979.* Norman: University of Oklahoma Press, 1999.

Deloria, Vine, Jr., and Clifford M. Lytle. *The Nations Within: The Past and Future of American Indian Sovereignty.* Austin: University of Texas Press, 1984.

DeMallie, Raymond J. "American Indian Treaty Making: Motives and Meanings," *American Indian Journal* 3 (January 1977).

———. "Touching the Pen: Plains Indian Treaty Councils in Ethnohistorical Perspective." In *Ethnicity on the Great Plains,* edited by Frederick C. Luebke. Lincoln: University of Nebraska Press, 1980.

Denig, Edwin T. "Of the Sioux." *Bulletin of the Missouri Historical Society* 7, no. 2 (1951).

De Voto, Bernard. *Across the Wide Missouri.* Boston: Houghton Mifflin, 1947.

———. "The Anxious West." *Harper's Magazine,* December 1946.

———. *The Course of Empire.* Boston: Houghton Mifflin, 1952.

———. "The West Against Itself." *Harper's Magazine,* January 1947.

Dippie, Brian W. *The Vanishing American: White Attitudes and U.S. Indian Policy.* Middletown: Wesleyan University Press, 1982.

Dobyns, Henry F. *Their Number Become Thinned: Native American Population Dynamics in Eastern North America.* Knoxville: University of Tennessee Press, 1983.

Doherty, Robert. *Disputed Waters: Native Americans and the Great Lakes Fishery.* Lexington: University Press of Kentucky, 1990.

Donaldson, Thomas. *The Public Domain.* Washington, D.C.: GPO, 1884.

Drinnon, Richard. *Keeper of Concentration Camps: Dillon Myer and America Racism.* Berkeley: University of California Press, 1987.

Drury, Clifford M., ed. *First White Women over the Rockies*. Glendale: Arthur H. Clark, 1965.

Duran, Bonnie, with Eduardo Duran and Maria Yellow Horse Brave Heart. "Native Americans and the Trauma of History." In *Studying Native America: Problems and Prospects*, edited by Russell Thornton. Madison: University of Wisconsin Press, 1998.

Ellis, Joseph. *American Sphinx: The Character of Thomas Jefferson*. New York: Knopf, 1997.

———. *His Excellency, George Washington*. New York: Knopf, 2004.

Erbstosser, Martin. *The Crusades*. New York: Universe, 1979.

Fenton, William Nelson. *The Great Law and the Longhouse: A Political History of the Iroquois Confederacy*. Norman: University of Oklahoma Press, 1998.

Fite, Emerson, and Archibald Freeman. *A Book of Old Maps: Delineating American History*. Cambridge: Harvard University Press, 1926.

Fitzharris, Tim. *The Wild Prairie: A Natural History of the Western Plains*. New York: Oxford, 1883.

Flanders, Henry. *The Lives and Times of the Chief Justices of the Supreme Court of the United States*, vol. 2. New York: James Crockcroft, 1878.

Fort Berthold Agency Report of 1943. Aberdeen, S.D.: Bureau of Indian Affairs, Regional Office, 1944.

Frémont, J. C. *Report of an Exploring Expedition to the Rocky Mountains in the Year 1842, and to Oregon and North California in the Years 1843–1844*. Washington, D.C., 1845.

Friesema, H. Paul, and Charles S. Matzke. "Socio-Economic and Cultural Effects of the Garrison Dam upon Members of the Three Affiliated Tribes of Fort Berthold Indian Reservation: A Report to the Joint Tribal Advisory Commission." May 1986 (on file with the author).

Garrison, George P. "Westward Extension." In *The American Nation*, edited by Albert B. Hart. New York, 1906.

Garrison, Tim Alan. *The Legal Ideology of Removal: The Southern Judiciary and the Sovereignty of Native American Nations*. Athens: University of Georgia Press, 2002.

Getches, David H. "Conquering the Cultural Frontier: The New Subjectivism of the Supreme Court in Indian Law." *California Law Review* 84, no. 6 (December 1996).

———. *The New Resource Wars: Native and Environmental Struggles Against Multinational Corporations*. Boston: South End, 1993.

Getches, David H., Charles F. Wilkinson, and Robert A. Williams, Jr. *Cases and Materials on Federal Indian Law*, 5th ed. St. Paul: Thompson/West, 2005.

Gibbon, Colonel John. *Last Summer's Expedition Against the Sioux and Its Great Catastrophe.* Bellevue, Neb.: Old Army, 1970.

Gibson, Arrell Morgan. "The Great Plains as a Colonization Zone for Eastern Indians." In *Ethnicity on the Great Plains,* edited by Frederick C. Luebke. Lincoln: University of Nebraska Press, 1980.

Goetzmann, William. *Exploration and Empire: The Explorer and the Scientist in the Winning of the American West.* New York: Knopf, 1966.

Gowans, Fred. *Rocky Mountain Rendezvous: A History of the Fur Trade Rendezvous, 1825–1840.* Rev. ed. Layton, Utah: Gibbs-Smith, 2005.

Gray, William H. *A History of Oregon, 1792–1849.* Portland: Harris, Holman, 1870.

———. "The Unpublished Journals of William H. Gray." *Whitman College Quarterly* 16 (1913).

Grijalva, James. "The Assertion of Natural Resource Damage Claims by Indian Tribal Trustees." *Environmental Claims Journal* 4, no. 2 (Winter 1991–1992).

Hafen, LeRoy R. *Broken Hand: The Life of Thomas Fitzpatrick, Mountain Man, Guide, and Indian Agent.* Denver: Old West, 1931.

Hafen, LeRoy R., and Francis Marion Young. *Fort Laramie and the Pageant of the West, 1834–1890.* Glendale, Calif.: Arthur H. Clark, 1938.

Harmer, Ruth Mulvey. "Uprooting the Indians." *Atlantic Monthly,* March 1956.

Hart, Henry Cowles. *The Dark Missouri.* Madison: University of Wisconsin Press, 1957.

Hastings, L. W. *The Emigrants' Guide to Oregon and California.* Glendale, Calif.: Arthur Clarke, 1932.

Henry, Alexander, and David Thompson. *The Manuscript Journals of Alexander Henry and of David Thompson,* vol. 1. Edited by Elliott Coues. New York: Francis P. Harper, 1897.

Hibbard, Benjamin H. *A History of the Public Land Policies.* Madison: University of Wisconsin Press, 1965.

Hill, Burton S. "The Great Indian Treaty Council of 1851." *Nebraska History,* 1956.

Hill, George W. "Rural Migration and Farm Abandonment." Washington, D.C.: Federal Relief Administration, 1935.

Hitchcock, Ethan Allen. *A Traveler in Indian Territory: The Journal of Ethan Allen Hitchcock.* Edited by Grant Foreman. Cedar Rapids, Iowa: Torch, 1930.

Hobson, Charles F. *The Great Chief Justice: John Marshall and the Rule of Law.* Lawrence: University of Kansas Press, 1996.

Holder, Preston. *The Hoe and the Horse on the Plains: A Study of Cultural Development Among North American Indians*. Lincoln: University of Nebraska Press, 1970.

Holt, P. M. *The Age of the Crusades: The Near East from the Eleventh Century to 1517*. London: Longman, 1986.

Horseman, Reginald. *Expansion and American Indian Policy, 1783–1812*. East Lansing: Michigan State University Press, 1967.

Hulbert, Archer Butler. *Forty-Niners: The Chronicle of the California Trail*. Boston: Little, Brown, 1931.

Hunt, Constance, with Verne Huser. *Down by the River: The Impact of Federal Water Projects and Policies on Biological Diversity*. Foreword by Jay D. Hair. Washington, D.C.: Island, 1988.

The Indian Removals. 5 vols. Introduction by John M. Carroll. Reprint of Document 512 of the U.S. Senate, 23rd Congress, 1st sess., correspondence and debates. New York: AMS, 1974.

Ivison, Duncan, with Paul Patton and William Sanders, eds. *Political Theory and the Rights of Indigenous Peoples*. London: Cambridge University Press, 2000.

Jackson, Donald. *Voyages of the Steamboat Yellowstone*. Norman: University of Oklahoma Press, 1978.

Jackson, Helen Hunt. *A Century of Dishonor: A Sketch of the United States Government's Dealings with Some of the Indian Tribes*. New York: Harper and Brothers, 1881.

Jefferson, Thomas. *The Writings of Thomas Jefferson*. Edited by Albert E. Bergh. Washington, D.C.: Thomas Jefferson Memorial Association, 1907.

Jones, Dorothy V. *License for Empire: Colonialism by Treaty in Early America*. Chicago: University of Chicago Press, 1982.

Jones, Terry, and Alan Ereira. *Crusades*. New York: Facts on File, 1995.

Josephy, Alvin, Jr. *The American Heritage History of the Congress of the United States*. New York: McGraw-Hill, 1975.

———. *Now That the Buffalo's Gone: A Study of Today's American Indians*. New York: Knopf, 1982.

———. *Red Power: The American Indian's Fight for Freedom*. New York: American Heritage, 1971.

Kappler, Charles, ed. *Indian Treaties, 1778–1883*. New York: Interland, 1972.

Karnes, Thomas L. *William Gilpin, Western Naturalist*. Austin: University of Texas Press, 1970.

Ketcham, Ralph. *James Madison*. New York: MacMillan, 1971.

Killoren, John J. *"Come, Blackrobe": De Smet and the Indian Tragedy*. Norman: University of Oklahoma Press, 1994.

Kreyche, Gerla. *Vision of the American West*. Lexington: University of Kentucky Press, 1989.

Kvasnicka, Robert, and Herman J. Viola. *The Commissioners of Indian Affairs, 1824–1977*. Lincoln: University of Nebraska Press, 1979.

Lawson, Michael. *Dammed Indians: The Pick-Sloan Plan and the Missouri River Sioux*. Norman: University of Oklahoma Press, 1982.

Lazarus, Edward. *Black Hills, White Justice: The Sioux Nation Versus the United States, 1775 to the Present*. New York: HarperCollins, 1991.

Lewis, Meriwether, and William Clark. *Original Journals of the Lewis and Clark Expedition*. New York: Dodd, Mead, 1904.

———. *The Journals of Lewis and Clark*. Vols. 1–2. Edited by Gary E. Moulton. Lincoln: University of Nebraska Press, 2001.

Limerick, Patricia Nelson. *The Legacy of Conquest: The Unbroken Past of the American West*. New York: W. W. Norton, 1987.

Limerick, Patricia Nelson, Clyde A. Milner II, and Charles Rankin, eds. *Trails: Toward a New Western History*. Lawrence: University Press of Kansas, 1991.

Linderman, Frank. *American: The Life Story of a Great Indian, Plenty-coups, Chief of the Crows*. New York: John Day, 1930.

Locke, John. *An Essay Concerning Human Understanding*. Edited by A. S. Pringle-Pattison. London: Oxford University Press, 1924; orig. pub. 1690.

———. *Essays on the Law of Nature*. Edited by W. von Leyden. Oxford: Clarendon, 1954.

———. *Of Civil Government*. London: J. M. Dent and Sons, 1943.

———. *Second Treatise of Government*. Edited by Thomas P. Peardon. Indianapolis: Bobbs-Merrill, 1952.

Lowe, Percival G. *Five Years a Dragoon, '49 to '54: And Other Adventures on the Great Plains*. Norman: University of Oklahoma Press, 1965.

Lyons, Oren, John Mohawk, Vine Deloria Jr., Laurence Hauptman, Howard Berman, Donald Grinde Jr., Curtis Berkeley, and Robert Venables. *Exiled in the Land of the Free: Democracy, Indian Nations, and the U.S. Constitution*. Santa Fe, N.M.: Clear Light, 1992.

McCabe, Joseph. *Crises in the History of the Papacy*. New York: Putnam Sons, 1916.

McCullough, David. *John Adams*. New York: Simon and Schuster, 2001.

McMurtry, Larry. *Oh What a Slaughter: Massacres in the American West, 1846–1890*. New York: Simon and Schuster, 2005.

McNickle, D'Arcy. *Native American Tribalism*. London: Oxford University Press, 1973.

Malone, Dumas. *Thomas Jefferson and the Rights of Man*. Boston: Little, Brown, 1951.

Manypenny, George. *Our Indian Wards*. Cincinnati: Robert Clark, 1880.

Martin, Calvin, ed. *The American Indian and the Problem of History*. New York: Oxford University Press, 1987.

Mason, Joseph, ed. *The Papers of James Madison*. Charlottesville: University Press of Virginia, 1985.

Masters, Joseph G. *Stories of the Far West: Heroic Tales of the Last Frontier*. Boston: Ginn, 1935.

Mattes, Merrill J. *The Great Platte River Road*. Lincoln: Nebraska State Historical Society, 1969.

Matthews, Richard K. *If Men Were Angels: James Madison and the Heartless Empire of Reason*. Lawrence: University of Kansas Press, 1995.

Mayer, Hans Eberhard. *The Crusades*. London: Oxford University Press, 1965.

Meadows, Paul. *John Wesley Powell: Frontiersman of Science*. Lincoln: University of Nebraska Press, 1952.

Merk, Frederick. *Manifest Destiny and Mission in American History: A Reinterpretation*. New York: Alfred A. Knopf, 1963.

Meyer, Roy. "Fort Berthold and the Garrison Dam." *North Dakota State Historical Society* 35 (1968), nos. 3–4.

——. *Santee Sioux: United States Indian Policy on Trial*. Lincoln: University of Nebraska Press, 1967.

——. *The Village Indians of the Upper Missouri*. Norman: University of Oklahoma Press, 1972.

Miller, Lee. *From the Heart: Voices of the American Indian*. New York: Knopf, 1995.

Miller, Leslie A. "The Battle That Squanders Billions," *Saturday Evening Post*, May 14, 1949.

Miner, H. Craig. *The Corporation and the Indian*. Columbia: University of Missouri Press, 1976.

Morgan, Arthur E. *Dams and Other Disasters: A Century of the Army Corps of Engineers in Civil Works*. Boston: Porter Sargent, 1972.

Neihardt, John G. *Black Elk Speaks*. Lincoln: University of Nebraska Press, 1979.

New American State Papers: Indian Affairs. 13 vols. (Reorganized from Gales and Seaton's *American State Papers*.) Introduction by Loring B. Priest. Wilmington: Scholarly Resources, 1972.

Newland, Mary Reed. *St. Thomas Aquinas.* New York: American RDM, 1967.

Nies, Judith. *Native American History: A Chronology of a Culture's Vast Achievements and Their Links to World Events.* New York: Ballentine, 1996.

Nixon, Richard M. *The Public Papers of the Presidents of the United States.* Washington, D.C.: Federal Register Division, National Archives and Records Service, General Services Administration, 1975.

Olson, James. *History of Nebraska.* Lincoln: University of Nebraska Press, 1965.

O'Sullivan, John L. "The Great Nation of Futurity." *Democratic Review* 6 (1839).

Parker, Samuel. *Journal of an Exploring Tour Beyond the Rocky Mountains, Under the Direction of the American Board of Commissions for Foreign Missions, in the Years 1835, '36, and '37.* Ithica: Mack, Andrus, and Woodruff, printers, 1840.

Pearce, Roy Harvey. *The Savages of America: A Study of the Indian and the Idea of Civilization.* Baltimore: Johns Hopkins University Press, 1953.

Pelzer, Louis, ed. *Prairie Logbooks: Dragoon Campaigns to the Pawnee Villages in 1844, and to the Rocky Mountains in 1845.* Chicago: Caxton Club, 1943.

Peters, Virginia Bergman. *Women of the Earth Lodges: Tribal Life on the Plains.* Norman: University of Oklahoma Press, 1995.

Peterson, Merrill. *Thomas Jefferson and the New Nation.* New York: Oxford University Press, 1970.

Powell, John Wesley. *Report on the Lands of the Arid Region.* Washington, D.C.: GPO, 1879.

———. *Seeing Things Whole: The Essential John Wesley Powell.* Edited by William deBuys. Washington, D.C.: Island, 2001.

Powers, H. H. "The Ethics of Expansion." *International Journal of Ethics* 10 (1900).

Pratt, Julius W. "John L. O'Sullivan and Manifest Destiny." *New York History* 14 (1933).

Prucha, Francis Paul. *American Indian Treaties: The History of a Political Anomaly.* Berkeley: University of California Press, 1994.

———. *The Great Father: The United States Government and the American Indians.* 2 vols. Lincoln: University of Nebraska Press, 1984.

———. *Indian Policy in the United States.* Lincoln: University of Nebraska Press, 1981.

Putnam, Robert. *The Naming of America: Early Sea Charts.* New York: Abbeville, 1983.

Raban, Jonathan. *Bad Land: An American Romance.* New York: Vintage, 1996.

Read, James H. *Power Versus Liberty: Madison, Hamilton, Wilson, and Jefferson*. Charlottesville: University Press of Virginia, 2000.

Reid, Bernard J. *Overland to California with the Pioneer Line: The Gold Rush Diary of Bernard J. Reid*. Edited by Mary McDougall Gordon. Palo Alto: Stanford University Press, 1983.

Reisner, Marc. *Cadillac Desert*. New York: Penguin, 1986.

Ridgeway, Marian. *The Missouri Basin's Pick-Sloan Plan: A Case Study*. Champaign-Urbana: University of Illinois Press, 1955.

Riemer, Neal. *James Madison: Creating the American Constitution*. Washington, D.C.: Congressional Quarterly, 1986.

Riley-Smith, Jonathan. *The Oxford History of the Crusades*. London: Oxford University Press, 1995.

Robinson, Doane. *A History of the Dakota or Sioux Indians*. Minneapolis: Ross and Haines, 1974.

Ronda, James. *Lewis and Clark Among the Indians*. Lincoln: University of Nebraska Press, 1984.

Sandoz, Mari. *The Battle of the Little Big Horn*. Philadelphia: J. B. Lippincott, 1966.

———. *The Beaver Men*. Lincoln: University of Nebraska Press, 1964.

———. *The Buffalo Hunters: The Story of the Hide Men*. New York: Hastings House, 1954.

Schleifer, James T. *The Making of Tocqueville's Democracy in America*. Chapel Hill: University of North Carolina Press, 1980.

Schlesier, Karl H., ed. *Plains Indians, A.D. 500–1500: The Archeological Past of Historic Groups*. Norman: University of Oklahoma Press, 1994.

Sides, Hampton. *Blood and Thunder*. New York: Doubleday, 2006.

Smet, Pierre-Jean de. *Life, Letters, and Travels of Father Pierre-Jean de Smet, S.J., 1801–1873*. Edited by Hiram Martin Chittenden and Alfred Talbot Richardson. New York: Arno, 1969.

———. *Western Missions and Missionaries*. New York: J. B. Kirker, 1863.

Smith, G. Hubert. *The Explorations of the La Vérendryes in the Northern Plains, 1738–1743*. Edited by W. Raymond Wood. Lincoln: University of Nebraska Press, 1980.

Stegner, Wallace. *The American West as Living Space*. Ann Arbor: University of Michigan Press, 1988.

———. *Beyond the Hundredth Meridian*. Boston: Houghton Mifflin, 1953.

———. *Marking the Sparrow's Fall: Wallace Stegner's American West*. New York: Henry Holt, 1948.

————. *Where the Bluebird Sings to the Lemonade Springs.* New York: Random House, 1992.

Streeter, Floyd Benjamin. *Prairie Trains and Cow Towns: The Opening of the Old West.* New York: Devin Adair, 1963.

Suarez, Francisco, S.J. *Selections from Three Works of Francisco Suarez: On Laws and God the Lawgiver.* Introduction by James Brown Scott. New York: Oceana, 1964.

Sunder, John. *Fur Trade on the Upper Missouri, 1840–1865.* Norman: University of Oklahoma Press, 1965.

————. *Joshua Pilcher: Fur Trader and Indian Agent.* Norman: University of Oklahoma Press, 1968.

Terrell, John Upton. *Black Robe: The Life of Pierre-Jean De Smet, Missionary, Explorer, Pioneer.* New York: Doubleday, 1964.

————. *Land Grab: The Truth About "The Winning of the West."* New York: Dial, 1972.

Territorial Papers of the United States, vols. 1–28. Washington, D.C.: GPO, 1952.

Textor, Lucy E. *Official Relations Between the United States and the Sioux Indians.* Palo Alto: Stanford University Press, 1898.

Thayer, James Bradley. *John Marshall.* New York: DaCapo, 1974.

Tocqueville, Alexis de. *Democracy in America.* Translated by Henry Reeve. Rev. ed. New York: P. F. Collier, 1900.

Triplett, Colonel Frank. *Conquering the Wilderness.* New York: Thompson, 1883.

Tyler, Lyman S. *A History of Indian Policy.* Washington, D.C.: Department of the Interior, 1973.

————. *Indian Affairs: A Paper on Termination with an Attempt to Show Its Antecedents.* Provo: Institute of American Indian Studies, 1964.

Utley, Robert M. *Frontiersmen in Blue: The United States Army and the Indian, 1848–1865.* Lincoln: University of Nebraska Press, 1984.

————. *The Indian Frontier of the American West, 1846–1890.* Albuquerque: University of New Mexico Press, 1984.

Van de Mark, Dorothy. "The Raid on the Reservations." *Harper's Magazine*, March 1956.

VanDevelder, Paul. "Cauldron of Life." *Audubon Magazine*, July–August 2004.

————. *Coyote Warrior: One Man, Three Tribes, and the Trial that Forged a Nation.* New York: Little, Brown, 2004.

————. "In the Name of the Fathers." *Stanford Magazine*, May 2005.

————. "A Native's Sense of the Earth." *Native Americas Journal*, Spring 2001.

Van Tramp, John C. *Prairie and Rocky Mountain Adventures.* Columbus: Gilmore and Brush, 1860.

Verano, John W., and Douglas H. Ubelaker, eds. *Disease and Demography in the Americas.* Washington, D.C.: Smithsonian, 1992.

Vestal, Stanley. *Short Grass Country.* Edited by Erskine Caldwell. Westport, Conn.: Greenwood, 1946.

Victor, Frances Fuller. *The River of the West.* Hartford: Columbian, 1870.

Vidal, Gore. *Inventing a Nation.* New Haven: Yale University Press, 2003.

Wallace, Anthony F. C. *Jefferson and the Indians: The Tragic Fate of the First Americans.* Cambridge: Belknap Press, Harvard University Press, 1999.

Walsh, Margaret. *The American Frontier Revisited.* London: MacMillian, 1981.

Washburn, Wilcomb E., ed. *The American Indian and the United States: A Documentary History.* 4 vols. New York: Random House, 1973.

———. *Red Man's Land, White Man's Law.* New York: Charles Scribner's Sons, 1971.

Washington, George. *The Papers of George Washington: Colonial Series.* 10 vols. Edited by W. W. Abbot. Charlottesville: University Press of Virginia, 1983–1995.

Weatherford, Jack. *Native Roots: How the Indians Enriched America.* New York: Crown, 1991.

Webb, Walter Prescott. "The American West: Perpetual Mirage," *Harper's Magazine,* May 1954.

———. *The Great Plains.* New York: Houghton Mifflin, 1936.

Weinberg, Albert K. *Manifest Destiny: A Study of Nationalist Expansionism in American History.* Baltimore: Johns Hopkins University Press, 1935.

Welch, James, with Paul Stekler. *Killing Custer: The Battle of the Little Bighorn and the Fate of the Plains Indians.* New York: W. W. Norton, 1994.

West, Elliott. *The Contested Plains: Indians, Goldseekers, and the Rush to Colorado.* Lawrence: University Press of Kansas, 1998.

Wexler, Alan. *Atlas of Westward Expansion.* New York: Facts on File, 1995.

Wheat, Carl I. *Mapping the Trans-Mississippi West: Vol. 1, The Spanish Entrada to the Louisiana Purchase, 1540–1804.* San Francisco: Institute of Historical Cartography, 1957.

White, Edward G. *The Marshall Court and Cultural Change, 1815–1835.* New York: MacMillan, 1988.

White, Kevin, ed. *Hispanic Philosophy in the Age of Discovery.* Washington, D.C.: Catholic University Press, 1997.

Wilkins, David E. *American Indian Sovereignty and the U.S. Supreme Court: The Masking of Justice.* Austin: University of Texas Press, 1997.

Wilkinson, Charles F. *American Indians, Time, and the Law: Native Societies in Modern Constitutional Democracy.* New Haven: Yale University Press, 1987.

———. *Crossing the Next Meridian: Land, Water, and the Future of the West.* Washington, D.C.: Island, 1992.

———. "The Headwaters of the Public Trust: Some Thoughts on the Source of the Traditional Doctrine," *Environmental Law* 19 (1989): 425.

Will, George, and J. J. Spinden. *The Mandans: A Study of Their Culture, Archaeology, and Language.* Cambridge: Peabody Museum, 1906.

Williams, Robert. *The American Indian in Western Legal Thought: Discourses of Conquest.* New York: Oxford University Press, 1990.

Wills, Gary. *James Madison.* New York: Times, 2002.

Wilson, Gilbert L. "Notes on the Hidatsa Indians." Anthropological Papers, vol. 56, pt. 2. Washington, D.C.: American Museum of Natural History, 1979.

Wilson, James. *The Earth Shall Weep.* New York: Grove, 1998.

Wischmann, Lesley. *Frontier Diplomats: The Life and Times of Alexander Culbertson and Natoyist-Siksina'.* Spokane: Arthur H. Clark, 2000.

Wood, Mary Christina. "Protecting Tribal Harvests." Speech delivered at the Environmental Protection Agency's Region 10 Tribal Leader Summit, at the Umatilla Indian Reservation, Umatilla, Washington, August 22, 2006 (www .law.uoregon.edu/faculty/mwood/speech.php).

Wood, Raymond. *Historical Overview of the Fort Clark State Historic Site.* Bismarck: State Historical Society of North Dakota, 1999.

Wood, Raymond, and Thomas Thiessen. *Early Fur Trade on the Northern Plains: Canadian Traders Among the Mandan and Hidatsa Indians, 1738–1818.* Norman: University of Oklahoma Press, 1985.

LETTERS AND MEMORANDA

Aandahl, Governor Fred G. Letter to Martin Cross, April 2, 1946.

Adams, John Quincy. Letter to Albert Gallatin, December 26, 1847, Adams Papers, Massachusetts Historical Society.

Brown, B. Gratz [and A. B. Chambers]. "The Fort Laramie Treaty of 1851, According to Letters from the Editor, Published in *The Missouri Republican,* St. Louis, Missouri, August 8, 1851, to November 30, 1851." Columbia, Mo.: Missouri Historical Society, 1956.

Brown, Orlando. Letter to Thomas Fitzpatrick, August 16, 1849, National Archives, Office of Indian Affairs, Letter Sent.

Burdick, Usher L. Letter to Martin Cross, May 4, 1953.

Case, Ralph. Letter to Martin Cross, December 27, 1945.

———. Letter to George Gillette and tribal council, January 21, 1947.

———. Expense account, tribal delegation in Washington, January 17, 1947.

Cohen, Felix. Letter to Amos Lamson, Omaha Tribal Council, May 12, 1950.

Cross, Martin. Letter to Mrs. Alfred Zuger, January 21, 1947.

———. Telegram to Senator William Langer, March 13, 1950.

———. Letter to son Crusoe, July 10, 1951.

———. Letter to son Crusoe, September 24, 1951.

———. Letter to Sioux Tribes on termination, December 22, 1951.

———. Letter to Robert Yellowtail, May 1953.

———. Letter to W. W. Short, February 24, 1953.

———. Letter to John Shaw, June 23, 1954.

———. Letter to *Harper's Magazine*, April 25, 1956.

———. Letter to Marilyn and Kent Hudson, March 25, 1963.

Calhoun, Secretary John C. Letter to President Monroe, January 24, 1825, Office of Indian Affairs, Letters Received, 1825.

Clark, William. Letter to Secretary of War Barbour, March 1, 1825, Office of Indian Affairs, 1825, American State Papers, Indian Affairs, Letters Received.

Curry, James. Letter to Senator Zales N. Ecton, October 1, 1952.

Dix, John A. Letter to Martin Van Buren, May 16, 1846, Martin Van Buren Papers, Library of Congress.

Fitzpatrick, Thomas. Letter to Lieutenant J. W. Abert, February 5, 1846, National Archives.

———. Letter to Lieutenant J. W. Abert, May 12, 1846, National Archives.

———. Letter to Superintendent Thomas H. Harvey, October 6, 1848, Commissioner of Indian Affairs, Annual Reports (1848), 471–472.

———. Letter to D. D. Mitchell, March 15, 1850, National Archives, St. Louis Superintendency, Office of Indian Affairs, Letters Received.

———. Letter to D. D. Mitchell, September 24, 1850, Commissioner of Indian Affairs, Annual Reports (1850), 48, 55–56.

———. Letter to Harvey, December 18, 1847, National Archives, Office of Indian Affairs, Letters Received.

———. Letter to Harvey, October 19, 1847, National Archives, Office of Indian Affairs, Letters Received.

———. Letter to Superintendent Cummins, November 21, 1853, National Archives, Commissioner of Indian Affairs, Annual Report, 1853.

Fort Berthold Superintendent's personal log. 1907–1912 (on file with author).

Fort Berthold Bulletins (biweekly newsletters). January 1950–August 1954.

Foster, W. G. Letter to Martin Cross and Senator Milton Young, March 11, 1950.

Garrison Dam Dedication Ceremony. Guest list and agenda, June 10, 1953.

George, Frank. Letter to NCAI tribal chairmen, September 26, 1952.

Krueger, Representative Otto. Letter to Martin Cross, December 28, 1953.

Lea, Commissioner Luke. Letter to D. D. Mitchell, May 26, 1851, National Archives, Office of Indian Affairs, Letters Sent, v. 42.

Lewis, Orme. Letter to Senator Arthur Watkins, March 13, 1953.

McNickle, D'Arcy. Letter to Martin Cross, November 20, 1945.

———. Letter to Martin Cross, May 1946.

Manypenny, George. Letter to Alfred Cummins, May 5, 1853, Office of Indian Affairs, Letters Sent.

Medill, William. Letter to Central Superintendency nominating Thomas Fitzpatrick to head new Indian agency on the Upper Platte, National Archives, Records of the Office of Indian Affairs, Letters Received, Upper Platte, B-2757/1846.

———. Letter to Upper Platte confirming Fitzpatrick's appointment, National Archives, Office of Indian Affairs, Letters Received, Upper Platte, S-4038/1846.

Mitchell, David D. Letter to Commissioner William Medill, June 1, 1849, National Archives, Office of Indian Affairs, Letters Received, St. Louis Superintendent.

———. Letter to Commissioner Orlando Brown, October 13, 1849, National Archives, Commissioner of Indian Affairs, Annual Report, 1849.

———. Letter to Commissioner Luke Lea, March 18, 1850, National Archives, Office of Indian Affairs, Letters Received, 1850.

———. Letter to Commissioner Luke Lea, September 14, 1850, Commissioner of Indian Affairs, Letters Received, 1850.

———. Letter to Commissioner Luke Lea, March 22, 1851, National Archives, Office of Indian Affairs, Letters Received, 1851.

———. Letter to Luke Lea, October 25, 1851, National Archives, Office of Indian Affairs, Letters Received, 1851.

Myer, Dillon. Letter to all regional BIA superintendents on termination, August 1952.

Pick, Lewis. "Transcript of meeting with Three Affiliated Tribes on Garrison Dam, at Elbowoods High School," May 27, 1946, Archives, Four Bears Museum, Three Affiliated Tribes.

Quinn, R. W. Letter to Warren Spaulding, BIA, September 21, 1951.

Schulte, Q. R. Letter to Martin Cross, October 14, 1954.

Shane, Ralph M. Letter to Col. H. Hille, Army Engineers, March 16, 1955.

Short, W. W. Letter to Martin Cross, March 5, 1953.

Smet, Pierre-Jean de. Letter Books, Jesuit Missouri Province Archives.

Three Affiliated Tribes. Corporate Charter. Ratified, April 24, 1937.

———. Constitution and bylaws, approved, June 29, 1936.

———. Report on meeting with BIA in Washington, March 15–28, 1953.

Wheeler, General R. A. Letter to George Gillette, December 3, 1947.

Yellowtail, Robert. Letter to Martin Cross, April 4, 1953.

———. Letter to Martin Cross, April 7, 1953.

———. Open letter to Indian tribes. May 1952.

Young, Senator Milton R. Letter to Martin Cross, January 20, 1947.

———. Letter to Martin Cross, May 7, 1953.

———. Letter to Martin Cross, May 27, 1953.

Zimmerman, William. Acting Indian Commissioner's statement and remarks to the Tribal Business Council of the Three Affiliated Tribes, at Washington, D.C., January 21, 1948.

GOVERNMENT DOCUMENTS

Abert, J. W. *Journal of Lieutenant J. W. Abert, From Bent's Fort to St. Louis, 1845.* Senate Executive Documents, 438, 29th Congress, 1st sess.

"Background Data Relating to the Three Affiliated Tribes of the Fort Berthold Reservation Located in the State of North Dakota." Bureau of Indian Affairs Report. Washington, D.C.: GPO, 1954.

Chapman, Oscar. Transcript of "Lieu Lands" Meeting Between BIA, Martin Cross, Army Engineers, Bureau of Reclamation, Felix Cohen, in Chapman's office, on December 16, 1946. Washington, D.C.: Department of the Interior, 1946.

Civil Functions of the War Department (also *Lieu Lands for Fort Berthold*). U.S. Public Law 374. 79th Congress, 2nd sess. *U.S. Statutes at Large* 60, pt. 1, May 2, 1946.

Commissioner of the General Land Office, Annual Report, November 26, 1851.

Commissioner of Indian Affairs, Annual Reports to Congress, 1848–1856.

Congressional Globe, 29th Congress, 2nd sess. December 16, 1846.

Congressional Globe, 29th Congress, 2nd sess. January 15, 1847.

Congressional Globe, 30th Congress, 1st sess. January 12, 1848.

Congressional Globe, 30th Congress, 1st sess. July 10, 1848.

Eisenhower, Dwight. Speech Made on Public Law 280 and Termination at Low-
ery Air Force Base, Denver, Colorado, in August 1953. Reprinted in the Pine
Ridge News bulletin, Pine Ridge, South Dakota, September 1, 1953.

Emory, W. H. "Notes of a Military Reconnaissance." *H. Ex. Doc. 41*, 30th Congress, 1st sess., 1851.

Establishing State Jurisdiction over Indian Nations in Civil Disputes. U.S.
Public Law 280. 83rd Congress, 1st sess. *U.S. Statutes at Large 67*, August
15, 1953.

Executive Orders Relating to Indian Reservations, 1855–1922. Wilmington:
Scholarly Resources, 1975.

Flood Control Act of 1944. U.S. Public Law 534. 78th Congress, 2nd sess. *U.S.
Statutes at Large 58*, pt. 1, December 14, 1944.

Fort Berthold Taking Act. U.S. Public Law 437. 81st Congress, 1st sess. *U.S.
Statutes at Large 63*, pt. 1, October 29, 1949.

General Allotment Act (Dawes Act), ch. 119, 24 Stat. 388 (1887).

Indian Appropriations Act of 1892. U.S. Public Law 437. In *Documents of
American Indian Diplomacy: Treaties, Agreements, and Conventions,
1775–1979*, ed. Vine Deloria Jr. and Raymond J. DeMallie. Norman: University of Oklahoma Press, 1999.

Jackson, Andrew. *Message from the President of the United States to the Two
Houses of Congress.* 23rd Congress, 1st sess., 1833, H. Doc. 1, vol. 1, Serial
Set 254.

Kearney, S. W. "Report of a Summer Campaign to the Rocky Mountains." Senate
Executive Documents 1, 29th Congress, 1st sess., 1849.

Macgregor, Gordon. Missouri River Basin Investigations. "Attitudes of the Fort
Berthold Indians Regarding Removal from the Garrison Reservoir Site and
Future Administration of Their Reservation." Department of the Interior,
Washington, D.C.: GPO, August 1947.

———. Missouri River Basin Investigations 2 (supplement no. 1). "Social and
Economic Impacts of Garrison Dam on the Indians of the Fort Berthold Reservation." Department of the Interior, Washington, D.C.: GPO, 1947.

———. Missouri River Basin Investigations 60. "The Resources, People and
Administration of Fort Berthold Reservation." Department of the Interior,
Washington, D.C.: GPO, August 1948.

———. Missouri River Basin Investigations 67. "The Indians and the Pick-Sloan
Plan." Department of the Interior, Washington, D.C.: GPO, November 1948.

Missouri Basin Inter-Agency Committee. *Report on Adequacy of Flows in the
Missouri River.* Department of Interior, Omaha, 1951.

Missouri River: A Letter from the Secretary of War; Referred to the Committee on Rivers and Harbors, February 5, 1934. 73rd Congress, 2nd sess., as ordered by the Flood Control Act of January 21, 1927. Washington, D.C.: GPO, 1935.

Myer, Dillon. Speech on Termination to the Western Governors' Conference at Phoenix, Arizona, December 9, 1952. Documents of the Commissioner of Indian Affairs, Washington, D.C.: GPO, 1952.

Reclamation Act of 1939. U.S. Public Law 76-260. 76th Congress, 1st sess. *U.S. Statutes at Large* 53, pt. 2, August 4, 1939.

Replacing Lieu Lands Conditions with Cash Settlement. U.S. Public Law 296. 80th Congress, 1st sess. *U.S. Statutes at Large* 61, pt. 1, July 31, 1947.

"Report on the Platte River Road." Senate Executive Documents 94, 34th Congress, 1st sess.

Roosevelt, Franklin. Letter to Congress on Desirability of Missouri Valley Authority. *Congressional Record,* September 21, 1944. Washington, D.C.: GPO, 1945.

U.S. Congress. Representative Usher Burdick charges the Army Corps of Engineers with unconstitutional taking of Fort Berthold, and violating treaties. 83rd Congress, 1st sess., *Congressional Record* 99, pt. 3, April 20, 1953. Washington, D.C.: GPO, 1954.

———. Senator Barry Goldwater speaking against termination legislation. 86th Congress, 1st sess., *Congressional Record,* March 9, 1959. Washington, D.C.: GPO.

U.S. Department of Interior. *Conference with Delegation from Fort Berthold Tribal Council on March 20, 1953,* from the files of Homer Jenkins, program officer, and Ross Landon, program counsel. Meeting chaired by Warren Spaulding, deputy commissioner of the Bureau of Indian Affairs.

———. Lieu lands press release, December 4, 1946.

U.S. General Accounting Office. *Descriptive Data on Garrison Diversion Unit and Other Reclamation Projects, RED-76-80,* March 5, 1976. Washington, D.C.: GPO, 1976.

U.S. House. Congressman James Murray speaking on the need for a complete revision of federal Indian policy. 85th Congress, 2nd sess., *Congressional Record,* April 17, 1958. Washington, D.C.: GPO, 1958.

———. Congressman Lee Metcalf speaking on proposed revision of federal Indian policy and P.L. 280. 85th Congress, 2nd sess., *Congressional Record,* April 17, 1958. Washington, D.C.: GPO, 1958.

———. Congressman William Lemke speaking on the injustice of the Ft. Berthold Takings Act. 81st Congress, 1st sess., *Congressional Record,* October 20, 1949. Washington, D.C.: GPO, 1950.

———. *The Pick Plan.* 78th Congress, 2nd sess., House Doc. No. 475 (1944).

———. *Report on House Resolution 108 Authorizing the Committee on Interior and Insular Affairs to Conduct an Investigation of the Bureau of Indian Affairs.* H.R. Report 2680, September 20, 1954. Washington, D.C.: GPO.

———. *Report on the Investigation into the Massacre of Cheyenne Indians,* January 10, 1865. (Also, see Vine Deloria Jr., *Of Utmost Good Faith.*)

U.S. House Committee on Interior and Insular Affairs. *Garrison Unit Joint Tribal Advisory Committee: Hearings on H.R. 2414 to Implement Certain Recommendations.* 102d Congress, 1st sess., October 30, 1991, November 4, 1991.

———. *Hearing with BIA Director Dillon Myer on Indian Attorneys and Per Capita Payments to Enrolled Members of Three Affiliated Tribes.* 82nd Congress, 2nd sess., April 5, 1952.

———. *Hearing on H.R. 7068: Provisions in Connection with the Construction of the Garrison Diversion Unit.* 85th Congress, 1st sess., October 30, 1957.

———. *Hearing on Provisions in Connection with the Construction of the Garrison Diversion Unit.* 86th Congress, 2nd sess., June 10, 1960.

———. *Hearing on Provisions in Connection with the Construction of the Garrison Diversion Unit.* 88th Congress, 2nd sess., February 20, 1964.

U.S. House Committee on Public Lands. *Providing for the Ratification of a Contract for the Purchase of Certain Indian Lands.* 81st Congress, 1st sess., May 9, 1949 (H. Rep. 544).

U.S. House Subcommittee of the Committee on Indian Affairs. *Investigation of Indian Bureau: Hearings on H. Res. 166.* 78th Congress, 1st sess., July 22–August 8, 1944.

U.S. House Subcommittees on Indian Affairs of the Committee on Public Lands. *Providing for the Ratification by Congress of a Contract for the Purchase of Certain Indian Lands Under H.J. Res. 33.* 81st Congress, 1st sess., April 29–30, May 2–3, 1949.

U.S. Senate Committee on Appropriations. *Hearing on War Department Civil Functions Appropriation Bill of 1948.* 80th Congress, 1st sess., July 16, 1947.

U.S. Senate Committee on Interior and Insular Affairs. *Presentation of Final Report of the Garrison Unit Joint Tribal Advisory Committee (JTAC).* 100th Congress, 1st sess., November 19, 1987.

———. *To Provide for the Return to the Former Owners of Certain Lands Acquired in Connection with the Garrison Dam Project of Mineral Interests in Such Lands: Hearing on S. 536 and S. 746.* 84th Congress, 1st sess., March 28, 1955.

U.S. Senate Committee on Irrigation and Reclamation. *Hearing to Establish a Missouri Valley Authority.* 79th Congress, 1st sess. (1945), 109.

U.S. Senate and House, joint hearing of the Senate Select Committee on Indian Affairs, the Senate Committee on Energy and Natural Resources, and the House Committee on Interior and Insular Affairs. *Final Report and Recommendations of the Garrison Unit Joint Tribal Advisory Committee.* 100th Congress, 1st sess., March 30, 1987.

U.S. Senate Select Committee on Indian Affairs. *Authorizing the Three Affiliated Tribes of Fort Berthold to File Claim for Damages in the Delay of Payment for Lands Claimed to Have Been Taken in Violation of the U.S. Constitution.* 96th Congress, 2nd sess., June 25, 1980 (S. Rept. 833).

——. *Hearing on the Three Affiliated Tribes and Standing Rock Sioux Tribal Equitable Compensation Act of 1991* (S.B. 168). 102d Congress, 1st sess., April 12, 1991.

——. *Hearings on Termination of Federal Trust Responsibility over Indian Lands, and H.R. 108.* 83rd Congress, 1st sess., July 18–August 1, 1953. Transcripts reprinted in *The American Indian and the United States,* edited by Wilcombe E. Washburn, Smithsonian Institution (New York, Random House, 1973).

——. *Implementing Recommendations of the Garrison Unit Joint Tribal Advisory Committee.* 102d Congress, 1st sess., November 26, 1991 (S. Rept. 102-250).

——. *Missouri River Basin: Conservation, Control, and Use of Water Resources of the Missouri River Basin in Montana, Wyoming, Colorado, North Dakota, South Dakota, Nebraska, Kansas, Iowa, and Missouri, with full report by Secretary of the Interior Harold L. Ickes on Bureau of Reclamation Plan for Basin Development.* 78th Congress, 2nd sess., May 5, 1944 (S. Rept. 191).

——. *Protesting the Construction of Garrison Dam: Hearing on S.J. Res. 79 to Establish a Joint Committee to Study Claims of Indian Tribes and to Investigate the Administration of Indian Affairs.* 79th Congress, 1st sess., October 9, 1945.

——. *Survey of Conditions Among the Indians of the United States.* 78th Congress, 1st sess., June 11, 1943 (S. Rept. 310).

——. *Three Affiliated Tribes and Standing Rock Sioux Just Compensation Act.* 100th Congress, 1st sess., March 30, 1987 (S. Rept. 249).

U.S. Senate Subcommittee on Water and Power of the Committee on Energy and Natural Resources. *Hearings in the Field to Ascertain the Impact of Garrison*

Dam and Lake Sakakawea on Local Communities. 101st Congress, 1st sess., August 25, 1989, October 9, 1989.

U.S. Weather Bureau. *Kansas-Missouri Floods of June–July 1951.* Technical Paper No. 17. Washington, D.C.: GPO, 1952.

ACKNOWLEDGMENTS

The legion of people who helped midwife this book are deserving of free trips to Borneo and Prague and St. Barts, a trek in Nepal, a mariachi serenade, and a lifetime's supply of Junior Mints and free passes to whatever A-list movies tickle their funny bones. Alas, praises and heartfelt gratitudes will have to suffice. This time.

As with many books, this one started out as a casual comment made over a lunch of linguini primavera and Caesar salad between my agent, Joe Vallaley, and my editor, Jonathan Brent. In time, their idea decided it wanted to be a book, and soon that idea grew into a proposal. Though it took a few months to worry the edges into proper shape, we never second-guessed the original notion. Jonathan Brent's unflagging enthusiasm for this story, buoyed and reinforced by generous and encouraging letters from my readers, has been an inspiration from the beginning. I never doubted for a moment that this story was in the best possible hands.

When I think about the many scholars whose insights and hard work contributed to this book, people such as Frederick Merk, Annie Abel, Charles Wilkinson, Raymond J. DeMallie, James Ronda, Vine Deloria Jr., Robert Williams Jr., Raymond Cross, and so many others, I imagine this story sitting atop a pyramid with a very broad base. That base also includes the hundreds of nameless and faceless stenographers who, across two centuries, have transcribed many millions of pages of transcripts, letters, and testimony heard in government agencies and committee rooms in Congress. As I read the letters that were received by various government agencies in the early 1800s, blindness seemed near, yet I marveled at the loyal and tireless scribes whose pens so carefully recorded thousands of letters into the government's official letter books. You served us well, and it is an honor and a privilege to add one stone to that pyramid, that monument to our collective narrative, in your names.

There is not enough stardust, chocolate, or praise to adequately thank or reward my masterful manuscript editor, Phillip King, or the numerous and far-flung archivists and research librarians who helped me assemble the myriad pieces of this story. Those of you at the Library of Congress, and those laboring at archives everywhere, continue to amaze and humble me with your talents, your knowledge, and your dedication. In particular, I'd like to thank Jim Davis at the North Dakota Heritage Center, historian Marilyn Hudson and Calvin Grinnell at the Four Bears Museum at Fort Berthold, archivist Sandra Lowry at the Fort Laramie National Historic Site, Sara Przybylski at the Missouri Historical Society, and Ellen Thomasson at the Missouri Historical Museum. None of this happens without you.

Then there are those unofficial helpers who turn drudgery into laughter, not to mention the many kind readers who have taken the time to write me notes and letters of encouragement: I thank you. To Carlos and Michelle and Lynn, Brent, Ryan, Paul, and Candace, Ted, Malcolm, and Raymond, your loyalty and friendship has humbled me with countless unconditional acts of kindness. I am deeply grateful to my father, Frank VanDevelder, for his eagle eye, and to Judge Gerald VandeWalle, John Byrne, Thomas Birdbear, Kurt Peters, Greg Munro, Mary Braun, Blake Rodman, Janet Daley, Eric Eberhard and Don Whorton, for their generous spirits and wise suggestions.

In the end, I hope this book will be a lasting tribute to the resilience of the many remarkable people who lived the story recorded on these pages. To members of the Mandan, Hidatsa, Crow, Arikara, Sioux, Cheyenne, Assiniboin, Arapaho, Shoshone, and Blackfeet tribes, many of whom were brave enough to share the painful details of their stories with me, I am forever in your debt. All of us are forever in your debt. Thank you.

And to my mother and father, Frank and Mary VanDevelder, and to my wife and daughter, Brenda and Ellie, to whom this book is dedicated, it was your day-to-day laughter, compassion, and unwavering devotion to justice that fused many disparate elements into that brilliant pole star, that beacon of kindness, love, and decency, that gave me comfort and a true course to follow on the darkest of nights.

INDEX

Indian Non-Intercourse Act
(1790), 53, 56, 80
and Manifest Destiny, 142–150
and Mexican War, 145, 146
and Removal Act, 109, 112
removal debates, 107, 108, 123,
124
and states' rights, 43, 47, 56, 57,
60, 64, 83, 101
treaty making, first era, 209, 210
treaty making, second era, 211
trust obligations to treaty tribes,
40–42, 64
U.S. Constitution, 32, 40, 43, 49, 50,
51, 52, 56–61, 64, 66, 92, 96,
102, 105–107, 113, 115, 121–127,
144, 149, 210, 229
challenges to, 64, 96
Cherokee and, 105–107, 121–124
Constitutional Convention, 42, 44,
48–50, 190, 256, 257
Indian Commerce Clause, 50, 57,
58, 106
and Indian problem, 50–52, 56
and Indian treaties, 40, 50, 105,
210
Madison and, 43–48
and Manifest Destiny, 149
and states' rights, 45, 47, 53,
57–59
supremacy clause, 50, 102, 105,
210, 256
U.S. Senate, 89, 138, 199, 205, 239
U.S. Supreme Court, 40, 41, 50, 55,
109, 111, 112, 114, 115, 116, 120,
122, 176, 209, 238
Cherokee v. Georgia, 54, 55, 57,
60, 114–118
establishing federal Indian law,

role in, 109–112, 114–118,
121–124
Jackson and, 124–125
Johnson v. McIntosh, 55, 109, 115,
120
*Three Affiliated Tribes v. Wold
Engineering*, 238
Worcester v. Georgia, 55, 121–124
See also Marshall, John
Upper Missouri River, 2, 69, 171, 194,
228
Urban II (pope), 69

Van Buren, Martin, 123, 146
Vasquez, Louis, 129
Vattel, Emmerich de, 49, 74
Vestal, Stanley, 225
Village Indians (Mandan, Hidatsa,
and Arikara), 199, 201, 231
Virginia, state of, 56
Vitoria, Francisco de, 74–77, 84, 110,
121
"On the Indians Lately Discov-
ered," 74, 110

Walker, Amasa, 31
Wallace, Anthony, 92
War of 1812, 59, 61
Washakie (Snake), 164, 183, 189
Washington, George, 115, 124, 226
as army general, 45, 53, 81–82
Farewell Address, 82–83, 107
and federalism, 45, 82–83, 107
as land speculator, 77–79
and peace with Indian nations, 52,
53, 56, 81–82, 83
as president, 51–52, 81
and tribal sovereignty, 56, 60,
81–82, 83–84, 95, 124